TOWARD A PLASTIC CONCEPTION OF SCALE

In recent scientific and technological research, the concept of scale has been addressed using two main approaches. On one hand, scale is presented as an ontological fact that organizes matter in a Russian-doll structure from the infinitely small to the infinitely large. On the other hand, scale is posited as a methodological tool that manages data within a defined spatial frame to access an extracted section of reality. These approaches, however, have proved either overwhelming and thus useless, or reductive and therefore biased in their representation of the world and social relations within it.

Scale is neither a given fact nor an imposed methodological frame. Contrary to what Google Earth and other representational tools seem to imply, things are not only related in a zoom-in, zoom-out manner. Scale is not transparent and space does not exist simultaneously across scales.

In the twentieth century, conventional city-frame analysis of urbanization proposed a narrow view of the development of urban regions. This way of looking at Brussels, for example, shows the hollowing out of the center to the benefit of the suburbs. A broader examination of the city, however, within the complex of Antwerp and Ghent – or what has been termed the BAG Flemish Diamond – highlights that this network of megapolises has actually become denser and attracted economic activities and population flows from the larger region of northern Europe. In this case, Brussels, within BAG, appears as an extraordinary centralization of activity.

To overcome the limitations of both the Russian-doll and the detached spatial-frame approaches, volume 4 of New Geographies advances the concept of the plasticity of scale to highlight that a geographic scale has the propensity to undergo deformations given certain dynamics. Scale is not a fixed environment within which events unfold; rather, it is the unfolding of events that produces a certain scale. Scale is a tool to understand relationships, negotiations, and tensions between actors in space. It is plastic because it is a network of dynamic relationships that expands and contracts through the interaction of objects and people. For example, the iconic Euralille project has recast the relations of this city to other European centers, not only in terms of physical distance but also in relation to a regional political project and economic infrastructure. A malleable map of Europe that deforms geographical distances between Lille and other European cities to reflect the impact of high-speed rail exemplifies the plasticity of the European scale.

In particular, Scales of the Earth proposes to address representations of "one-world" through the notion of plastic scale as an alternative to homogenizing assumptions about global space. Globalization discourse tends to be subsumed under the two conventional approaches to scale described earlier; a plastic conception of scale, in contrast, would offer unexplored opportunities to design the Earth through a careful mapping of the relationships (continuities and discontinuities) between people and objects. Rather than approaching scale under the banner of the global, Scales of the Earth seeks to focus on the material and spatial underpinnings of scale, whose implications are yet to be fully elaborated, to achieve an effective design approach.

– El Hadi Jazairy
Editor-in-Chief, Scales of the Earth, New Geographies 4

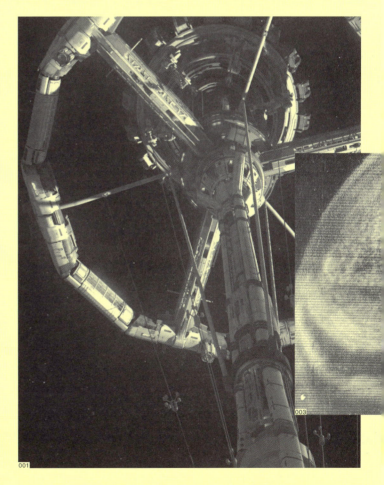

001. drexfiles.files.wordpress.com/2009/06/phaeton_concept_angle_01_v01.jpg
002. www.nasaimages.org/download.php?mid=nasaNAS~20~20~120328~22
   7027&file=GPN-2000-001588.jpg&src=http%3A%2F%2Fmm04.
   nasaimages.org%2FMediaManager%2Fsrvr%3Fmediafile%3D%2FJP2K%2F
   nasaNAS-20-NA%2F121566%2FGPN-2000-001588.jp2%26x%3D0%26y
   %3D0%26height%3D1215%26width%3D3061%26level%3D0
003. http://www.photolib.noaa.gov/bigs/spac0100.jpg

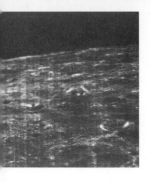

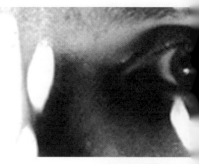

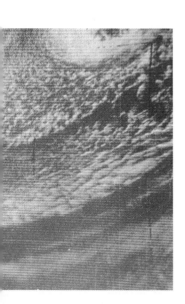

004. *2001: a Space Odyssey*, 1968. Courtesy Warner Brothers Entertainment
005. photolib.noaa.gov/bigs/spac0199.jpg
006. photolib.noaa.gov/bigs/spac0265.jpg
007. photolib.noaa.gov/bigs/spac0107.jpg

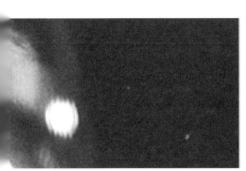

008. 3.bp.blogspot.com/_4c4umiCddtA/TBzYiTPjBgI/AAAAAAAAE6c/XmxbHMEn8tw/s1600/tbm.jpg

009. bbso.njit.edu/Images/daily/images/wfullb.jpg

010. anonymous surveillance camera

011. thelivingmoon.com/45jack_files/04images/Echelon/Navy-Radome-1.jpg

012. photolib.noaa.gov/bigs/spac0175.jpg

018. photolib.noaa.gov/bigs/spac0291.jpg

019. photodocuments.com/ProfessionalInterest/ProfIntrestJPGs/05-Miami-Stadium.jpg: courtesy usmicromap.com

020. nasaimages.org/download.php?mid=nasaNAS~4~4~11857~113887&file=PIA04347.
jpg&src=http%3A%2F%2Fmm04.nasaimages.org%2FMediaManager%2Fsrvr%3Fmediafile%3D%2FJP2K%
2FnasaNAS-4-NA%2F14135%2FPIA04347.jp2%26x%3D0%26y%3D0%26height%3D3200%26width%3D2
895%26level%3D0

021. courtesy El Bee, New York

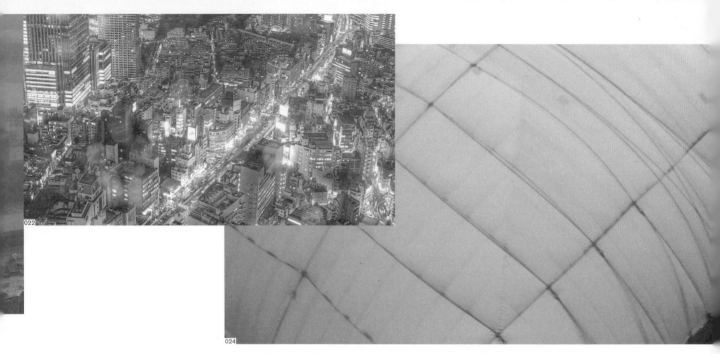

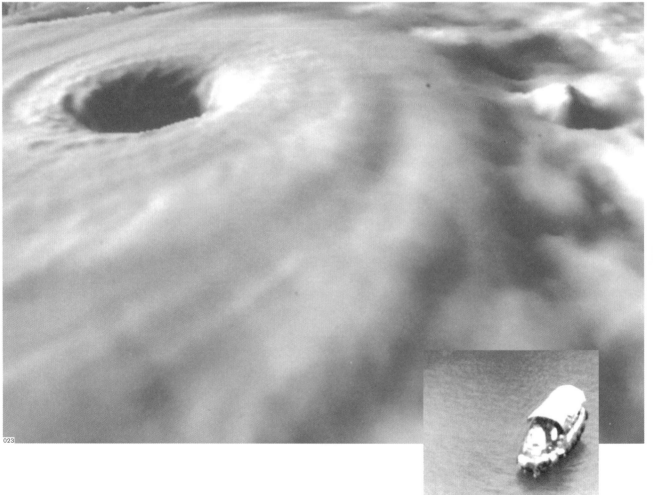

022. farm1.static.flickr.com/137/322152193_f1ab23b927_o.jpg

023. photolib.noaa.gov/bigs/spac0289.jpg

024. courtesy El Bee, Hong Kong

025. courtesy El Bee, Hong Kong

026. wyes.org/programs/localprod/nightlife/nightlife_pix.html
027. courtesy usmicromap.com
028. courtesy EL Bee, Hong Kong
029. courtesy EL Bee, Hong Kong
030. courtesy EL Bee, Hong Kong
031. thompsonsanders.com/Assets/RB%20%New/Leyte-01-1100.jpg

034

032

EDITOR-IN-CHIEF
El Hadi Jazairy

EDITORIAL BOARD
Gareth Doherty
Rania Ghosn
Antonio Petrov
Stephen Ramos
Neyran Turan

ADVISORY BOARD
Bruno Latour
Mohsen Mostafavi
Antoine Picon
Hashim Sarkis
Charles Waldheim

EDITORIAL ADVISOR
Melissa Vaughn

GRAPHIC DESIGN
Thumb

New Geographies 4: Scales of the Earth
Copyright 2011 President and Fellows of Harvard College
All rights reserved. No part may be reproduced without permission

Printed in Hong Kong by Regal Printing
Logo design by Jean Wilcox

ISBN: 9781934510278
www.gsd.harvard.edu/newgeographies

New Geographies has been made possible by the generous funding of the Aga Khan Program at the Harvard University Graduate School of Design. The editors also thank the GSD and GSD Alumni for their support.

Established in 2003, the main aim of the Aga Khan Program at the GSD is to study the impact of development on the shaping of landscapes, cities, and regional territories in the Muslim world and to generate the means by which design at this scale could be improved. The program focuses on the emerging phenomena that characterize these settings and on issues related to the design of public spaces and landscapes, environmental concerns, and land use and territorial settlement patterns. The process entails a study of their current conditions, their recent history (from World War II to the present), and, most important, the exploration of appropriate design approaches.

The Harvard University Graduate School of Design is a leading center for education, information, and technical expertise on the built environment. Its departments of Architecture, Landscape Architecture, and Urban Planning and Design offer masters and doctoral degree programs and provide the foundation for its Advanced Studies and Executive Education programs.

All attempts have been made to trace and acknowledge the sources of all images. Regarding any omissions, contact New Geographies, c/o Publications, Harvard University Graduate School of Design, 48 Quincy Street, Cambridge Massachusetts 02138.

New Geographies is distributed by Harvard University Press.

032. courtesy El Bee, Houston
033. emeraldinsight.com/fig/2720070603002.png
034. myspace.com/galwayartscentre

CONTENTS

Image essay by Thumb

ROBIN KELSEY IS SHIRLEY CARTER BURDEN PROFESSOR OF PHOTOGRAPHY IN THE HISTORY OF ART AND ARCHITECTURE DEPARTMENT AT HARVARD UNIVERSITY. HE IS THE AUTHOR OF *ARCHIVE STYLE: PHOTOGRAPHS AND ILLUSTRATIONS FOR U.S. SURVEYS, 1850 TO 1890*, AND CO-EDITOR, ALONG WITH BLAKE STIMSON, OF *THE MEANING OF PHOTOGRAPHY*. HE IS AT WORK ON TWO NEW BOOKS — ONE ON PHOTOGRAPHY AND CHANCE AND THE OTHER ON PHOTOGRAPHY IN THE UNITED STATES DURING THE COLD WAR.

REVERSE SHOT

EARTHRISE AND BLUE MARBLE IN THE AMERICAN IMAGINATION

On December 24, 1968, while *Apollo 8* was orbiting the moon, the earth came into view. The crew used its Hasselblad camera with a telephoto lens to take three photographs, one in black and white and two in color. After the astronauts returned, NASA rotated one of the color photographs 90 degrees, and the resulting "*Earthrise*" image quickly became an icon. Four years later, in December 1972, as *Apollo 17* approached the moon, the crew took a series of color photographs, including one depicting the whole earth without a terminator. Known as "the *Blue Marble*" photograph, it was also reoriented prior to distribution: taken with Antarctica at the top of the image, it was rotated 180 degrees before NASA released it. These two photographs, *Earthrise* and *Blue Marble*, are the most celebrated of all NASA images.[1] They have become symbols of the precious beauty of the earth, the shared home and fate of all humanity, the emergence of ecological thinking, and the wonders achieved by the Apollo space program. In this article, a historical review of the meanings of these photographs leads to reflections on their significance now.

Before photographs of the earth from space were made, they were anticipated and desired. By 1950, the astronomer Fred Hoyle had predicted, "Once a photograph of the Earth, taken from the outside, is available, we shall, in an emotional sense, acquire an additional dimension."[2] Hoyle imagined that this new dimension would reinforce a sense of common humanity. He explained, "once let the sheer isolation of the Earth become plain to every man whatever his nationality or creed, and a new idea as powerful as any in history will be let loose. And I think this not so distant development may well be for good, as it must increasingly have the effect of exposing the futility of nationalistic strife."[3] Others joined Hoyle in suggesting that the photographic capture of the earth would release a momentous recognition of the planet's finitude and isolation. In 1966, Stewart Brand, a young Stanford graduate and counterculture entrepreneur, sold buttons and posters that read, "Why haven't we seen a photograph of the whole Earth yet?" The slogan, ingeniously calibrated to harness the youthful suspicion of the times, recast the quest for photographs of earth from space as a demand that the political establishment, bent on secrecy and embroiled in international conflict, surrender a sign of terrestrial wholeness. As Brand recalls, he believed that "the sight of the entire planet, seen at once, would be quite dramatic and would make a point that Buckminster Fuller was always ranting about: that people act as if the earth is flat, when in reality it is spherical and extremely finite, and until we learn to treat it as a finite thing, we will never get civilization right."[4]

Not everyone anticipated the production of an image of earth from space in such hopeful terms. Hannah Arendt, in her remarkable 1963 essay, "The Conquest of Space and the Stature of Man," argued that the epistemology of modern science had long rehearsed the astronaut's distant view of earth. That view, she asserted, corresponded to the Archimedean point that modern science, seeking in its quest for universal laws to move beyond anthropocentric experience and geocentric idiosyncrasy, had exalted as its privileged vantage. The push of science past sensation and embodiment to mathematical understandings of invisible phenomena, such as the mind-bending behavior of subatomic particles, had distanced scientific inquiry from earthly life. In her words, "It was precisely by abstracting from these terrestrial conditions, by appealing to a power of imagination and abstraction that would, as it were, lift the human mind out of the gravitational field of the earth and look down upon it from some point in the universe, that

modern science reached its most glorious and, at the same time, most baffling achievements." According to Arendt, through the effort to put humans, not merely instruments or robots, into space "man hopes he will be able to journey to the Archimedean point which he anticipated by sheer force of abstraction and imagination."[5]

Arendt thus raised the possibility that the effort to propel men into space stemmed from a desire to reintegrate science and humanity. The cold detachment with which modern science had been examining the earth would, in an astronaut so positioned, give way to embodied perception. Science had passed from a Newtonian mechanics anchored in the everyday experience of apples falling from trees to a quantum mechanics based on bizarre invisible particles that defy the laws of probability. In the prospect of the astronaut, the scientific worldview that had estranged knowledge from the body and the earth would, as if to fulfill a kind of prophecy, return to human sensory experience. Such reasoning may help explain why of all the marvelous images from space that NASA has produced, many taken by satellites, the two most celebrated are photographs taken by humans. Only photographs taken by humans could signify our bodily arrival, our actual presence, at the extraterrestrial vantage that had underwritten the scientific imagination.

For Arendt, however, this imagined moment offered a false reassurance. Writing under the pall of totalitarianism and nuclear aggression, she interpreted this destined reintegration of scientific mindset and human experience as in fact the subordination of the latter to the former. The astronaut, weightless, squeezed into a tiny capsule, surrounded by an airless void, would not return science to the sensory fundamentals of human life. Instead, embodiment would be subjected to the severe demands of a society given over to scientific ambition. It would be forced to abide by the disregard for corporeal experience that was the prophecy's initial premise. Indeed, the moment would be received, not as a means of mending the rift between science and earthly life, but rather as, to use Arendt's description of the popular reception of *Sputnik I*, yet another "step toward escape from men's imprisonment to the earth."[6] If we accept her view, the notion that the sensorially rich and life-giving earth could constitute a prison is a stark index of modernity's madness.

For Arendt, the quest to occupy the Archimedean point was vain as well as misguided. An astronaut in the vicinity of the moon might occupy such a point with respect to the earth, but science had larger worlds to consider. As Arendt put it, "All [man] can find is the Archimedean point with respect to the earth, but once arrived there and having acquired this absolute power over his earthly habitat, he would need a new Archimedean point, and so *ad infinitum*."

In December 1968, Arendt's unease did not stop the mainstream American press from greeting *Earthrise* rapturously. After a year marked by urban riots, campus unrest, the assassinations of Martin Luther King, Jr., and Robert Kennedy, a deepening distrust of official representations of the war in Vietnam, and escalation in the war's violence and casualties, the image confirmed a widespread feeling of global fragility and seemed to promise the dawning of a new consciousness of human commonality and ecological embeddedness. Although many characterized the timing in redemptive terms (a frequently quoted telegram received by the astronauts read, "Thanks for saving 1968"), the flip side was the irony of progressives receiving such a compelling sign of their utopian aspirations at the very moment when those aspirations were being crushed.

Viewed in the context of the race to the moon, the whole-earth images bore deeper ironies. An image anointed as a sign of universal humanity and ecological fragility had emerged from an intensely militarized international rivalry and a space program every bit as environmentally profligate as the society that produced it (the Apollo missions' *Saturn V* rockets burned through 15 tons of kerosene per second in their initial stage of ascent, and shed orbiting junk afterward). [7]

The notion of the earth being "our home" was repeated ad nauseam by white males who seemed oblivious to the restricted gender and race of "our" representatives in space, and to the irony of exalting an image of "our home" that was produced at enormous financial cost at a time when so many social needs "at home" were going unmet. Gil Scott-Heron brilliantly critiqued this blindness in his 1970 song, *Whitey on the Moon*, which begins with the lines:

> A rat done bit my sister Nell
> (with Whitey on the moon)
> Her face and arms began to swell
> (and Whitey's on the moon)
> I can't pay no doctor bill
> (but Whitey's on the moon)
> Ten years from now I'll be paying still
> (while Whitey's on the moon). [8]

No one anticipated the implications of the whole-earth photographs more presciently than Brand, who put *Earthrise* on the cover of the fall 1969 edition of his *Whole Earth Catalogue* (the inaugural 1968 edition bore a satellite image of the earth). For Brand, these images were symbolic of a new economy that would respect ecological limits and yet reward entrepreneurial verve. The whole earth was a precious home requiring care but also a global village generating new networks for the exchange of information and personal goods. The *Whole Earth Catalogue*, subtitled "Access to Tools," linked the image of the earth to new distributive systems, and its global approach to information and product dissemination foreshadowed the powers of the Internet.[9]

By the Reagan years, the utopian promise of the whole-earth photographs had largely succumbed to ideology as usual. In March 1985, Yaakov Jerome Garb, in the pages of *Whole Earth Review*, a periodical founded by Brand that bore *Blue Marble* on its cover, critiqued these images by locating them within an ideology of geographical conquest and graphic control. Garb decried the flattening of the planet, both literally as a photographic surface and figuratively as an instrumental sign bereft of enchantment. He saw the view of earth from space as "an impoverished image that symbolizes and perpetuates an impoverished world view." According to him, such images invite the imposition of cartographic order, an impulse "symptomatic of our culture's profound estrangement from the realities of organic life on Earth." His disillusionment was hastened by the kitschy appropriation of the whole-earth motif by commercial interests; images of the whole-earth as light bulb, as beach ball, and as early video-game icon illustrate his article. Many progressives of the time shared Garb's distress. Indeed, a tenor of disillusionment characterizes the entire March 1985 issue of the Whole Earth Review, which includes a short seethe by Brand entitled "Environmentalism as Poison?" that pondered the incapacity of the environmental movement to generate radical change.

In the mid-1990s, when the hotbed of critique had moved from the coffeehouse to the academy, two scholarly articles analyzed *Earthrise* and *Blue Marble* with more historical rigor. In 1994, Denis Cosgrove wrote an essay that situated these photographs in both "one-world" (human universality) and "whole-earth" (ecological fragility) ideologies. Both ideologies, he noted, shifted the popular imagination from the ostensible purpose of the Apollo missions to investigate the moon to the implications of the astronauts' gaze backward.

As Cosgrove argued, for those following Hoyle and adopting the "one-world" approach, this gaze was a reminder of our common humanity and the artificiality of geopolitical boundaries. Astronaut Frank Borman reported in the December 23, 1968, issue of *Newsweek*, "When you're finally up at the moon looking back at the earth, all those differences and nationalistic traits are pretty well going to blend and you're going to get a concept that maybe this is really one world and why the hell can't we learn to live together like decent people." Two days later, Archibald MacLeish opined in the *New York Times*, "To see the earth as it truly is, small and blue and beautiful in that eternal silence in which it floats, is to see ourselves as riders on the earth together." In the wake of the Apollo missions, the link between optical distance and common humanity became a popular motif, often mixed with religious sentiment. In 1985, while Garb was decrying the descent of the whole-earth image into kitsch, singer-songwriter Julie Gold penned the ballad "From a Distance," which explicitly associated the view of earth from space ("the world is blue and green") with divine oversight ("God is watching us") and common purpose ("From a distance we are instruments / marching in a common band").

For proponents of "one-earth" symbolism, the gaze back to earth was a reminder of the planet's finitude, exceptionality, and ecological vulnerability. Once again, the astronauts provided a gloss. Bill Anders, generally credited with taking *Earthrise*, remarked, "I think that all of us subconsciously think that the Earth is flat or at least almost infinite. Let me assure you that, rather than a massive giant, it should be thought of as the fragile Christmas-tree ball which we should handle with considerable care." [10] Time and again, the environmental movement has circulated the NASA earth photographs to cash in on their pictorial connotations of a delicate and bounded beauty. The Earth Day flag designed by John McConnell features *Blue Marble* against a blue background.

For Cosgrove, the two ideological uses of *Earthrise* and *Blue Marble*, although superficially contradictory (one is anthropocentric, the other ostensibly not), share fundamental features. According to him, both suppress the cultural and historical specificity of their assumptions, and both exemplify "the Apollonian urge to establish a transcendental, univocal, and universally valid vantage point from which to sketch a totalizing discourse." [11] Following through with Arendt's critical forecast, Cosgrove concludes that the two images, as understood within these ideological frameworks, "draw upon and extend ideas of human territoriality that have deep historical, geographical, and cultural roots in Western imaginings." [12]

In 1997, Kevin McGuirk, in an effort to come to terms with a book-length poem by A. R. Ammons entitled *Sphere: The Form of a Motion*, analyzed the whole-earth photographs in a similar vein.[13] McGuirk characterized the image of the whole earth as "a perfect cipher," whose allegedly timeless meanings "can be shown to be contextual, historical, and contradictory." [14] Like Cosgrove, he traced the whole-earth image to the history of geographical expansionism and the urge to take optical control over new territory. According to McGuirk, "the whole earth image continues to be read as self-evidently a benign source of knowledge that might contribute both to world peace and to 'saving the earth,' despite its symbolic relation to the history of Western knowledge and colonialism, its material connection to the massive technological apparatuses of a post-war imperial power, and its ambiguities as an interpretable text."[15] He traces the romantic idealization of the whole-earth image to Emerson's figure of the "transparent eyeball."[16] For McGuirk, the image of the earth, contained and complete within itself, promises an immanent meaning, an ontological fullness that displaces the specificities of history and discourse.[17]

In light of this brief history of their reception, what might *Earthrise* and *Blue Marble* mean now? Should Cosgrove's and McGuirk's critiques still govern our understanding of these images? As powerful as these critiques continue to be, I think we should perhaps not align *Earthrise* and *Blue Marble* so readily with the ideological histories and apparatuses that produced them. Historically, these images have radical aspects, and Cosgrove's and McGuirk's critiques may owe more to them than either author acknowledges.

A key source of historical tension in these images is the clouds. Although critics of the photographs often treat them as though they were aerial photographs taken to a higher degree, they are not. Most aerial photography is taken through cloudless air to depict terrain with uniform clarity. The practice suppresses the very existence of a turbulent, moisture-laden atmosphere and brings aerial photography into alignment with the cartographic imagination, which excludes clouds from maps and globes. The vantage from space thwarted this habit and thus yielded unfamiliar images. After NASA released *Blue Marble*, a writer for the *Chicago Tribune* wrote: "Wispy clouds add an unreal touch over the deep-blue seas and brown continent."[18] The curious phrase, "an unreal touch," speaks to the tactile disturbance of geographical expectation. For the writer, only the relatively fixed components of the terrestrial ecosystem, the seas and the land, qualify as real. The clouds that have discomfited the geographical gaze become, in this moment of fanciful recuperation, fairy gauze over the earth.

The prominence of clouds surfaced in the conversations between the *Apollo 8* astronauts and Mission Control. While the spacecraft orbited the moon, Borman said: "I certainly wish we could show you the earth. It is a beautiful, beautiful view, with predominantly blue background and just huge covers of white clouds, particularly one very strong vortex up near the terminator." In this description, the covering clouds have become the figure, and the oceans mere background. In a similar way, astronaut James Lovell, when Mission Control asked him to describe the colors of earth, responded:

> Okay. For colors, waters are all sort of a royal blue; clouds, of
> course, are bright white; the reflection off the earth is – appears
> much greater than the moon. The land areas are generally a brownish
> – sort of a dark brownish to light brown in texture. Many of the vorti-
> ces of clouds can be seen of the various weather cells. A long band
> of – it appears cirrus clouds that extend from the entrance of the
> Gulf of Mexico going straight out across the Atlantic. The terminator,
> of course, cuts through the Atlantic Ocean right now, going from
> north to south. Southern Hemisphere is almost completely clouded
> over, and up near the North Pole there is quite a few clouds.[19]

Asked to talk about colors, Lovell spends much of his time talking about the bright white clouds that cover most of the earth he can see. The photographic apparatus may have flattened out the earth into a disc, but this was not the flatness of the map. The turbulent atmosphere, so thin that it hewed to the earth like a skin, had become inseparable from the globe.

The clouds, one might say, had taken the place of the usual overlay for the earth, namely the cartographic grid. As Cosgrove has written of *Blue Marble*, "Freed of graticule, names, and human boundaries, [the photograph] represents an earth liberated from cultural constrictions and apparently at liberty to clothe itself anew

in the natural hues of water, earth, and the softest veils of atmosphere."[20] This sartorial freedom, of course, was perfect for the countercultural times. While American youth were stripping off the rigid attire of their parents and donning loose, swirling bell-bottoms and tie-dyed T-shirts featuring spontaneous bursts of color, or donning nothing at all and showing off their natural hues, the earth evidently engaged in a parallel surface liberation. In this sense, these images now have a specific historical character. Like the Lava Lamp, they speak to the stressful conjunction in the 1960s of technological innovation and organicist dreams.[21]

Rather than link these photographs directly to cartography and aerial surveying, I would associate them with the Western landscape tradition. In that tradition, going back to Constable and Turner and their Dutch predecessors, the roiling forms of clouds were aesthetically exalted. The English romantics, rebelling against the ossifications of the academy, found in clouds a source of freshness and spontaneity. Since then, clouds have often signified the aleatory processes of nature that evade the determinations of system or will. In the 1920s, the photographer Alfred Stieglitz, feeling accused by the critic Waldo Frank of using "hypnotism" to manipulate his portrait sitters, turned to clouds as a subject to demonstrate that his photography could aesthetically depict the unmasterable.[22] Stieglitz and his romantic forebears thus surrendered control only to more splendidly exert it: their understanding of clouds made the motif a perfect foil for virtuosic efforts to fix and construe the ineffably dynamic.

As Hubert Damisch has argued, the use of clouds as a means of thwarting optical systemization and challenging artistic skill has roots extending further back in the Western tradition.[23] According to him, the Renaissance, in inventing the geometric matrix of linear perspective, dialectically generated its opposite in what he designates as *cloud*, a signifying motif for which clouds are the everyday reference. For Damisch, the semiotic instability of *cloud*, its capacity to integrate or disintegrate pictorial structure, gave the motif its power.[24] Painted clouds could demarcate or signify the heavenly realm, or they could operate as an optical blockage. For example, Correggio, in painting domed ceilings, fashioned "solid-looking clouds" that did not mediate between the earthly and heavenly realms, as clouds in Renaissance painting often did, but rather blocked the sky ("the sky of the astronomers," writes Damisch), thus setting physics and metaphysics into a modern opposition.[25]

The clouds in *Earthrise* and *Blue Marble* intervened in this history in curious ways. By obscuring most of the land and sea, they deflected the cartographic impulse to optically master the surface of the planet and recalled the rebellion of clouds in the Western tradition of depiction. Modifying the formula that Damisch devised to understand Correggio's cupola paintings, the clouds in the NASA photographs blocked the astronaut's charting gaze. Circa 1970, this blockage corresponded not to the split between physics and metaphysics but instead to that between the instrumental ambitions of modern science and an ecological understanding of the earth. These photographs thus became symbols for the environmental movement not simply because the earth looked beautiful, small, and fragile but also because the impenetrable cloud layer had seemingly restored the planet's veil of mystery before the eye of science.

In light of the subsequent developments in earth science and ecology, however, the photographs have taken on a very different meaning. By depicting the polymorphous turbulence of clouds as itself a kind of surface, a swirling layer of white, these photographs forecast the diachronic mapping of the atmosphere that the development of chaos theory and computer modeling have facilitated in recent years. In this way, they figure the subjection of meteorological and climatological phenomena to the very scientific determinations that those phenomena were once thought to discomfit. As it happens, this process of subjection was already under way when the photographs were taken; NASA had begun by the late 1960s to use satellites to improve weather observation and prediction. We might say, then, that the very blockage by the clouds of geographical scrutiny in *Earthrise* and *Blue Marble* marked a shift toward the integration of atmosphere and terrestrial surface, making clouds a subject of mapping, and collapsing an old opposition between the cloud and the grid. In recent years, we have witnessed parallel developments, namely a growing dependence of the environmental cause on scientific findings, and a surge of environmental concern among the scientific community. Thus the ideological opposition that cloud and grid once signified has also largely collapsed. Green protesters cite data-driven climatological models, and scientists take seriously the notion of the earth as a sensitive entity governed internally by interdependence.

The ecological significance of *Earthrise* and *Blue Marble* derived not only from clouds but also from distance.[26] The distance between the Apollo spacecraft and the earth was quantitatively so much greater than the distance entailed by ordinary aerial photography as to produce qualitatively different images. It not only secured the depiction of the earth as a bounded planet and made cloud cover unavoidable but it also rendered humanity invisible. In this regard as well, these images sidled up less to the geographic imagination, which had always been fascinated with human settlements and encounters, than to the idealizations of landscape. By the late 1960s, the environmental movement had embraced a landscape aesthetic that represented the natural world as if humans had never arrived. As Rebecca Solnit has argued, landscape photographers led by Ansel Adams, who was at the zenith of his fame and influence during the Apollo era, had mastered the norms of the nature calendar, which featured soaring peaks and tranquil glades but prohibited signs of human beings and their history[27] While this prohibition obliged nature photographers to turn away from backpackers, houses, trails, and airplanes in making their idealized images of an earthly Eden, the Apollo astronauts secured this "virgin nature effect" simply through distance and the limits of their telephoto lenses. In the era of the Apollo missions, the earth in these photographs thus paradoxically represented both "our home" and the unpopulated Eden that the environmental moment had been imagining terrestrial essence to be. These views served as the perfect images for the environmental imagination because of their insistence—through both the distancing of the viewer and the resulting invisibility of civilization—that a condition of nature's beauty and wholeness was the negation of human presence. The Whole Earth photographs can thus signify for us that the desire for planetary escape that Arendt associated with modern science characterized the environmental movement equally well. Both pursuits were predicated on a fantasy of not belonging.[28]

Perhaps the most questionable aspect of the critical literature on *Earthrise* and *Blue Marble* is a tendency to underplay the radical significance of their retrospection. The critics, in an effort to locate these images within a history of territorial expansion and geographical prospect, tend to finesse the problem that the imperial gaze, almost by definition, did not look back. To be sure, the nationalistic drive behind the Apollo program supports suspicions that these photographs asserted American control over the earth in toto, but the eradication of signs of empire in images that ostensibly include its centers of power throws a wrench into any neat ideology critique

along these lines. In these iconic NASA photographs, the centers of imperial power disappear into an equalizing representation of terrestrial colors and forms. In the production of *Blue Marble*, one of astronauts reported to Mission Control, "the continent of Africa dominates the world right now."[29] This egalitarian vantage, albeit compromised by the reorientation of the images to fit conventional expectations, is the progressive germ that Hoyle anticipated and others hailed, and the critiques of recent histories do not account for it adequately.

There was also something unsettling for science itself in this backward glance. Arendt, in her effort to situate the vantage from space within a dehumanizing history of scientific inquiry, brilliantly characterized the drive to put men in space as a doomed effort to occupy the Archimedean point, but she failed to anticipate the salutary effects that pursuing such a vain hope might deliver. Once an astronaut occupied what was imagined as the Archimedean point, that point would lose either a measure of its reality (because the impossibility of embodying it would become more conspicuous) or a measure of its impersonal authority (because as a point embodied it would become only one human vantage among others). In the years since the Apollo missions, both effects have more or less come to pass. There has been a widespread recognition that scientists, even when acting or writing in the name of science, remain subject to personal bias and ideological partisanship, as well as a corresponding weakening of belief in the possibility of disembodied scientific objectivity. These developments are, of course, largely independent of NASA's photography, but the popularity of *Earthrise* and *Blue Marble* may have contributed their small share to the shift.

The fact that human astronauts took these photographs is crucial to their retrospective power. They emerged from within an unprecedented spatial relationship and reversed the elemental human act of celestial observation. The viewer of these images cannot help but imagine her or himself as both observer and observed. *Earthrise* offers a particularly remarkable instance of reversal. The surface of the moon stands in for the terrestrial landscape, while the earth takes the part of the moon. The reversal even tripped up Anders as he spoke from the spacecraft to Mission Control: "The horizon here is very, very stark. The sky is pitch black, and the earth—or the moon, rather, excuse me—is quite light; and the contrast between the sky and the moon is a vivid, dark line."[30] Elsewhere the record of communications between the astronauts and Mission Control exhibits a playful fascination with this reversal. For example, there is this exchange between Borman and his interlocutor in Houston:

> CC "Yes. They told us that there is a beautiful moon out there."
> CDR "Now I was just saying that there's a beautiful earth out there."
> CC "It depends on your point of view."
> CDR "Yes."[31]

These exchanges diverge fundamentally from the history of the geographical gaze associated with territorial expansion and imperial ambition. They do not exemplify "the Apollonian urge to establish a transcendental, univocal, and universally valid vantage point from which to sketch a totalizing discourse." Instead, they open out to a basic understanding of positional relativity ("it depends on your point of view") upon which the ideology critiques of these images have relied. Although the photographs of earth from space have been subject to ideology and conventional pressures, including their reorientation prior to dissemination, and have been subject to conversion into kitsch, they nonetheless have fruitfully destabilized the relation of observer to observed.

The retrospection of these images has taken on new meaning in light of the troubled post-Apollo history of NASA. Whereas writers on the Apollo program in the late 1960s imagined that we would soon see permanent lunar stations, interplanetary travel, and other extensions of human settlement in the solar system, we have seen no such things. The trips to the moon remain the far reach of human presence beyond the earth. From this historical perspective, images such as *Earthrise* and *Blue Marble* loom far larger as achievements of the Apollo program than one might have anticipated when they were made. The program was an extravagant and swaggering display of national might, determination, and ingenuity that has thus far failed to extend imperial settlement to extraterrestrial quarters. But it helped to define the earth as an ecosystem and enacted a celestial relativization of human position memorialized in images that, rightly understood, remind us of the limits of both vantage and embodiment.

This article is dedicated to the memory of Denis Cosgrove, whom I knew only electronically but am grateful enough for that.

NOTES

1. In 2008, to celebrate NASA turning fifty, the Air and Space Museum ranked the fifty "most memorable" images from the agency's history. *Blue Marble* was number one, and *Earthrise*, number two. *Air & Space Magazine*, November 1, 2008.
2. Fred Hoyle, *The Nature of the Universe* (New York: Harper & Brothers, 1950), 9. The book is a transcription of lectures.
3. Ibid., 10.
4. Stewart Brand, "Photography Changes our Relationship to Our Planet," Click! Photography Changes Everything, a Smithsonian Photography Initiative, http://click.si.edu/Story.aspx?story=31, accessed 23 May 2010.
5. Hannah Arendt, "The Conquest of Space and the Stature of Man," *The New Atlantis* 18 (Fall 2007): 43–55.
6. Arendt uses this quotation at the start of the prologue to *The Human Condition* to characterize the mass appeal of Sputnik 1.
7. On the fuel burning rate, see "Saturn V is the Biggest Engine Ever Built," *Popular Mechanics*, April 2003.
8. On the occasion of the moon landing, Charles Evers, the mayor of Fayette, Mississippi, made a similar critique in prose in the pages of the *New York Times*. See "Reactions to Man's Landing on the Moon Show Broad Variations in Opinions," *New York Times*, July 21, 1969.
9. See Steve Jobs, commencement address at Stanford University, June 12, 2005 (Remarking that the *Whole Earth Catalogue* "was sort of like Google in paperback form, thirty-five years before Google came along").
10. Quoted in Oran W. Nicks, ed., *This Island Earth* (Washington, D.C.: NASA, 1970), 14. This quotation also appears in Cosgrove, 284.
11. Denis Cosgrove, *Apollo's Eye: A Cartographic Genealogy of the Earth in the Western Imagination* (Baltimore: John Hopkins University Press, 2001), 288.
12. Ibid., 289.
13. Kevin McGuirk, "A. R. Ammons and the Whole Earth," *Cultural Critique* 37 (Autumn 1997). Cosgrove is not cited in the article.
14. Ibid., 133.

15. Ibid., 139-140.
16. Ibid., 139.
17. Ibid., 142-143.
18. "One Last View of Earth," *Chicago Tribune*, December 24, 1972.
19. NASA, *Apollo 8: Technical Air-to-Ground Voice Transcription*, December 1968, Tape 37, p. 8.
20. Cosgrove, 278.
21. On the Lava Lamp, see Jennifer Roberts, "Lucubrations on a Lava Lamp: Technocracy, Counterculture, and Containment in the Sixties," in Jules David Prown and Kenneth Haltman, eds., *American Artifacts: Essays in Material Culture* (East Lansing: Michigan State University Press), 2000.
22. Alfred Stieglitz, "How I Came to Photograph Clouds," in *Stieglitz on Photography*, ed. Richard Whelan (New York: Aperture, 2000), 235-237.
23. Hubert Damisch, *A Theory of /Cloud/: Toward a History of Painting*, tr. Janet Lloyd (Stanford: Stanford University Press, 2002).
24. See, for example, ibid., 156-157.
25. Ibid., 174-175.
26. Cosgrove acknowledged, "Perhaps the sheer distance of the Earth in these images, which obscures their cartography and renders them almost tenable constitutes the challenge that they present to the gaze." Cosgrove, 289.
27. Rebecca Solnit, "Uplift and Separate: The Aesthetics of Nature Calendars," *Art Issues* 50 (Nov./Dec. 1997), 14-17.
28. For more on this contradiction within the environmentalist imagination, see Robin Kelsey, "Landscape as Not Belonging," in James Elkins and Rachael Ziady DeLue, eds., *Landscape Theory* (New York: Routledge, 2008), 203-213.
29. *Apollo 17* commander Eugene Cernan to Mission Control. *Apollo 17*, Tape 6/8, 66, AS17_TEC.PDF.
30. *Apollo 8*, Tape 57, p. 7 AS08_TEC.PDF.
31. *Apollo 8*, Tape 57, p. 1 AS08_TEC.PDF.

Blue Marble, 1972. NASA.

NICHOLAS DE MONCHAUX IS AN ARCHITECT
AND URBANIST WHOSE WORK CONCERNS THE NATURE OF
CITIES. HE IS ASSISTANT PROFESSOR OF ARCHITECTURE
AND URBAN DESIGN AT UNIVERSITY OF CALIFORNIA,
BERKELEY. DE MONCHAUX'S DESIGN WORK AND CRITICISM
HAVE BEEN PUBLISHED IN *ARCHITECTURAL DESIGN*, *LOG*,
THE NEW YORK TIMES, AND *NEW YORK TIMES MAGAZINE*.
DE MONCHAUX'S ARCHITECTURAL HISTORY OF THE LUNAR
EXTRAVEHICULAR GARMENT, *SPACESUIT: FASHIONING
APOLLO*, WILL APPEAR IN SPRING 2011 FROM MIT PRESS.

CITIES AND CYBERNETICS

"The techniques that are going to put a man on the Moon are going to be exactly the techniques that we are going to need to clean up our cities," declared Hubert H. Humphrey in remarks at the Smithsonian in 1968.[1] The vice president's remarks were no simple comparison of difficulty; rather, they were indicative of a deliberate effort to shift the interplanetary-scaled techniques, staffing, and equipment of "space-age management" to the nation's cities.[2]

The notion that expertise gained in NASA should be so extended was an article of faith among NASA's founders. "We are going to spend 30–35 billion dollars pushing the most advanced science and technology," NASA administrator James Webb wrote on taking office in 1961, and "endeavoring in every way possible to feed back what we learn into the total national economy."[3] From the outset of the space race, Webb argued for the importance of space-borne ideas for the social and physical landscape of the nation, emphasizing "the best ways of utilizing the tremendous developments of science and technology in what might be called a total-community-workable-plan kind of concept."[4] "It is incumbent on us, while achieving our specific mission objectives," Webb reminded colleagues in 1962, "to make available to citizens generally the specific practical benefits which can flow from a research and development program of this magnitude."[5] The spread of such optimism is characterized by a 1968 *Science* editorial; "In terms of numbers of dollars or of men, NASA has not been our largest national undertaking, but in terms of complexity, rate of growth, and technological sophistication it has been unique. It may turn out that the most valuable spin-off of all will be human rather than technological: better knowledge of how to plan, coordinate, and monitor the multitudinous and varied activities of the organizations required to accomplish great social undertakings"[6]

This logic was soon rendered explicit; in June 1962, thirty-five NASA officials and military-industrial executives were invited by Wayne Thompson (city administrator of Oakland, California, and president of the International City Managers' Association) to discuss areas of shared interest, in particular: "Can a national program of space exploration be applicable to the daily tasks of the men and women who live and work in our central cities? [And] how may [such] new knowledge… be used to seek answers to the critical issues facing expanding urban populations?"[7]

Out of this meeting came a March 1963 conference on "Space, Science, and Urban Life," supported by NASA and the Ford Foundation, in cooperation with the University of California and the City of Oakland. "It is imperative," declared Thompson in the conference's introduction, "that we depart from time-worn traditions and concepts and adopt space-age techniques to cope with the problems of our space-age cities."[8]

The specific nature of these techniques was the subject of presentations by figures ranging from federal luminaries James Webb and Jerome Weisner to Martin Meyerson, Director of the Harvard-MIT Joint Center for Urban Studies, and Burnham Kelly, Dean of the School of Architecture at Cornell. While discussions in the meeting ranged from communication to automation and biotechnology, conclusions gravitated toward systems analysis and management techniques as holding particular promise for urban problems.[9]

This conclusion – that urban problems could be best tackled through systems-engineering methods, and particularly their use of information – contained another, more fundamental assertion: that cities themselves could be understood, like complex weapons, as flows of information and feedback. Mirroring the origins of the "cyborg" concept in lunar mission research,[10] the city became a system of controls that could be retuned and amplified to better serve "space-age" reality.

"A city is primarily a communication center, serving the same purpose as a nerve center in the body. It is a place where railroads, telephone and telegraph centers come together, where ideas, information and goods can be exchanged." So wrote Norbert Wiener in a December 18, 1950, opinion piece in *Life* magazine.[11] Along with several MIT collaborators, Weiner's main contribution to the issue was a pictorial essay advocating better highways and ring-roads, as well as dispersal of resources, to help guard U.S. cities against the atomic attack. Wiener's piece was a small part of a very public debate in the late 1940s and 1950s advocating the "dispersal" of American cities – defensive suburbanization – as a bulwark against atomic attack. While of secondary import to economic and social forces in the physical development of America's postwar suburbs,[12] the dispersal debate had a lasting impact on the culture and vocabulary of postwar planning. First, it introduced the notion of a collaborative cadre of experts shaping urban form – academic figures such as Wiener, but also government and industry elites. Second, it (re)introduced the notion of the city as a scientific subject, abandoning the exclusively biological models of urbanity common since the nineteenth century in favor of ideas of information flow and feedback, which Wiener's new science of cybernetics had shown to be shared by both natural and manmade controls.[13]

By the early 1960s, texts such as *A Communications Theory of Urban Growth* and *The Cybernetic Approach to Urban Analysis* proclaimed the city as a "cybernetic system… an information handling machine." [14] New institutions such as the Urban Systems Laboratory at MIT sought to extend the reach and specificity of the cybernetic urban model. Along with several recruits from RAND,[15] the center's faculty included digital computing pioneer Jay Forrester. Forrester would soon publish his own work on cybernetic urban simulation, titled *Urban Dynamics*.[16] Although allowing that the text made little or "no reference to [previous] urban literature,"[17] the book used cybernetic simulations of complex urban processes to forcefully advocate new, "scientific" approaches to planning. While confining its scope to a macroscopic urban scale, the book was especially influential among architects interested in a "rational," systems-based approach to design in cities.[18]

CITIES AND SPACECRAFT, 1966-1974

"Although comparing a city to a spaceship may seem absurd," ventured a 1967 joint NASA-HUD report, "both are inventions produced by men. The speed with which spaceships have been built makes many men wonder why progress in urban affairs has not been accelerated, too." [19]

The document, entitled Science and the City, was the result of a three-week session on "Science and Urban Development" at Woods Hole, Massachusetts, organized by NASA and the newly formed Department of Housing and Urban Development (HUD) in the summer of 1966. The Woods Hole Conference, as well as the action-oriented language of its resulting report, marked a shift from simply imagining a translation of the military-industrial systems approach, grounded in cybernetics, to urban policy, to direct efforts at implementation. Unlike the 1963 conference, where top NASA officials met with politicians and local officials, the 1966 meeting included equal numbers of government, industrial, and federal representatives, and came at a time when ugly urban riots, public failures of previous "renewal" schemes, and congressional pressure led President Lyndon Johnson to propose (in a message accompanying the Demonstration Cities and Metropolitan Development Act of 1966) "that we focus all the techniques and talents within our society on the crisis of the American city."[20]

A year earlier, Senator Gaylord Nelson (D-Wis) introduced a bill (S.2662) proposing that $125 million be provided to state and local governments "to design computer programs that would test various solutions for urban woes with the same logic used in designing moon rockets."[21] By 1968, RAND, the Santa Monica think-tank that had established the basis for Cold War simulation (and worked closely with Air Force General Bernard Schreiver and others in laying the conceptual foundations of systems management), had opened an office in Manhattan under contract to the John Lindsay administration.

Especially as late 1960s defense budgets sacrificed aerospace spending for the escalating costs of the war in Vietnam, the movement of NASA employees and contractors from the frontiers of space to the "urban frontier"[22] became an exodus. During the summer of 1971, the Department of Labor and HUD funded intensive summer schools at UC Berkeley and MIT to retrain aerospace employees in

The cover of the concluding report from the 1966 HUD-NASA conference at Woods Hole, MA. University of California, Berkeley Libraries.

"A model of a hypothetical space craft equipped with the components of a nuclear rocket propulsion," a design by Harold Finger from the Lewis Research Center, 1961. Finger's work on nuclear-propelled interplanetary spacecraft would form the basis of the *Discovery* spacecraft in Stanley Kubrick's *2001: A Space Odyssey*. NASA Image C-52113, Courtesy NASA Lewis Research Center.

techniques of urban management. Organized by the National League of Cities and the U.S. Conference of Mayors, the programs focused on "how to apply systems thinking in a new milieu."[23] Placement programs matched graduates of the programs to mayor's offices, city planning departments, and budget offices around the country; within a year, 80 percent of graduates were working in urban government.[24]

UNITED SYSTEMS ASSOCIATES

In June 1968, George Washington University, RAND spinoff Systems Development Corporation, and North American Rockwell (builder of the *Saturn V*) organized a "Conference on the Urban Challenge." Speaking to the group, General Schreiver laid out his own vision of systems thinking and urban expertise; recently retired, he announced that during his last years of service, "I began to realize that many of the problems we faced in the Air Force in the research, development, and production of our weapons systems were similar to the problems facing our cities. I also became convinced that the solutions we devised in the Air Force to our technical and management problems were applicable to the problems of our cities."[25]

With Simo Ramo and Dean Wooldrige (founders of TRW), General Schreiver had invented a new kind of organization in the 1950s – the military-industrial-academic collaboration, brought together by the "systems manager." Schreiver, as commander of the Air Force's Western Development Division, developer of the nation's first ICBMs, was himself the ur-systems manager – in the words of a glowing *Time* magazine profile in 1957, "Tomorrow's Man."[26] Having helped found the military-industrial complex, Schreiver by 1968 was assembling a new kind of collaboration, "a consortium of eight to ten leading companies… aimed at being able to do a city-system study and then to execute a program based on that study… a city rehabilitation."[27]

Schreiver's partners in the (for profit) "city rehabilitation" venture included Lockheed, Northrop, and Raytheon. The company was called "Urban Systems Associates," or USA. Beyond Schreiver's own account, the venture's origin can be traced to the general's enlistment as a consultant to the Department of Housing and Urban Development, closely following his retirement from the Air Force in 1966, where he served as an adviser to HUD's founding secretary, Robert Weaver.

OPERATION BREAKTHROUGH

As with the enlistment of Bernard Schriever, some of the most literal translations of expertise and procedure from a military-industrial to urban context came at HUD, the cabinet-level urban department founded by Lyndon Johnson in 1966. Even after the loss of the Great Society's sponsor in the White House, the transfer of military-industrial insight to HUD continued.

"Creating a safe, happy city is a greater challenge than a trip to the moon," NASA and HUD's Science and the City report had proposed, "because urban housing is more complex than a rocket… Its ever-changing problems, nevertheless, can be attacked in the same logical way we have gone about exploring the universe."[28]

In January 1969, Harold Finger, NASA Associate Administrator for Organization and Management, was called to a late-night meeting at HUD. George Romney, Richard Nixon's HUD Secretary, invited Finger to join his administrative team;[29] leaving NASA, Finger became HUD's first Assistant Secretary for Urban Technology and Research in March 1969.

Finger would later confess that he had no qualifications in urban or social policy ("I really don't know how they learned of me").[30] Before joining NASA's administration in 1967, he had for a decade served as head of NACA, then NASA's programs in nuclear propulsion

research. While Finger's initial work had focused on nuclear propulsion for airplanes – including the installation of a working nuclear reactor in a Convair B-36 "peacemaker" bomber [31]– his later research focused on nuclear-powered interplanetary spacecraft; these prototypes would form the basis for the *Discovery* spacecraft in Kubrick's *2001: A Space Odyssey*.[32] Discussions around Finger's recruitment by Secretary Romney in late 1968 directly referenced "turmoil in the cities – riots, real problems,"[33] and the continued need for a "systems approach."

The largest project overseen by Finger was the multimillion-dollar "Operation Breakthrough." Instead of "piecemeal" solutions, Operation Breakthrough attempted to address the country's urban crisis through "new total systems for constructing and marketing" urban homes and communities.[34] Instead of segregating populations based on race and income, Breakthrough sought to catalyze prefabricated, mixed-income housing construction that would allow the US housing industry to "break through" to innovations in standardization, systemization and mass production, and enable the country to "break through" its own sense of urban malaise.[35]

Despite his lack of specific qualifications, Finger's expertise was embraced by both aerospace firms – which sought to enter the construction and transportation sectors – and the building industry itself, where a fascination with the possibilities of "systems building" was one of the main legacies of the space program in American architectural culture.

Unlike foreign innovators, such as the British Archigram, the American architectural press had elevated none of the physical artifacts of the space race as worthy of architectural imitation. Instead, the focus was on systems management with prefabricated, expandable architectural "systems."[36] Operation Breakthrough was the most ambitious program of this type. Its goals were "the application of technology," and in particular, "prefabrication, heavier mechanization… modular standards… integration" and the direct involvement of "aerospace corporations" and conglomerates "in revolutionizing the landscape of American building." [37]

To advance Operation Breakthrough, Finger recruited a range of personnel from military-industrial backgrounds, and actively consulted his former superiors such as James Webb and Thomas O. Paine.[38] Instead of being managed "helter-skelter,"[39] Operation Breakthrough was directed from an aerospace-style "control room" in Marcel Breuer's new HUD headquarters. There the systems management that Bernard Schreiver founded was applied directly to the creation of model American neighborhoods.

Under an aerospace model of procurement, companies such as Alcoa, Bechtel, and Martin-Marietta proposed hundreds of prototype housing systems. Of these, twenty-two were funded for full development, including proposals by Lockheed, General Electric, and TRW. In the first years of the program, these systems were used to build 2,800 units on nine test sites from Jersey City to Kalamazoo, incorporating innovations not only in prefabricated constructions but in site systems such as waste management and pneumatic trash collection, with particular emphasis given to "blighted" areas.[40] Once site planning and fabrication were underway, shared computing facilities with the Department of Defense were used to develop and modify modular housing designs according to structural, tectonic, hydrological, and even social variables.[41]

Whereas Operation Breakthrough sought in principle to integrate its digitally inflected fabric into existing urban settings, a final set of urban proposals favored the creation of urban form from scratch. "The *de novo* city is a very exciting concept," said Litton Industries' Roy Ash in 1966. Litton was one of the largest, most admired, and most lucrative companies in America. "Litton Shoots for the Moon,"[42] a 1958 *Fortune* cover story had said, as the company began a process of acquisition and expansion that was to make it the first major post-war conglomerate.

Citing "too many problems... all of them interrelated," in addressing existing urban contexts, Litton Industries called for "integrating the urban problem... raising it to a higher level." Ash raised the prospect of Litton-built new towns in a 1966 *Fortune* magazine interview as one of the main prospects for extending the firm's "systems management capability."

"By 1970," Ash explained, "we think that we'll be able to build a city that is adequate for 25,000 and has prospects of growing to 500,000. By 1990 we will be designing cities for a million people with the prospect of growing to five million."

"Don't worry," Ash demurred slightly, "the systems management work involved in getting a one-million population city in business overnight is probably more sophisticated... than the work required to get to the moon." But, he concludes, "this whole business of military command-and-control systems has considerable potential."[43]

SLIPPERY WATER
Litton's appraisal of "too many" interrelated problems in existing contexts may have been stated to advance the notion of systems planning, but the appraisal would apply equally to the actual outcome of the many attempts to institute its tenets in the city.

Despite trumpeted technological successes – such as the introduction of "slippery water" into the city's fire hoses[44] – the New York City RAND Institute, one of the most public collaborations between military-industrial management and urban government, met increasing resistance from the government, and people, of its host city. At its peak, the Institute had commanded four floors of midtown office space, a staff of sixty consultants, and $75 million in city contracts. Starting in the early 1970s, however, the institute became subject to increasing criticism, from both city financial officials (such as Lindsay's eventual successor, Comptroller Abraham Beame), and the many communities affected by the policies RAND shaped with its (often confidential) recommendations to the city. There is a "growing unwillingness," on the part of communities, admitted RAND Director Peter Szanton in 1970, to "accept decisions which affect their lives but which they have no part in making."[45] With the city council dismissing RAND reports as "curiously irrelevant"[46] to the practice of city government, contracts were reduced in scope; the institute finally closed in 1974. (Also closing in 1974 was MIT's Urban Systems Laboratory, again for lack of funding.[47])

Urban System Associates, the consortium founded by Bernard Schriever in 1967, encountered parallel difficulties in raising interest for its systems-management services from urban clients. While extended negotiations took place over its participation in a San Francisco urban redevelopment proposal and a regional water plan in Arizona, no consulting contracts were signed by the consortium, and Schriever – uncharacteristically – "admitted defeat," dissolving the consortium more than two years after its public launch. Reflecting later, Schriever observed, "Though the need for a systematic approach to urban development exists, unfortunately its application today is extremely difficult. The key problem is that social and psychological phenomena cannot be rigorously posed in mathematical terms... due [in part] to the lack of a meaningful data base."[48]

Yet much work continued, with the acquisition and interpretation of urban data its particular focus. Los Angeles, which 1964's *The Cybernetic Approach to Urban Analysis* had praised for both its "early and pioneering efforts to use automation in the form of computers as

a tool of city planning," and its "application of cybernetics to urban problem-solving,"[49] continued to fund its digital Community Analysis Bureau through the 1970s. And "Urban Systems Divisions" continued in think-tanks such as RAND and its spinoff Systems Development Corporation.[50] The legacy of this work in today's geospatial data tools is palpable – if not quite its military-industrial origins.[51]

SURVEYING BREAKTHROUGH
Operation Breakthrough – the largest and most detailed project to implement systems management in the creation of urban fabric – met its own complex set of challenges. The first of these were both social and political. While several hundred cities initially volunteered to be sites for the experimental program, at least one finalist site was abandoned when community objections to the mixed-income component of Breakthrough's proposals became too vociferous.[52] Politically, too, the shift in construction methods proposed by Breakthrough – from on-site work divided by craft, to assembly-line efforts by mostly non-union labor – met resistance from labor unions; this political volatility led to some areas of the country being considered untenable for the proposed construction.[53]

Further problems were economical and technological. While a significant impetus behind Breakthrough had been perceived cost inefficiency in existing "helter-skelter" construction, many of the manufactured housing systems produced to create Breakthrough communities failed to accomplish any savings over conventional methods. Despite HUD Secretary Romney's prediction that, within five years of Breakthrough, "two-thirds of all the housing built in this country will be basically factory-made,"[54] by 1976 only five of the twenty-two systems developed for Breakthrough were still being produced.

A final set of technological difficulties involved the advanced infrastructural systems installed on Breakthrough sites, in particular the sophisticated systems deployed to accommodate refuse. At the Jersey City Breakthrough site, a 1978 HUD study found that persistent faults in a pneumatic trash system produced a 46 percent failure rate, with predictably malodorous results.[55] The Nixon administration shut down Operation Breakthrough a year later. (Harold Finger had departed HUD in 1972, becoming a spokesperson for General Electric's nuclear power business.)

Assessing the program in 1976, a General Accounting Office report concluded that Operation Breakthrough "did not accomplish its objectives."[56] Of the industry experts surveyed by the GAO, less than a third thought that Breakthrough had even made a "minor contribution."[57] (It should be noted decades later, however, that the extension of aerospace techniques to building forecast by Breakthrough has become standard practice, at least in certain architectural contexts.[58])

"THE SHATTERED IMAGE OF LITTON INDUSTRIES"
As for Litton Industries' plans to enter the city-construction business, they fell prey to larger problems between the perception and reality of the company's systems-management culture. The December 1, 1969 issue of *Forbes* magazine featured a cover image of broken glass, and the headline "The Shattered Image of Litton Industries." "Much of the glamour" of Litton, *Forbes* reported, "is gone. And for good reason."[59] After almost fifteen years of a continual rise in its earnings, Litton shocked Wall Street in January of 1968 with the revelation that earnings would be 'substantially lower' than expected. The only public explanation for the sudden change in fortune was "earlier deficiencies of management personnel."[60]

The reverberations extended beyond Litton's own future and were taken by Wall Street to indicate that the conglomerate strategy pioneered by Litton did not necessarily lead to the efficiencies of scale, interrelationships, and "synergy" promoted by the firm. "Litton was the sacred cow of these… companies," one broker commented, "but yet they stumbled. Who's to say the others aren't equally vulnerable?" "What is clearer almost daily," Forbes lamented, "is the considerable distance between concept and reality at Litton."[61]

Despite Litton's public failings the particular expertise of its management team continued to play a prominent role in public affairs. Roy Ash, author of Litton's city-building scheme, moved on to a central role in the Nixon administration, serving first as the head of a task force on government reorganization that proposed a massive (and ultimately unsuccessful) "synergistic" reorganization of the executive branch.[62] In a second Nixon term, Ash became Director of the White House Office of Management and Budget. His "new, expanded role" was a sweeping mandate from Nixon to survey and evaluate "all government programs now in existence," with a special focus on welfare and urban revitalization efforts.[63]

DEATH AND LIFE

This legacy of failure on the one hand, and continued influence on the other, makes the systems movement in architecture and urban planning particularly worthy of attention.

When, in the last chapter of her 1961 opus *The Death and Life of Great American Cities*, "The Kind of Problem a City Is," urban activist Jane Jacobs sought to articulate a metaphor for urban planning distinct from the "collection of file drawers"[64] she abhorred, she turned to recent work at the Rockefeller Institute, which had provided her with funding and an office to assemble her manuscript. There her neighbor, Warren Weaver, was composing an essay for the foundation's 1958 annual report that identified new thinking in the natural sciences, describing what Weaver termed "organized complexity." (The frontispiece to Weaver's essay was a model of the newly discovered DNA structure.)[65] Heavily quoting from Weaver's essay, Jacobs makes a case for the special affinity between urban landscapes and complex biological systems. Invoking the example of a single urban park, she submits that any attempt to isolate the variables, however many, leading to the success or failure of an urban enterprise is inherently dubious; those variables are "too numerous and interconnected."

Contrast such an analysis with NASA and HUD's 1967's *Science and the City*: "The city, too, consists of systems and sub-systems… We have experts on the operation of social as well as physical *black boxes*. Their talents and skills, however, have usually been brought together on urban problems helter-skelter, rather than *by a systems approach*."[66] Weaver's 1958 essay on science and complexity was circumspect when it came to envisioning "black boxes" in nature, referring, for example, to the problem of "dissectabilty": "Between the living world and the physical world, there is a critical distinction as regards dissectability. A watch spring can be taken out of a watch and its properties usefully studied apart from its normal setting. But if a heart be taken out of a live animal, then there is a great limitation on the range of useful studies which can be made."[67]

As to the contrast between living and electromechanical systems studied in situ, Weaver offers a further caution that is itself, in retrospect, wildly optimistic: "The significant problems of living organisms are seldom those in which one can rigidly maintain… variables. Living things are more likely to present situations in which a half-dozen, or even several dozen quantities are all varying simultaneously and in subtly interconnected ways. And often they present

situations in which some of the essentially important quantities are either non-quantitative, or at any rate have eluded identification or measurement." While the insights of cybernetics on feedback and homeostasis help us understand the nature of natural systems, their actual function and complex relationships remain, as Jane Jacobs remarked of the dynamics surrounding a single urban space, "as slippery as an eel."[68]

While presciently dismissive of attempts to "reduce biology… to physics,"[69] Weaver's mention of a daunting "dozen" of variables in a given natural system would itself prove a gross oversimplification. The revolution in biological science foretold by Weaver has – if anything – vastly increased our appreciation for the proliferating complexity of nature.

To take one example, Weaver refers to the newly discovered DNA molecule as the "blueprint of life" – implying, as many mistakenly believe, a systematic connection between base pairs and biological form directly analogous to the contractual documents governing architectural construction.[70] In reality (to borrow Weaver's own words) there is much that "eludes identification or measurement." Indeed, it has recently been asserted, "although mutational change [that is, change in genetic instructions] is needed for phenotypic change [change in the visible architecture of life], the two are simply not related."[71] Or, in other words, "Genes may have an effect on the phenotype, but this effect strongly depends on other genes."[72] Our own body's "blueprints," it transpires, do not perform directly, or even transitively, but rather through a complex web of shifting relationships, disturbed even by our own observation of them. (For example, the use of X-ray crystallography, discussed at length by Weaver as a revelatory technique, led through the necessity of solidifying DNA into crystals to the mistaken belief that a single genetic strand produced a single protein form. Recent advances in both microscopy and simulation have shown this to be far from the case).[73]

SPACE SETTLEMENTS

Although Operation Breakthrough had, at best, a minor impact on the earthbound housing industry, a final footnote to its space-age origins is provided by a post-Apollo strategic plan for U.S. space stations, Space Settlements: A Design Study. Produced by NASA's Ames research center, the 1975 study identifies systems developed for Breakthrough as "especially suitable for building in space."[74]

Drawing on the same space-station research borrowed by Kubrick's *2001: A Space Odyssey*, the habitat proposed by Ames would house 10,000 astronauts, optimized by age and gender and "settled by persons from Western industrialized nations."[75] In the renderings accompanying the proposal, the components of systems building are seen in perhaps their only truly native soil: a perfectly managed, balanced world entirely subject to "principles from government and industry." As in a renaissance utopia, it is only in a celestial realm that man steps above the more complex realities of his own, multilayered nature.

Opposite: A rendering from the 1975 NASA Ames study "Space Settlements," showing modular building components deployed for residential use within the artificial gravity of a toroidal space station located at Lagrange point five between the Moon and Earth. Richard D. Johnson and Charles Holbrow, Eds. *Space Settlements; A Design Study* NASA SP-413 (Washington, DC: Scientific and Technical Information Office, National Aeronautics and Space Administration, 1977) 49

NOTES

1 "HHH on the Space Program," *Aerospace Technology*, vol. 21, no. 24 (May 20, 1968): 19. Excerpts from a speech given on May 7, 1968, at the Smithsonian Institution, Washington, D.C., on the awarding of the Robert J. Collier Trophy

2. See James E. Webb, *Space Age Management: The Large-Scale Approach*, McKinsey Foundation lecture series (New York: McGraw-Hill, 1969).

3. James E. Webb, NASA administrator, to E.F. Buryan, July 18, 1961, James E. Webb Papers, Harry S. Truman Library, Independence, MO.

4. James E. Webb, NASA administrator, memorandum for Mr. Stoller, April 23, 1962, Webb papers.

5. James E. Webb, NASA administrator, memorandum for Directors, NASA Field Centers, Western Operations Office and North Eastern Office, the Industrial Applications Program, September 19, 1962, Webb papers.

6. Wolfe Dael, "The Administration of NASA," *Science* 1968;163:753.

7. National Aeronautics and Space Administration, *Conference on Space, Science, and Urban Life* proceedings of a conference held at Oakland, California, March 28-30, 1963, supported by the Ford Foundation and the National Aeronautics and Space Administration in cooperation with the University of California and the City of Oakland (Washington, D.C., Office of Scientific and Technical Information, National Aeronautics and Space Administration, 1963), ix,

8. Ibid., 1.

9. A cogent analysis and context is provided by Jennifer Light, *From Warfare to Welfare: Defense Intellectuals and Urban Problems in Cold War America* (Baltimore: Johns Hopkins University Press, 2003), 111-112. See also R. Launius, "Managing the Unmanageable: Apollo, Space Age Management and American Social Problems," *Space Policy* 24 (2008), 158–165.

10. See Nathan S. Kline, and Manfred Clynes, "Drugs, Space, and Cybernetics: Evolution to Cyborgs" Symposium on psychophysiological aspects of space flight, and Bernard E. Flaherty. *Psychophysiological Aspects of Space Flight* (New York: Columbia University Press, 1961).

11. Norbert Weiner, Karl Deutsch, and Giorgio di Santillana "The Planners Evaluate Their Plan," analysis of the "Weiner defense plan for cities," *Life* vol. 29, no. 25, December 18, 1950, 85

12. See Jennifer Light, *From Warfare to Welfare*, chapter 3, "Cybernetics and Urban Renewal," and Peter Galison, "War against the Center," in Antoine Picon, and Alessandra Ponte, eds. *Architecture and the Sciences: Exchanging Metaphors.* Princeton Papers on Architecture, 4. (New York, N.Y.: Princeton Architectural Press, 2003.)

13. Light, *From Warfare to Welfare.*

14. Richard Meier, *A Communications Theory of Urban Growth* (Cambridge, MA: Joint Center for Urban Studies, 1962). At the time, Meier was a nuclear chemist-turned-planner based at the Harvard-MIT Joint Center for Urban Studies; he later moved to UC Berkeley's College of Environmental Design. Leland M. Swanson and Glenn O. Johnson, The Cybernetic Approach to Urban Analysis (Los Angeles: University of Southern California 1964), 10.

15. Such as Robert Levine and Thomas Schelling

16. Jay W. Forrester, *Urban Dynamics* (Cambridge: MIT Press, 1969).

17. Ibid., x.

18. *AD*, November 1971.

19. U.S. Department of Housing and Urban Development, *Science and the City* (Washington, DC: U.S. Government Printing Office, 1967).

20. Lyndon B. Johnson, Special Message accompanying the Demonstration Cities and Metropolitan Development Act of 1966, http://www.presidency.ucsb.edu/ws/index.php?pid=27682 accessed December 12, 2009

21. Cited in Jennifer S. Light, *From Warfare to Welfare*, 119. Senator Nelson's full remarks appear in *Congressional Quarterly*, October 18, 1965. He would go on to be the sponsor of the legislation instituting Earth Day.

22. U.S. Department of Housing and Urban Development (1967), *Science and the City*, 8.

23. Arthur Naftalin and Richard W. Gable, Aerospace Orientation Program, University of California, *Adapting Professional Manpower from Aerospace to Urban Government: Project Syllabus*, California, August 6   September 3, 1971.

24. William L. C. Wheaton, Warren W. Jones, and Warren H. Fox. *Adapting Professional Manpower from Aerospace to Urban Government: Final Report, Aerospace Orientation Program.* (Springfield, VA: National Technical Information Service, 1972). See also Light, Jennifer, *From Warfare to Welfare*, 121.

25. General Bernard A. Schreiver (ret), "Rebuilding Our Cities for People," transcript of remarks given at the Conference on the Urban Challenge, June 19–21, Warrenton, Virginia, *Air Force and Space Digest*, 51: 8, August 1968, 64.

26. "The Bird and the Watcher" *Time*, April 1, 1957.

27. Schreiver, *Rebuilding Our Cities for People*, 66

28. U.S. Department of Housing and Urban Development, *Science and the City*, 8.

29. Finger was invited to choose between this position and one equivalent to his administrative role at NASA. Harold Finger, interview with the author, January 11, 2010.

30. NASA oral history interview with Harold Finger, p. 61.

31. This 1954 installation placed a 1,000-kilowatt nuclear reactor and a massive, lead-lined crew compartment in a B-36 airframe. The compartment had lead and rubber walls several feet thick, and pilots gazed through foot-thick yellow protective glass. The light from this glass gave a sickly cast to the standard gray interior of the plane, which was painted lavender to compensate. See Dennis R. Jenkins, *Convair B-36 "Peacemaker,"* Warbird Tech Series, no. 24 (North Branch, MN: Specialty Press, 1999).

32. Harold Finger, interview, also Frederick Ordway III, interview with the author, June 15, 2006. Ordway, former assistant to Werner Von Braun at NASA's Marshall Spaceflight Center, was hired as an assistant to Kubrick on the production.

33. Ibid., 62

34. Promotional material, Operation Breakthrough, National Archives Record Group 207-HUD-MPF, Still Pictures and Photograph Collection, National Archives at College Park, College Park, MD.

35. For an extended discussion of this theme, see Colin Davies, *The Prefabricated Home* (London: Reaktion Books, 2005). Davies briefly discusses Operation Breakthrough on pages 82-83

36. See, for example, *Architectural Design*, November 1971, special issue on "systems approach to building" edited by Building Systems Design, Inc.

37. *The Impact of Social and Technical Change in Building: A Report to the National Bureau of Standards, the Institute for Applied Technology.* Washington, DC: Building Systems Development, Inc., August 1, 1967.

38. Harold Finger, NASA History Office/JSC Interview, 62. Aiming to preserve good relations, Finger favored military and aerospace personnel in staffing over his former colleagues at NASA. Harold Finger author interview.

39. Ibid.

40. U.S. Department of Housing and Urban Development *Operation Breakthrough… Now* (Washington, DC: U.S .Government Printing Office, 1974).

41. See Llwelyn-Davies Associates, *Operation Breakthrough: An Evaluation Framework for Site Planning* (New York: Llwelyn-Davies Associates, 1970).

42. William B. Harris, "Litton Shoots for the Moon," *Fortune* April 1958, 114-119, #206, #208, #210, #212.

43. Daniel Seligman and T.A. Wise, interview with Litton Industries President Roy Ash and Senior Vice President Harry Gray, "How Litton Keeps It Up, the View from Inside," *Fortune*, September 1966, 152-153, 180-182.

44. "Councilmen Ask Changes in Hiring of Consultants" *New York Times*, October 29, 1970, 1.

45. "The Men Who Tell City, How to Run the City" *New York Times*, July 8, 1970, 40.

46. "Garelik Calls RAND Study Of City's Police a Failure" *New York Times*, October 7, 1970, 55.

47. Light, *From Warfare to Welfare*, 121.

48. Paul Dickson. *Think Tanks* (New York: Atheneum, 1971), 216.

49. See Leland M. Swanson and Glenn O. Johnson, *The Cybernetic Approach to Urban Analysis* (Los Angeles: University of Southern California 1964).

50. Light, *From Warfare to Welfare*, 121.

51. On the unacknowledged military-industrial history of Geographic Information Systems, or GIS, see Neil Smith, "History and Philosophy of Geography: Real wars, Theory Wars," *Progress in Human Geography*, 1992: 16; 257.

52. Harold Finger, interview with author.

53. *Operation Breakthrough: Lessons Learned About Demonstrating New Technology, Department of Housing and Urban Development, Department of Commerce: Report to the Congress* (Washington, DC: U.S. General Accounting Office, 1976), 25.

54. HUD, *Operation Breakthrough... Now*, 1974, 2.

55. Jack Preston Overman, Terry G. Statt, and David A. Kolman, *Operation Breakthrough: Site Waste Management Systems and Pneumatic Trash Collection*, utilities demonstration series, vol. 4 (Cincinnati, OH: Environmental Protection Agency, Office of Research and Development [Office of Energy, Minerals, and Industry], Municipal Environmental Research Laboratory, 1978).56. United States, *Operation Breakthrough: Lessons Learned*, ii.

56. *Operation Breakthrough: Lessons Learned*, ii.

57. Ibid., 23.

58. The CATIA aerospace design system, manufactured by French Aerospace giant Dassault, was first used by architect Frank Gehry in the late 1980s, its use, and its derivatives, have spread widely, William J. Mitchell, See "A Tale of Two Cities: Architecture and the Digital Revolution," *Science*, 285, 5429 (August 6, 1999), 839-841.

59. "Litton's Shattered Image," *Forbes*, December 1, 1969, 26.

60. *Wall Street Journal*, January 29, 1968, 25.

61. "Litton's Shattered Image."

62. "Nixon to Seek Restructured Government," *Washington Post*, January 22, 1971, A1.

63. "Shake-Up for the Team," *New York Times*, December 3, 1972, E1.

64. Jane Jacobs, *The Death and Life of Great American Cities* (New York: Vintage, 1961), 428-447.

65. Warren Weaver, "A Quarter-Century in the Natural Sciences," *Annual report*. (New York: Rockefeller Foundation, 1958), 1-91. See section 1, "Science and Complexity."

66. U.S. Department of Housing and Urban Development, *Science and the City*, "A Quarter-Century in the Natural Sciences."

67. Weaver, "A Quarter-Century in the Natural Sciences," 9.

68. Jacobs, *The Death and Life of Great American Cities,* 433.

69. Weaver, "A Quarter-Century in the Natural Sciences." 37.

70. See, for example, *US News & World Report*, Special Report on Craig Venter, "The Blueprint of Life" (October 31, 2005).

71. Marc Kirschner and John Gerhart, "Evolvability," in *Proceedings of the National Academy of Sciences of the United States of America*, vol. 95 (July 1998): 8, #420–27.

72. J. de Visser, G.M. Argan, et al., "Perspective: Evolution and Detection of Genetic Robustness," *Evolution: International Journal of Organic Evolution*, vol. 57, no. 9 (September 2003): 1959.

73. See Joram Piatigorsky, *Gene Sharing and Evolution: The Diversity of Protein Functions.* (Cambridge, MA: Harvard University Press, 2007).

74. Richard D. Johnson and Charles Holbrow, eds., *Space Settlements: A Design Study*, NASA SP-413 (Washington, DC: Scientific and Technical Information Office, National Aeronautics and Space Administration, 1977), 49.

75. Ibid., 51.

Shared HUD/DOD computing facilities, deployed for site-planning and system analysis during Operation Breakthrough. Image 207_MPF-199-22, Record Group 207, National Archives at College Park, College Park, MD

STUART ELDEN IS A PROFESSOR OF POLITICAL GEOGRAPHY AT DURHAM UNIVERSITY IN THE UK. HE IS THE AUTHOR OF, MOST RECENTLY, *SPEAKING AGAINST NUMBER: HEIDEGGER, LANGUAGE, AND THE POLITICS OF CALCULATION AND TERROR AND TERRITORY: THE SPATIAL EXTENT OF SOVEREIGNTY.* HE IS CURRENTLY COMPLETING A HISTORY OF THE CONCEPT OF TERRITORY.

THE SPACE OF THE WORLD

Globalization remains a significant research topic across the social sciences and humanities. Yet despite attention within geography, a coherent analysis of the relation between globalization, space, and territory remains lacking. At the same time, philosophers have attempted to think the notion of the world, particularly in terms of it being something that precedes the extension of economic, political, and cultural phenomena across the globe. These philosophical accounts, however, have often remained frustratingly detached from the global forces actively reshaping the world, its constituent states and territories. Where philosophical ideas have been employed in analysis, this has often been at the expense of sufficient nuance. One example would be the widespread adoption of the term "deterritorialization" to describe globalization, when at most what is being observed is a remaking of spatial relations. Continuities between the state-territorial modern world and globalization cannot be properly conceived because the conditions that made both possible are poorly understood.

This essay is the outline of a project that seeks to bridge these divergent literatures to undertake a philosophical investigation of the relation between territory and globalization. It is conceived as the third part of an informal "trilogy" of books on different aspects of the question of territory. The first part was an investigation of the question of territory in relation to the "war on terror": *Terror and Territory: The Spatial Extent of Sovereignty*.[1] The second, nearly complete, offers a broad-scale history of the concept of territory in Western thought under the working title of *The Birth of Territory*. The first is the political book; the second is the historical one. The book I will outline here is the philosophical study, which will interrogate the space of the world.

The Space of World orientates itself around a range of debates and thinkers within the European tradition of philosophy and political theory. The key authors that will be analyzed are Eugen Fink, Kostas Axelos, Henri Lefebvre, Jean-Luc Nancy, Alain Badiou, Quentin Meillassoux, and Peter Sloterdijk. While Fink and Axelos have had some work translated in the past; they largely remain to be discovered in English-speaking scholarship. The central works are Fink's *Spiel als Weltsymbol* and Axelos's *Le jeu du monde*, which are untapped philosophical resources for thinking about the world, and the process of *mondialisation*, becoming-world.[2] Axelos rightly contends that that globalization is a kind of *mondialisation* without the world.[3] Lefebvre advances many of their ideas in a more explicitly political analysis.[4] Jean-Luc Nancy's important work has raised some key issues in such an account of the creation of the world.[5] Badiou is now a major figure in translation, with his *Logics of Worlds* translated in 2009 and his ex-student Meillassoux's book *After Finitude* the year before.[6] As yet the majority of scholarship on their work, especially within geography, has been overwhelming positive, not recognizing the problems of their mathematical ontology.[7] Sloterdijk is the subject of an extensive and ongoing program of translation, including his three-volume masterwork *Sphären*, forthcoming with Semiotext(e).[8] He has also been the focus of some critical attention.[9]

Key questions to be investigated include asking how the world became an object of thought. How was this related to its becoming an object of practice? What potential is there for rethinking the way the world is constructed without simply falling into mechanistic, technocratic ways of rendering? To think the world of globalization forces us to realize that this is not a transcending of spatial or territorial problems, but rather their reconfiguration. Territory – understood as the political corollary of calculative space, as a political technology – offers us insight into the world scale or the notion of the worldwide. In Lefebvre's terms, *l'échelle mondiale* is not the same as *le niveau globale*, the world scale is distinct from the global or general level. The process of globalization is an acceleration of the understanding of space and time as coordinates on a three- and four-dimensional grid. The determination of space and time as calculative, and extension as the primary characteristic of material nature, is to make it amenable to science through geometry and measure more generally. A difference of degree rather than an ontological transformation is thus the way to grasp the spatiality of globalization.

The planned book proceeds not through a thematic approach – globalization of politics, of economy, of culture – nor through thinker-based chapters, but is led by problematics. Taking up questions or issues – violence, fossils, earth, wound, volume, and play – it intends to raise a wide range of philosophical, political, and historical issues about how we think of the world, the globe, and beyond. It enables a thinking of such diverse themes as religion, relation, ecology, disasters and crises, the air and the subsoil, the pragmatic and the poetic. How do philosophical resources help to make sense of the global forces reshaping the world?

VIOLENCE

How does violence relate to the world? Does it make sense to speak of a violent world or a world of violence? Is the violence a process directed toward the world, or the things that constitute it, or is violence inherent in the world or particular ways of grasping the world? Is the world itself violent? Is the violence to be understood in terms of brute force or some other degree? How does violence work in different ways at different scales or levels?

Max Weber famously defined the state as "that human community, which within a certain area or territory [Gebietes] – this 'area' belongs to the feature – has a (successful) monopoly of legitimate physical violence."[10] Yet violence is not simply a possession of the state, something that it exercises, but one of its conditions of possibility. The modern state requires a whole range of calculative, abstracting techniques that are shot through with violence. This is no more so than in the question of its territory, where creating a bounded space is already a violent act of exclusion and inclusion; maintaining it as such requires constant vigilance and the mobilization of threat; and challenging it necessarily entails a transgression.

As Henri Lefebvre described it, sovereignty implies "a space against which violence, whether latent or overt, is directed – a space established and constituted by violence." Yet Lefebvre argues that this is also found in its enthroning of "a specific rationality, that of accumulation, that of the bureaucracy and the army – a unitary, logistical, operational and quantifying rationality which would make economic growth possible and draw strength from that growth for its own expansion to a point where it would take possession of the entire planet."[11]

It is that relation between this specific rationality, its violence, and the things it makes possible that I want to explore under this theme. To what extent is the notion of the world itself a category of violence, before any mere extension of political, cultural, and economic phenomena across the surface of the globe? How does this help us to think the notion of the world, as something comprising, but clearly exceeding, the states into which it is divided? Are there ways of thinking of the world as something other than as scarred through violence, divided and partitioned? Should we understand the global system of capitalism, trade, and finance as itself violent?[12]

FOSSILS

Next I want to take the problem of fossils as a means of thinking through two questions: religion and relation. First, I want to investigate ways in which the discovery of fossils forced a realization that the world was much older than previously thought, and that the biblical account of Genesis could not be literally true. Or did God plant fossils to provoke man into heresy? This provides an opportunity to consider global religions.

The more substantive part of the chapter takes up the challenge posed by Quentin Meillassoux in his book After Finitude. Post-Kantian philosophy has based itself, in large part, on the question of the relation between human and world: not simply that what we know about the world is always filtered through our experience of it; but that what we experience of the world is subject to the way we experience it. The world is as it is for us. Meillassoux articulates a radical problem with this: how to understand the problem of the *arche*-fossil, those radioactive traces that predate any life on the earth, but not its existence. Correlationism is described as the thesis that things we observe are dependent on the observer in some way, or, more fundamentally, that humans and the world coexist. There is a necessary correlation between what is observed and that which observes. Correlationism is flawed, Meillassoux suggests, because *arche*-fossils show that there is a world of which we can have objective knowledge without there being any mediation between the knowledge and the observer, except at a several-million-year interval. While the explicit dating is meditated, the existence of these phenomena is not. Meillassoux suggests that correlationism, in all its variants, is a convenient way of avoiding having to account for the world as it is, prior to human access.

Meillassoux is problematic because he ends up returning to a mathematical foundation for the ontology of the world – based in large part on the work of Alain Badiou. But the question he asks poses a fundamental challenge to phenomenological and poststructuralist accounts of the world and its relation. His work has been linked to the "speculative realism" movement that includes thinkers like Graham Harman and Ray Brassier.[13] The return of realism, of objects and encounters that can be understood aside from the human experience or mediation of them, raises fundamental issues in terms of our sense of the world.

EARTH

How is the Earth divided, reformulated, fractured, and ruined? Under this theme I want to understand the question of its environment, and political orderings. I first look at the book published in 1950 by the fascist jurist Carl Schmitt, *The Nomos of the Earth*.[14] Drawing on the Ancient Greek meaning, Schmitt suggests that *nomos* means both a law and a division, arguing that "*Nomos* is the measure by which the ground and soil of the earth [*Grund und Boden der Erde*] in a particular order is divided and situated; it is also the form of political, social, and religious order determined by this process. Here, measure, order, and form constitute a spatially concrete unity."[15] Schmitt contends that it was only with the explorations of the late fifteenth century that the earth as a globe actually became tangible. Of course, even the Ancient Greeks knew the earth was a sphere, but it was not demonstrably shown through circumnavigation until Magellan's voyage of the early sixteenth century. Schmitt argues that "the new global image [*globale Raumbild*] required a new global spatial order," an order of the earth-as-ball [*Erdenballes*].[16]

If Schmitt's own ideas are indelibly stained with their political associations,[17] a number of thinkers coming in his wake have sought to understand these issues. These include Giorgio Agamben, Michael Hardt, and Antonio Negri. I investigate Agamben through the category of life and work on animals, which shows how important it is to realize that in life on Earth, in a populated world, humans are a tiny minority. Agamben problematically understands a fundamental division between the Greek terms of *zoe* and *bios*, which he then sees as rendered separate when humans are reduced to animality, to bare, or naked, life.[18] Rather than follow Hardt and Negri's call for an understanding of empire, a newly radical multitude or a resurgent commonwealth,[19] I want to go back to their other key inspiration, Gilles Deleuze and Félix Guattari. The relation between deterritorialization and reterritorialization, especially as outlined in their book *A Thousand Plateaux*, requires much more careful investigation if we are to use it to understand a new world Imperium.[20] *En passant*, the question of the earth allows the examination of a number of related questions, including environmental security, and the almost inconceivably major challenge of climate change.

WOUND

In one of his seminars on Freud, Jacques Lacan declared, "there is something originally, initially, profoundly wounded in the human relation to the world."[21] How should we react to global events, to local occurrences that through the media appear to the world, or genuinely huge ones such as the Boxing Day Tsunami? How was the financial crisis from 2007 to 2009 produced as global? What about global health crises, pandemics of contagion? Rather than the overused notions of terror, fear, or tragedy, here I want to think about the notion of the wound through horror, and the horrific.[22] Faced with the void, a tear in the fabric of the world, what is our sensibility, our attunement? Although there have been some interesting philosophical studies of horror, notably Julia Kristeva and Noël Carroll,[23] to explore these issues I will turn to the recent reengagement with the early twentieth-century writer H.P. Lovecraft.[24] Lovecraft's writings have received attention both within geography and philosophy, notably the issue of the journal *Collapse* on "Concept Horror,"[25] Lovecraft is an unpleasant writer – misogynist, racist, and deeply conservative – and his style of writing is often execrable. But he is interesting for a number of reasons. He discards ghosts, witches, and other stereotypes of horror, and instead puts humans as minor figures in a horrific world and universe.

Rather than the pale imitations of his style that can be found in countless writers, I want also to examine the contemporary writer who arguably shares more of his sensibility, China Miéville. Miéville offers alternative visions, other worlds. Two of his novels are particularly relevant here. In *The Scar*, the city is a flotilla of ships, a world that is detached and mobile, that has lost its bearings. In *The City and the City*, the place is one that folds back and over the other, where occupants of each occupy the same space, but different places, and where transgression is known as breach.[26] Miéville's work helps us to grasp what is so profoundly unsettling about horror, a sense that our connection to the world is ruptured, that space is out of joint. The concept of wound is interesting for other reasons, because the Greek for wound is *trauma*, and, as is well known, the German word *Der Traum* means dream. The closing part of this theme would look at the interesting work in international relations on the question of memory, wounds, and trauma, focusing on the book-length studies of Jenny Edkins and Maja Zehfuss.[27]

VOLUME

We all too often think of the spaces of geography as areas, not volumes. Territories are bordered, divided, and demarcated, but not understood in terms of height and depth. There are exceptions of course – Matthew Gandy's *Concrete and Clay* on the subterranean spaces of New York City, or Peter Sloterdijk's *Terror from the Air*, for which the original title is *Luftbeben*, "Airquake."[28] Such concerns are magnified in his major book *Sphären*. Similarly the Israeli architect Eyal Weizmann has shown how we must grasp the fractured spaces of the West Bank as three-dimensional, with tunnels, bridges, hilltops, and airspace as much as land, terrain, and walls.[29] There have also been a couple of recent books by geographers on the government of the air.[30]

In his philosophical theory of globalization, Sloterdijk offers a way of conceiving it in three registers, three epochs. The first was metaphysical globalization that can be traced back to Greek ontology; the second was the terrestrial, the globalization of imperialism and commercial trade routes, of Europe's conquest of the new world for markets and resources. It is the third that now needs to be investigated − what he calls the globalization of saturation, where technology and capitalism lead to the collapse of temporality into simultaneity, distance into proximity.[31]

How do questions of height change how we understand the space of the world? What happens if we think of the vertical as much as the horizontal? How does this work with the ideas of globalization that Sloterdijk investigates? Examples from below include resources of the subsoil, infrastructure projects, and tunnels. From above would include the importance of aerial photography in archaeology, surveillance and bombing in warfare, satellite images, and Google Earth. The world does not just exist as a surface; space is volumetric.

PLAY

In distinction to globalization, *mondialisation* can be understood as a process of becoming, a "becoming worldwide." The world needs to be understood as a whole, but as a whole made up of fragments, an event in thought. In thinking this process, this becoming, Axelos regularly cites the comment from Marx's doctoral thesis that suggests that "the world's becoming philosophical is at the same time philosophy's becoming worldly, that its realization is at the same time its loss."[32] In its becoming worldwide, that is, in its actualization or realization, philosophy is transcended and overcome. If Marx forms one end of the tradition drawn upon here, a fragment of Heraclitus forms the other. This is the fragment, which states that eternity, or time, *aion*, standing as a cipher for the world, is "like a child playing a game."[33] How then can the world be understood as deploying itself as a game, a *jeu*? *Le jeu du monde* can be translated as "the game of the world" or as "the play of the world." Axelos works with these and other meanings to show how the world can be understood only on its own terms, or in terms of its own rules, rather than on the basis of anything exterior to it. It is a question of internal relations and interplay. The making-worldly of phenomena through a logic implicit only to itself, and the claim that the world can be understood only through this continual process of becoming, is particularly brought into modern thought by Heidegger's suggestion that "world never is, but worlds."[34] Play is a cosmic symbol and a symbol of the cosmos. The play of the world is between the fragment and the whole.

All too often globalization is understood as a political or economic process, most discussion of which fails to comprehend the world or the globe over which this is extended. This is the case in both material and philosophical senses. Globalization does not refer the end of geography, but rather to its reconfiguration within existing terms. Territory continues into the worldwide. In Leibniz we find the claim that "*cum Deus calculat… fit mundus*"; "as God calculates, the world comes to be."[35] Heidegger's retranslation is that "as God plays, world comes to be."[36] The challenge is one of rethinking the way the world is constructed that does not simply fall into mechanistic, technocratic ways of rendering it as a whole, an object for thought and practice.

NOTES

1. Stuart Elden, *Terror and Territory: The Spatial Extent of Sovereignty* (Minneapolis: University of Minnesota Press 2009).

2. Eugen Fink, *Spiel als Weltsymbol* (Stuttgart: Kohlhammer 1960); Kostas Axelos, Le jeu du monde (Paris: Les Éditions de Minuit 1969).

3. Kostas Axelos, "*Mondialisation* without the World: Interviewed by Stuart Elden," *Radical Philosophy*, no. 130, 2005, 25-28.

4. Henri Lefebvre, De l'État (Paris: UGE, four volumes 1976-78); *State, Space, World: Selected Essays*, edited by Neil Brenner and Stuart Elden

(Minneapolis: University of Minnesota Press, 2009).

5. Jean-Luc Nancy, *La création du monde ou la mondialisation* (Paris: Galilée 2002).

6. Alain Badiou, *Logics of Worlds: Being and Event II*, translated by Alberto Toscano (London: Continuum 2009); Quentin Meillassoux, *After Finitude: An Essay on the Necessity of Contingency*, translated by Ray Brassier (London: Continuum 2008).

7. See, for example, J.D. Dewsbury, "Unthinking Subjects: Alain Badiou and the Event of Thought in Thinking Politics," *Transactions of the Institute*

of British Geographers, vol. 32, no. 4, 2007, 443-459; Ian Graham Ronald Shaw, "Sites, Truths and the Logics of Worlds: Alain Badiou and Human Geography," *Transactions of the Institute of British Geographers*, online advance publication, 2010. For a partial critique, see Stuart Elden, "Dialectics and the Measure of the World", *Environment and Planning A*, vol. 40, no. 11, 2008, 2641-2651.

8. Peter Sloterdijk, *Sphären* (Frankfurt: Suhrkamp, three volumes 1998-2004).

9. Sjoerd van Tuinen, ed., "Special Issue on Peter Sloterdijk," *Cultural Politics* vol. 3 no. 3, 2007; Stuart Elden, Eduardo Mendieta and Nigel

Thrift (eds.), "The Worlds of Peter Sloterdijk", *Environment and Planning D: Society and Space*, Vol. 27 no. 1, 2009; Stuart Elden (ed.), *Sloterdijk Now* (Cambridge: Polity, 2011).

10. Max Weber, "Politik als Beruf," in Gesammelte *Politische Schriften* (Tübingen: Mohr 1971), 510-511.

11. Henri Lefebvre, *The Production of Space*, translated by Donald Nicolson-Smith (Oxford: Blackwell 1991), 280.

12. See Slavok Žižek, *First as Tragedy, Then as Farce* (London: Verso 2009); and Christian Marazzi, *The Violence of Financial Capitalism*, translated by Kristina Lebedeva (New York: Semiotext(e) 2010).

13. Graham Harman, *Tool-Being: Heidegger and the Metaphysics of Objects* (Chicago: Open Court 2002); *Guerrilla Metaphysics: Phenomenology and the Carpentry of Things* (Chicago: Open Court 2005); Ray Brassier, *Nihil Unbound: Enlightenment and Extinction* (London: Palgrave 2007).

14. Carl Schmitt, *The Nomos of the Earth in the International Law of the Jus Publicum*, translated by G.L. Ulmen (New York: Telos Press 2003).

15. Ibid., 70, translation modified.

16. Ibid., 86, translation modified.

17. See Stuart Elden, "Reading Schmitt Geopolitically: Nomos, Territory and Großraum," *Radical Philosophy*, no. 161, May/June 2010, 18-26.

18. Giorgio Agamben, *Homo Sacer: Sovereign Power and Bare Life*, translated by Daniel Heller-Roazen (Stanford: Stanford University Press 1998); *The Open: Man and Animal*, translated by Kevin Attell (Stanford: Stanford University Press 2004).

19. Michael Hardt and Antonio Negri, *Empire* (Cambridge: Harvard University Press 2000); *Multitude: War and Democracy in the Age of Empire* (New York: Penguin Press 2004); Commonwealth (Cambridge: Harvard University Press 2009).

20. Gilles Deleuze and Félix Guattari, *A Thousand Plateaus: Capitalism and Schizophrenia*, translated by Brian Massumi (London: Athlone 1988).

21. Jacques Lacan, *The Ego in Freud's Theory and in the Technique of Psychoanalysis 1954-1955*, edited by Jacques-Alain Miller (New York: Norton 1988), 167.

22. See also Adriana Cavarero, *Horrorism: Naming Contemporary Violence* (New York: Columbia University Press 2008).

23. Julia Kristeva, *Powers of Horror: An Essay on Abjection*, translated by Leon S. Roudiez (New York: Columbia University Press 1982); Noël Carroll, The Philosophy of Horror or Paradoxes of the Heart (New York: Routledge 1990).

24. There are multiple editions of his books. See, for example, H.P. Lovecraft, *The Call of Cthulhu and Other Weird Stories*, edited by S.T. Joshi (London: Penguin 2002).

25. "Concept Horror," edited by Robin Mackay and Damian Veal, *Collapse*, vol. IV, 2008; James Kneale, "From Beyond: H.P. Lovecraft and the Place of Horror", *Cultural Geographies*, vol. 13, 2006, 106-126. See also Reza Negarestani, *Cyclonopedia: Complicity with Anonymous Materials* (Melbourne: re.press 2008).

26. China Miéville, *The Scar* (London: Pan Macmillan, 2002); *The City and the City* (London: Pan Macmillan, 2009). The latter is a more successful treatment of the idea of parallel cities than his earlier *Un Lun Dun* (London: Pan Macmillan, 2007).

27. Jenny Edkins, *Trauma and the Memory of Politics* (Cambridge: Cambridge University Press 2003); Maja Zehfuss, *Wounds of Memory: The Politics of War in Germany* (Cambridge: Cambridge University Press, 2007).

28. Matthew Gandy, *Concrete and Clay: Reworking Nature in New York City* (Cambridge: MIT Press, 2002); Peter Sloterdijk, Luftbeben: An den Quellen des Terrors, (Frankfurt: Suhrkamp, 2002); *Terror from the Air*, translated by Amy Patton and Steve Corcoran (New York: Semiotext(e), 2009).

29. Eyal Weizmann, *Hollow Land: Israel's Architecture of Occupation* (London: Verso, 2007).

30. Mark Whitehead, *State, Science and the Skies: Environmental Governmentality and the British Atmosphere* (Oxford: Wiley-Blackwell, 2009); Peter Adey, *Aerial Life: Spaces, Mobilities, Affects* (Oxford: Wiley-Blackwell, 2010).

31. As well as Sphären, see also *Im Weltinnenraum des Kapitals: Für eine philosophische Theorie der Globalisierung* (Frankfurt: Suhrkamp, 2005).

32. Karl Marx, *Writings of the Young Marx on Philosophy and Society*, edited by Loyd D. Easton and Kurt H. Guddat (New York: Doubleday, 1967), 62.

33. Hermann Diels, *Die Fragmente der Vorsokratiker: Griechisch und deutsch*, edited by Walther Kranz (Berlin: Weidmann, 6th edition, 1952), 162, fragment 52.

34. Martin Heidegger, *Wegmarken, Gesamtausgabe Band 9* (Frankfurt: Vittorio Klostermann, 1976), 164.

35. Gottfried Leibniz, *Die Philosophischen Schriften von Gottfried Wilhelm Leibniz*, edited by C.J. Gerhardt, Seven Volumes, Hildesheim: Georg Olms, 1961, vol VII, 191 n.

36. Martin Heidegger, *Der Satz vom Grund, Gesamtausgabe Band 10* (Frankfurt: Vittorio Klostermann, 1997), 167.

MARC ANGELIL IS A PROFESSOR AND DEAN AT THE DEPARTMENT OF ARCHITECTURE OF THE ETH ZURICH. HIS RESEARCH AT THE INSTITUTE OF URBAN DESIGN OF THE NETWORK CITY AND LANDSCAPE (NSL) ADDRESSES DEVELOPMENTS OF LARGE METROPOLITAN REGIONS. HE IS THE AUTHOR OF SEVERAL BOOKS, INCLUDING *DEVIATIONS* ON METHODS OF TEACHING AND *INDIZIEN* ON THE POLITICAL ECONOMY OF CONTEMPORARY URBAN TERRITORIES. HE IS A BOARD MEMBER OF THE HOLCIM FOUNDATION FOR SUSTAINABLE CONSTRUCTION.

CARY SIRESS IS AN ARCHITECT AND A TENURED FACULTY MEMBER IN ARCHITECTURE AND THEORY AT THE SCHOOL OF ARTS, CULTURE, AND ENVIRONMENT OF THE UNIVERSITY OF EDINBURGH AND VISITING PROFESSOR AT THE SCHOOL OF ARCHITECTURE AT THE UNIVERSITY OF NANJING IN CHINA. HE IS THE FOUNDING EDITOR OF THE NEW JOURNAL *ARCHITECTURE &*. FOLLOWING HIS GRADUATE STUDIES AT COLUMBIA UNIVERSITY IN NEW YORK, HE WAS INVOLVED IN TEACHING AND RESEARCH AT THE ETH ZURICH, WHERE HE COMPLETED HIS PH.D.

DISCOUNTING TERRITORY

LOGISTICS AS CAPITAL PRINCIPLE OF SPATIAL PRACTICES

Wal-Mart Supercenter on Karl-Marx-Strasse in Berlin, 2006 (Photograph Jesse LeCavalier)

Wal-Mart Supercenter interior view, Berlin, 2006 (Photograph Jesse LeCavalier)

Promotional map entitled "Wal-Mart Around the World" in both English and Chinese used by Wal-Mart Inc. in 2003

It never stops.
– Rollin L. Ford, 2006[1]

Imagine strolling down Karl-Marx-Strasse in Berlin on a shopping spree. After passing common names such as C&A, Hennes & Mauritz, and Woolworth, one arrives at the budget end of the strip dominated by a Wal-Mart Supercenter – an ostensibly firm anchor of commerce. A chance encounter of two giants – Marx and Wal-Mart – traces a diagram played out in real time on territory. Written here into the fabric of the city is a standoff between opposing ideologies: one promoting the unhindered spread of capital and the other recalling the historic call to arms for resisting capital exploitation.

But this clash is anything but obvious, for it is buried in the familiar trappings of consumption. We come up on a tangle of signs that are front stage to an otherwise unadorned box where banality prevails. Inside, the ubiquity of low prices serves to elevate cheapness to a higher level, never ceasing to remind customers of super deals available. Mass products are stacked in the cases in which they were delivered, underscoring the no-frills attitude that pervades the store. Though relaxed in appearance, the scene is underwritten by a formula casting utility as program. Control and the principle of cost-cutting marketeering are key to this blueprint that lays out an elaborate scheme linking low price to high profit as the Golden Rule. "High turnover and low overhead," goes the saying. With an efficient machinery perpetually running backstage, quantity is managed – the more, faster, and cheaper, the better.[2]

Such a business model remains unrivaled in its success, having reframed the worldwide flow of commodities and with it the modus operandi of the entire retail industry. The simple fact that one encounters Wal-Mart in Berlin is witness to the scale of the enterprise and the extent of its ambition. To drive the point home, a world map labeled in both English and Chinese is proudly exhibited in the company's headquarters in Bentonville, Arkansas, demonstrating to visitors the reach of the "Wal-Mart Effect," while clearly spelling out a politics of expansion. City by city, country by country, each conquest is displayed like a trophy in a case.[3] But national boundaries are nothing more than proverbial placeholders on a map used to plot the next move.

Other players in the game such as K-Mart and Target in the United States, or Aldi, Carrefour, and Metro in Europe, have followed suit in transcending those former geographies of politically bound place to span the globe in a new fluid market. In effect, a transnational landscape of corporate retail – one marked by dispersed regimes of logistics and supple distribution networks – is superimposed onto the more familiar mosaic map of nations. Hardly noticeable in their day-to-day functioning, the systems servicing this extensive retail web nevertheless leave their mark on the physiognomy of urban regions. Territory is reformatted in the process according to the placeless logic of hyper-rationalized movements of capital. In the venture of flexible accumulation, companies must remain agile in their response to changing market circumstances. As quickly as they move in, they might likewise move out. Take the case in Berlin; Wal-Mart has for now left the scene, as the situation did not work to the company's advantage. The company vacated the premises in 2006, discounting territory in its pursuit of strategic purpose elsewhere.[4]

War Logistics
Wal-Mart does not produce commodities *per se* but rather systems of distribution, including all the requisite administrative procedures for managing the global movement of goods. The attendant expertise to maintain such an overview is known within the industry as "logistics" and has by now gained the status of a full-fledged discipline. And here, the devil is in the detail. Whereas logistics circumscribes all aspects of corporate operations, from data compilation and analysis, planning, organization, implementation, and project steering to the control of flows of information, material, and commodities, it comes as no surprise that the term has its origin in the domain of military science.

Open any instruction manual devised to train the armed forces, and logistics is found alongside "strategy" and "tactic" as a central tenet of military engagement. "Victory is dependent upon the logistic problem," as stated in a textbook of the United States army, was published during the Vietnam War as to ensure the efficacy of that campaign.[5] Logistics, then as now, is the art of calculation, remaining vital to achieving supremacy with the most efficient means possible in any theater of operation.[6] For this reason, logistics has been appropriated by business in what amounts to a transfer of practice from state to the private sector, having become by now routine, if not a buzzword, for corporate management. And with the spread of a free-market ethos to all corners of the earth, this formula has likewise become omnipresent. Put bluntly, we are enmeshed in logistic networks. And given our current market-centered way of life, it would seem that "one never escapes the economy of war."[7]

In business lingo, logistics incorporate the six R's: right product, right time, right price, right place, right quantity, and right quality. This is the recipe for success, but one requiring discipline. Hence Wal-Mart's business structure is pervaded by military thinking, and by implication, all of its associated technologies. Not only is the company organized according to a strict hierarchy, with the command center in Bentonville administering all orders, but the firm also deploys the same reconnaissance measures, data management, and communication systems developed by the United States army both during and after the Cold War.

Even satellites make up part of Wal-Mart's strategic repertoire of information control. The Satellite Business Systems (SBS) – by Hughes Corporation, currently a subsidiary of the Defense, Space, and Security Division of Boeing – tracks all transactions across the globe. Rendered as a gadget suspended in space, the satellite is portrayed in all its innocence in promotional images to attract the interest of corporate customers. The image is telling, for it depicts the view from above as supreme in its territorial coverage. The all-seeing eye, performing as an essential relay in the steady stream of data flow, "handles more than one million customer transactions every hour, feeding databases estimated at more than 2.5 petabytes – the equivalent of 167 times the books in America's Library of Congress."[8] Given such an unrivalled vantage, the logistics industry constitutes invisible contours of power, while holding patent command over the edgeless geography of the global economy.

Back on the ground at the frontline – namely in the stores themselves where customers ultimately shop – the stock of available goods must be guaranteed. To this end, an efficiently functioning supply chain is required to link the place of production with that of consumption. It is here where Wal-Mart's contribution to the logistic revolution is most notable.[9] To maintain a strict economy between supply and demand, the principle known in the business as "just-in-time delivery" is implemented, whereby merchandise is produced only when needed. This in turn serves the "pull supply system" responding to demand with those commodities most desired. Eliminated in the process is the need for fixed storage of any sort. Instead, everything is on the move, with transportation performing as mobile warehouse. "It never stops," according to the head of the company's global information systems.

Aimed at reducing the degree of complexity within the overall system, logistics mandates methodically calibrated protocols that can be easily put into practice, summed up under the straightforward slogan "make it simple."[10] The tiers of management and company organization are scaled to a lean minimum, as is the assortment of products in the stores. Similarly, the standardization of all procedures aids the streamlining of the entire supply infrastructure as well as the electronic monitoring of goods. Last but not least, the operative axiom of Wal-Mart concerning simplicity at all cost extends to its facilities, whether Supercenter, distribution center, or data center.

Black Box

Different types of boxes are to be credited for the triumph of discount empires – from the cardboard box, to the shipping container, to the big box of buildings. In that all are standardized goes without saying, thus facilitating the most economic means of stacking, transporting, and displaying merchandise.

Starting with the cardboard box, contractually binding specifications for manufacturers are formulated in the most unambivalent terms. Box sizes are specified not only to consolidate packaging and thereby minimize space requirements but also to accommodate the norms of pallets, forklifts, conveyor belts, and robots. As the smallest unit in the system, boxes are comparable to pixels in the digital realm. Accordingly, goods must be tagged to be tracked. By now an industry standard, the Universal Product Code (UBC) is used for scanning goods both upon delivery and at point of purchase to close the loop of supply and demand.[11] Other technologies, some developed by the military, are being tested for large-scale application in the market. Wal-Mart, for example, is exploring the use of Radio Frequency Identification (RFID) to monitor every move of every box. Generally speaking, the very act of scanning and tracking sets off a chain reaction throughout the whole machinery, with satellite transponders communicating with supercomputers to relay a constantly updated overview of product activity. Automatic identification enables collection and analysis of information leading to a veritable geography of data. Maps are instantaneously drawn, then redrawn as soon as other parameters come in to profile shopping preferences, categorized by neighborhoods and regions. Mining data increases profits. Identifying patterns in this landscape of numbers, statistics, and

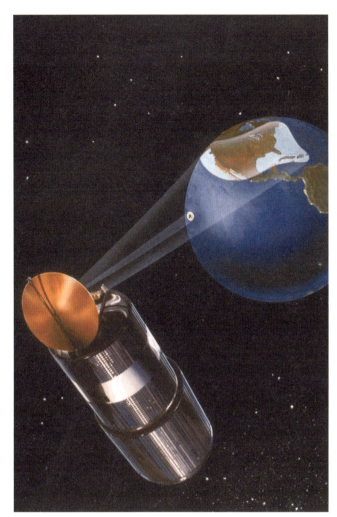

Rendering of Wal-Mart's communication satellite model SBS4 (from the Boeing corporate website)

Interior of Wal-Mart distribution center near Bentonville, Arkansas (promotional image from Wal-Mart)

graphs is key to the buildup of the specialized knowledge coveted by retailers to stay ahead. Even weather reports are factored into the equation as indicators of possible changes in consumer behavior.

Introduced in the 1960s, the next unit in the system catalyzed a transportation revolution. Nothing more than a simple metal box, the shipping container is characterized by some as the quintessential symbol of globalization, if not its core principle.[12] Yet containers did not appear overnight. The ur-scene of materials handling is marked by trial and error. A case in point is the pallet, which originated in the military. Promoted in the 1940s as "the war's secret weapon," the pallet made its way to the private sector when the concept was disseminated by the National Bureau of Standards in campaigns including trade magazines, newspapers, and educational films.[13] One movie in particular was called *Be Wise – Palletize*. Conceived as a means to reduce the amount of muscle needed to move merchandise, the pallet made possible the sheer volume of trade that has by now become worldwide fact. Down the line, shipping containers appeared amid debates about industry standards and appropriate dimensions for train, truck, and sea transport. This yielded the ISO-Norm for containers, which in turn determined the Twenty-Foot-Equivalent-Unit (TEU) capacity of freight vessels that specifies the maximum number of containers a ship can accommodate. Entire fleets and harbors had to be rebuilt in accordance with this standard. As with the cardboard boxes, this innovation transformed the way retail business was done. Here again, goods are tracked, but now in larger quantities. In one blow, the shipping container reduced the scale of the earth

CFO Jack Shewmaker pointing to map registering economic data on territory, *Wal-Mart Annual Report 1980*

Image entitled "This is a pallet!," from *Army Services Manual M703–4*, Washington D.C. 1943

Diagram of Yangshan Port container terminal, Shanghai 2007

and simultaneously increased that of the world economy.[14] And yet, with this new idea, cargo became more anonymous, an abstract thing hidden from view and only traceable with the proper scanning technology.[15]

The next scale up the chain is commonly referred to as "big box", a building type merging warehouse with store, and, like the cardboard box and shipping container, conceived as a standardized unit. As the name implies, bigness and simplicity rule. In the case of Wal-Mart, these buildings are under the purview of a Real Estate Division that employs hundreds of people with diverse expertise. Scattered throughout the landscape and surrounded by parking lots, the featureless facilities can cover an area of up to five acres. The company's entire fleet of buildings, including distribution centers, are determined by specification templates that spell out everything down to the last detail. Repeated *ad absurdum*, the same structure, the same cladding, the same fixtures are stamped out in succession, removing architecture from the equation to make way for pure enclosure. Only what has proven successful time and again to eliminate risk is integrated into Wal-Mart's blueprint. What you see is all you get. More to the point, what is interesting here is that the buildings' commonplace appearance serves to camouflage and, in effect, conceal the calculated intricacy of logistics machinery running nonstop. Not just cogs in the system, big boxes function as conduits for flows of information and commodities.[16]

Whether made of cardboard, metal, or any other material, the box is a principle that places a premium on performance rather than content. These units work analogously to what is known in the natural and behavioral sciences as a "black box", which designates any system or object understood solely in terms of input, output, and transfer capacity. What is here bracketed from view is the internal functioning of the box. Applied to the retail industry, this principle supports the prevalent bias in favor of opacity over transparency – *fiat nox* in place of *fiat lux* – that has ultimately become the operative program of discount retail. Companies vehemently protect their knowledge as classified intelligence in data centers guarded as one would a fortress. Whereas the Enlightenment might have promised the advance of lucidity, contemporary culture is no longer intelligible in these terms.[17] Quite the contrary, for we inhabit environments comprised of aggregated black boxes and characterized increasingly by stealth.

Real Estate

The public image portrayed by Wal-Mart is that of a conservative family business rooted in small-town values, epitomized by Sam Walton himself, who as company founder continues to serve as the firm's emblematic figurehead. His autobiography, *Sam Walton: Made in America*, is written in a plain, jovial style and sets down simple rules for running a successful enterprise. Especially revealing is his presentation of Wal-Mart's real estate strategy and its politics of spatial practice. With the motto "rolling out the formula," Walton explains his recipe for territorial expansion that rolls out store after store over the land.[18] The fact that the book has been translated into numerous languages, including Chinese, makes clear just how fertile the soil is for such a plan. Looking for potential new locations for stores, Walton examined urban patterns from the perspective of his private plane. Those areas not yet encroached upon by the city were of particular interest, as he was attempting to anticipate future corridors of growth. Instead of shopping for sites in the city, he headed out to the periphery, with no competition in sight. Basically, the agenda was to cover entire fringe regions with stores. "We saturated northwest Arkansas. We saturated Oklahoma. We saturated Missouri."[19]

Current practices have not strayed far from this original plan save for those updated by advances in data collection and communication technologies. After reconnaissance and only if a site is deemed worthy, a distribution center is planted deliberately near a highway intersection, guaranteeing the all-important connection for transport. Then the territory is peppered with branches within a circumference of several hundred miles. Conditions are negotiated with local municipalities and landowners to get the best deal on land prices, ensure tax incentives, and secure the provision of publicly funded infrastructure.

To eliminate competition, too many outlets are built, with the assumption of eventual attrition. Anything in the way is crushed. The first victims are usually the small shops in nearby towns, which cannot compete with the discount belt encircling them. Here territory is unmistakably discounted, resulting in what is often lamented in the press as "The Death of Main Street USA." The economic lifeblood of whole agglomerations is methodically sucked out in due course, and with it goes public space. Without question, the firm's objective is to establish an economic monopoly over a given region.

The next step is to remove those Wal-Mart stores that – according to the Darwinian "survival of the fittest" – do not yield the adequate quota of profit. What remains after the field

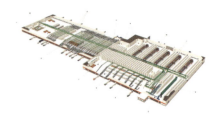

Illustration of a distribution center, "Supply Chain Management, Inc: System Overview," Dematic Corporation, 2008

Aerial photograph of Wal-Mart's distribution center in Alachua, Florida

Empty Wal-Mart Supercenter, Beaver Dam, Wisconsin (Photograph by Wilbur E. Selbrede)

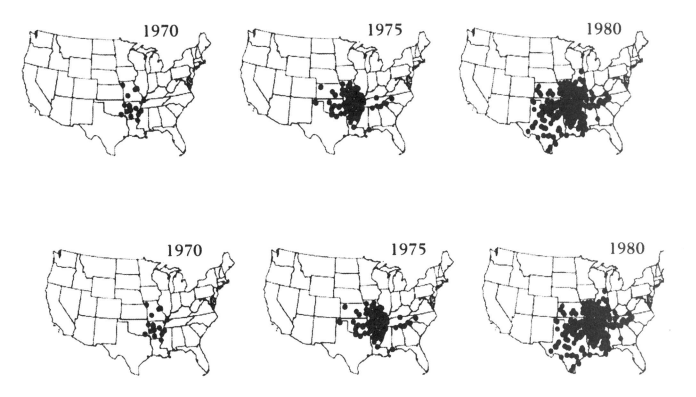

Map of Wal-Mart's territorial expansion from 1970 to 1995 by Emek Basker, University of Missouri

is selectively cleared are wastelands dotted with empty boxes, in turn giving rise to ghost towns on the edge of cities. It is clear that Wal-Mart's policy of cheap construction is also motivated by the fact that their stay is limited. Flexible accumulation engulfs not only the realm of commodity production and consumption but space itself.[20] This is the real state of real estate. Just as goods are mobile, locations are rendered transitory in the game of moving in and out. Place is temporary and architecture disposable. That something is lost on the way should come as no surprise. Social and spatial conditions are compromised, leaving those left behind to foot the bill.

Spatial Fix

A specter is haunting America. "The history of all hitherto existing society is the history of class struggles," proclaim Marx and Engels in *The Communist Manifesto*.[21] Whereas we encountered by chance the clash of mindsets on a street in Berlin, this confrontation is anything but geographically bound, now being most evident in the United States. In the land of market freedom, who would have thought that Wal-Mart would face fierce resistance? Those most affected by the downside of discount retail have assembled and begun to fight back in a manner recalling proletarian uprising. The company has come under attack in numerous lawsuits for accusations from human rights violations and denying worker benefits to the exploitation of female employees.

A documentary entitled *Wal-Mart: The High Cost of Low Price* captures this showdown, in a movie that Bentonville dismisses as an unwarranted rallying call.[22] The film documents the destruction of social bonds and urban space, revealing the hidden cost of this destruction played out not only on the edge of the city but also on the fringes of the legal system.[23] Story after story recount personal misfortune, community tragedy, and disaster visited upon place. One scene unfolds in the jurisdictions of commercial licensing and building permits. It is when Wal-Mart seeks approval to set up shop that it faces the stiffest opposition from local stakeholders, including neighborhood organizations, city officials, and clergy. The significance of territory and its very constitution come to the fore. A "war machine" of another sort is at work here, aiming to shatter the space of corporate logistics.[24] Activists fighting with the fervor of a guerilla movement try to re-appropriate the conditions of spatial production by galvanizing resistance as a means of holding position within territory. Space, however fragile, is forged in a geographical tug-of-war between parties, pitting tactics against strategy and vice versa. The film concludes with a call to arms, echoing the last sentence of the *Manifesto* "Working men of all countries unite!"

A rereading of Marx's and Engels's pamphlet, as suggested by David Harvey, uncovers another dimension of their plea.[25] Anticipating the current operational mechanisms driving world trade, the opening passages of the *Manifesto* offer a precise, if not prophetic, analysis of the relations between capital and territory so crucial to the contemporary global economy. With an acute sense of the scale of the capitalist project, Marx and Engels describe the advance of a vast machinery that conquers the world place by place, often with violent force. The drive of this machine knows no boundary. "The cheap prices of its commodities are the heavy artillery with which it batters down all Chinese walls."[26] What is described here is a spatial dynamic fueled by the development of technology and infrastructural networks that empower "industries whose products are consumed not only at home, but in every quarter of the globe."[27] These networks, of course, serve the logistic system of capital to enable unhindered flows of "materiel" and to ensure flexibility in its operational deployment. Territory plays a central role in this economic colonization, for "the accumulation of capital has always been a profoundly geographical affair."[28]

Yet another twist comes by way of capital's need to inflict crisis upon itself through the excessive accumulation of wealth, goods, and labor, which subsequently spawns repeated collapse of price and wage levels. Like a sorcerer no longer in control of the powers summoned by his spells, capitalism perpetually jeopardizes its own interests.[29] Destruction is inherent to the very buildup of capital. That such a destructive tendency depends on territory to destroy territory explains the perpetual summoning of spatial fixes to remedy the internal contradictions of the system. And the cycle continues by moving in and out of place. The current acceleration to push beyond limits in search for new markets churns up territory at an ever-faster pace, and with it produces increasingly volatile spatial relations. Nowhere are these relations more erratic than in the production of contemporary urban geographies.

With so much value granted to space, one wonders whether the situation could not be turned around. Rather than viewing urban space as a passive consequence, and thus victim, of capital, one could attribute to space an active role in reorganizing capital production, even if requiring cunning means to reorient economic processes toward more even geographical development. Here the city cannot be understood only as a physical object but moreover as a process instrumental in the production of relations, whether social, economic, or spatial. Viewing such relations as something still to be designed in more inclusive terms would amount to a devilish turn in the current orbit of capitalist cycles. Logistics would be appropriated to serve other ends, contributing to a seemingly improbable Wal-Marxian world.

Stills from Robert Greenwald's documentary film *Wal-Mart: The High Cost of Low Price*, Los Angeles, 2005

The authors would like to thank Jesse LeCavalier for his invaluable preparatory research that made this essay possible.

NOTES

1. Rollin L. Ford, Executive Vice President and Chief Information Officer for Wal-Mart Stores, Inc., "The Age of Wal-Mart: Inside America's Most Powerful Company," CNBC, 2006.

2. John Dicker, "The Growth Machine," *The United States of Wal-Mart* (London and New York: Penguin Books, 2005), 54-78.

3. Charles Fishman, *The Wal-Mart Effect* (New York: Penguin Press, 2006), 9.

4. Wal-Mart's attempt to establish the company's presence in Germany failed. The eighty-five stores were taken over by the German chain Metro in 2006. See *Neue Zürcher Zeitung*, "Wal-Mart zieht sich aus Deutschland zurück," July 29th, 2006.

5. James A. Huston, *The Sinews of War: Army Logistics 1775-1953* (Washington, D.C.: Office of Military History, United States Army, 1966), 435.

6. The term *logistics* has its etymological origin in the Greek adjective *logistikos*, meaning "proficient in the art of calculation."

7. Jacques Derrida, *Writing and Difference*, first published 1967 by Édition du Seuil, translated by Alan Bass (Chicago: The University of Chicago Press, 1979), 185.

8. "Data, Data Everywhere," *The Economist*, issue entitled "The Data Deluge and How to Handle It," February 27th-March 5th, 2010, 3.

9. Edna Bonacich und Khaleelah Hardier, "Wal-Mart and the Logistics Revolution," *Wal-Mart: The Face of Twenty-First-Century Capitalism*, edited by Nelson Lichtenstein (New York: The New Press, 2006), 170.

10. Dieter Brandes, *Die 11 Geheimnisse des ALDI-Erfolgs*, (Munich: Piper Verlag, 2006) 13.

11. Jesse LeCavalier, "Wal-Martians: Servo-Organisms and Information Transit," unpublished essay, ETH Zurich 2006.

12. Christian Seiler, "Editorial," *Du*, issue 733, *Container: Container: Das Prinzip Globalisierung*, (Zurich: Niggli Verlag, 2003) 7.

13. Monika Doman, "Be Wise—Palletize," *traverse*, 2009, issue 3, 26.

14. See Marc Levinson, *The Box. How the Shipping Container Made the World Smaller and the World Economy Bigger*, (Princeton: Princeton University Press, 2006).

15. "The interiors of these distribution centers are constituted by seemingly blank boxes and crates, the contents of which can only be accessed by workers with special 'eyes' in the form of their hand-held or 'wearable' scanners." John Harwood, Jesse LeCavalier, and Guillaume Mojon, *Standpunkte 01: This Will _ This* (Basel: Standpunkte, 2009), 29.

16. Ibid., 28.

17. See Peter Sloterdijk, "Erleuchtung im schwarzen Kasten – Zur Geschichte der Undurchsichtigkeit", *Der ästhetische Imperative* (Hamburg: Philo & Philo Fine Arts, 2007), 116.

18. Sam Walton with John Huey, *Made in America: My Story* (New York: Doubleday and Bantam Books, 1992 and 1993), 139-160.

19. Ibid., 141.

20. Ellen Dunham-Jones, "Temporary Contracts: On the Economy of the Post-Industrial Landscape," *Harvard Design Magazine*, Fall 1997, Issue 3.

21. Karl Marx und Friedrich Engels, *The Communist Manifesto* (1848) (New York: Labor News, 1968), 12.

22. Robert Greewald (director and producer), Wal-Mart: *The High Cost of Low Price*, Los Angeles, 2005.

23. See Ken Jacobs's research report, *Hidden Cost of Wal-Mart Jobs*, Center for Labor Research and Education, University of California Berkeley, 2004.

24. See the use of the concept of "the war machine" as described by Gilles Deleuze and Félix Guattari in *A Thousand Plateaus* (1980), (Minneapolis: University of Minnesota Press, 1987), 351-423.

25. David Harvey, "The Geography of Class Power" (1998), *Spaces of Capital: Towards a Critical Geography* (New York: Routledge, 2001), 369.

26. Marx and Engels, 18.

27. Ibid.

28. Harvey, 369.

29. Marx and Engels refer to the means of production as being "like the sorcerer, who is no longer able to control the powers of the nether world whom he has called up by his spells." See, 20.

Sam Walton and his personal plane.

STEPHEN GRAHAM IS

PROFESSOR OF CITIES AND SOCIETY AT THE GLOBAL URBAN RESEARCH UNIT IN NEWCASTLE UNIVERSITY'S SCHOOL OF ARCHITECTURE, PLANNING, AND LANDSCAPE. HIS RESEARCH ADDRESSES INTERSEC- TIONS BETWEEN URBAN PLACES, MOBILITY, TECHNOLOGY, WAR, MILITARIZATION, SURVEILLANCE, AND GEOPOLITICS. HIS BOOKS INCLUDE *TELECOMMUNICATIONS AND THE CITY* AND *SPLINTERING URBANISM* (BOTH WITH SIMON MARVIN), *THE CYBERCITIES READER*, *CITIES, WAR, AND TERRORISM*, *DISRUPTED CITIES: WHEN INFRASTRUCTURES FAIL*, AND *CITIES UNDER SIEGE: THE NEW MILITARY URBANISM*.

GLOBAL HOMELANDS SECURITY AND EXTRA- TERRITORI- ALIZATION

National borders have ceased being continuous lines on the earth's surface and [have] become non-related sets of lines and points situated within each country.[1]

Power itself goes nomadic.[2]

A striking aspect of the recent surge in efforts to surveil and secure the United States "Homeland" since the 2001 terrorist attacks has been the attempt by the U.S. State to extend its efforts beyond the territorial limits of North America toward transnational and even global scales. Just as ideas of international security are "coming home," to radically reorganize ideas of domestic urban life, so parallel efforts to continually demarcate risky and risk-free popula- tions, activities, and circulations are moving "out" from the local and national scales to colonize the infrastructures, systems, and circulations sustaining transnational capitalism.

Global mobilities are thus increasingly being policed in what James Sheptycki calls "informated space."[3] Such a dynamic parallels the Bushian logic of preemptive, colonial, and securocratic war, purportedly to shore up the safety of the domestic homeland by anticipat- ing and neutralizing threats as they build on the global frontier.[4] Thus many elements of the security apparatus of nations are now seeking to challenge long-standing Westphalian separa- tions of internal and external security along traditional geopolitical and civil/military lines. "The discourses that the United States and its closest allies have put forth asserting the necessity to globalize security have taken on an unprecedented intensity and reach," writes Didier Bigo. "This globalization is supposed to make national borders effectively obsolete, and to oblige other actors in the international arena to collaborate."[5]

Here we confront perhaps the ultimate point at which borders cease to be simply geo- graphic lines and filters between states and emerge instead as transnational, increasingly interoperable, systems or assemblages of control technologies strung out across the world's infrastructures, circulations, cities, and bodies. Rather than merely blockading territorial bor- ders, the imperative is to permanently anticipate, channel, and monitor flows and circulations so that proper ones can de demarcated from improper ones.[6] In the process, borders become transformed "from a two-dimensional line across an absolute space that divides inside and outside, to a transitional zone, defined by exceptional forms of government that blur estab- lished categories, jurisdictions and spaces."[7]

Attempts to securitize the systems, infrastructures, and circulations sustaining global capi- talism are inevitably urban and global at the same time. They are a response to the fact that transnational capitalism is anchored by a network of "global cities" that together constitute its strategic processes by organizing flows, exchanges, and circulations across transnational space. "More than ever, the reach of the city now stretches outward to a global scale."[8] In fact, it is possible to see such global or world cities themselves as "fluid machines" – "fixes" in space and time constructed to organize a vast and usually hidden universe of connection, process, and flow.[9] At the same time such cities orchestrate what I have termed elsewhere the new military urbanism.[10] As the dominant centers of corporate and financial power for the world's military-security-industrial complex, they are the brains of the global war machine itself.

Peter Taylor and colleagues at Lougborough University have mapped the transnational net- works of so-called "global cities," earmarking dominant hubs ("alpha" world cities), secondary centers ("beta" world cities) and peripheral cities that act as gateways between regions and the world economy ("gamma" world cities). The flows between these cities are at the heart of the drive to securitize the global systems and circulations sustaining transnational capitalism.

Advocates of the emerging transnational models of border security argue that traditional efforts at drawing and enforcing territorial borders are actually a problem rather than a solution.[11] This is because of the delays and costs they bring in the interruption of global flows. But it is also because they fail to allow flows and people to be systematically profiled, located, and tracked as they move around the world, *before* reaching the most vulnerable and strategic targets in and around the North's global cities. As we have seen, instead of merely policing flows across territorial borders, the emerging architectures of securocratic war and (attempted) control work to colonize the "seam" between war and crime and continually oscillate between the scales of the human body, via that of the port, airport, and Internet PC, to that of the city and of transnational capitalism itself.

New ideas of U.S. national security, in particular, are based on "defending forward" and "global defense in depth"[12] This new security doctrine is built on the argument that no matter how much money, technology, and militarized fencing is thrown at the problem of the securo- cratic filtering of the boundaries separating the United States from the rest of the world, such geopolitical ideas of security are rendered less and less useful in a world where the

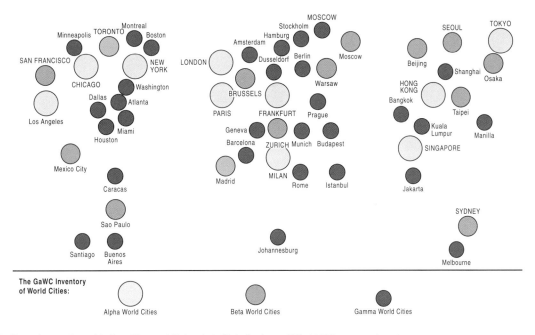

The GaWC Inventory of World Cities:

Alpha World Cities   Beta World Cities   Gamma World Cities

The World City Network as envisaged by Loughborough University's Globalization and World Cities research center

flows of the world continually work themselves *through* U.S. cities and regions via a myriad of infrastructural connections and systems. [13]

"Homeland" security is thus increasingly seen to be "an away game." "We don't want [identified security threats] to get in our airspace, on our land or close to our shoreline in the maritime domain," writes U.S. Navy Admiral Timothy Keating.[14] Instead, the U.S. national security state is "working very hard with the other regional combatant commanders so as to roll up the bad guys, capture or kill them and interrupt their attacks" long before they reach the continental margins of North America.[15]

Such an approach helps address the problem that "the imperatives of national security and global trade are in many ways conflicting projects"[16] if homeland security centers merely on erecting barriers – which translate into costs and delays – in the way of the circulations connecting the U.S. and the rest of the world. "U.S. prosperity – and much of its power – relies on its ready access to North America and global networks of transport, energy, information, finance and labor," Stephen Flynn argues. "It is self defeating for the United States to embrace security measure that isolated it from those networks."[17]

Those advocating the new doctrine also stress that terrorist threats, are already "within the wire"[18] of the transnational circulations that tie U.S. cities so intimately to the rest of the world: terrorists themselves already inhabit Western and U.S. cities; the tools they use to launch their attacks are close at hand within those cities; and their targets are the myriad "soft targets" that actually *constitute* those cities. Even when terrorists are located within colonial peripheries rather than the U.S. itself, their access to the transnational circuits of Internet, container, logistic, and air systems means that they can project attacks toward U.S. cities at any instant.

Containing Insecurity

Attempts to extend U.S. homeland security initiatives through worldwide systems of infrastructure, circulation and flow are already continuing apace.[19] A prime focus here is the extended archipelagos of "park"-style enclaves that together orchestrate the world's neoliberal divisions of labor and the trade flows that result.[20] A major Container Security Initiative, for example, is attempting to build a global architecture of control, covering the world's major sea container ports and the flows that link them.[21] The CSI aims "to push [America's] borders out and pre-screen containers in specially created security zones before they are loaded in foreign ports."[22] It is a major element within an effort to try and "secure the entire maritime supply chain, from the factory gate in a foreign country to the final destination of the product in the United States."[23]

The "global homeland" orchestrated through the extension of U.S. sovereignty as part of the U.S. VISIT initiative: Frankfurt airport, Germany.

The U.S. Department of Homeland Security now needs to control, police, and track movements within what it calls a "global security envelope."[24] By 2003, fifteen of the twenty-five major containers ports in the world had agreed, under considerable pressure from the U.S., to establish a global control CSI system. This theoretically allows containers to be continually tracked, reduces the potential for them to be tampered with in transit, and allows ports to keep delays for inspections to a minimum.

Crucially, this global securitization drive blends seamlessly into the 'forting up' of U.S. port spaces as security zones that are also being used to justify the suspension of normal labor and privacy rights in the name of 'national security'.[25] The re-imagination of U.S. and Canadian ports – and urban waterfronts – as key national security spaces has meant that they are being physically securitized as spaces of legal exception, enrolled into national systems of government power, and re-regulated in ways that dramatically undermine the labor rights of port workers.[26] Thus national security, at least in the ports, is conceptualized as almost interchangeable with the security of intentional trade flows."[27]

Global Biometric Regime

The globe shrinks for those who own it; for the displaced or the dispossessed, the migrant or refugee, no distance is more awesome than the few feet across borders or frontiers. [28]

In the airline and airport sectors, meanwhile, the purported motivation of U.S. homeland security efforts is to ensure that the "border guard [is] the last line of defense, not the first, in identifying potential threats."[29] The dream here is a system of interoperable "smart" borders sustaining the globalization of border control through preemptive risk management.[30] To this end, the U.S. has developed the well-known U.S. VISIT Program as a global extension of homeland security principles through the global airline system. Here we confront a second application of biometric attempts to objectively fix bodies and identities whilst coercing the United States' key partner nations to reorganize their national passport systems to biometric standards defined by the United States.[31] In the Enhanced Border Security and Visa Act of 2002, for example, the U.S. Congress imposed a requirement for the 27 countries organized within the U.S. Visa Waiver Program to begin using machine-readable passports incorporating both biometric and radio frequency tag technology.[32]

Nations or supranational blocs that failed to undertake these radical shifts were threatened with losing their coveted status within the U.S. visa-waiver system. "Our leveraging of America's visa waiver partners, in order to promote the use of the new ID technologies for purposes of national security," write Richard Pruett and Michael Longarzo of the U.S. Army War College, "may prove to be a paradigm for the coming age."[33] The passage-point architectures of overseas airports now display symbols of U.S. as well as domestic sovereignty.

1	Full name	28	Details of passengers on booking with a different itinerary
2	Gender	29	E-mail address
3	Date of birth	30	Ticket number and date of issue
4	Nationality	31	Any other information the ticket agent consider of interest
5	Type of travel document	32	Number on ticket
6	Travel document number	33	Reserved seat number
7	Issuing country of travel document	34	Date ticket issued
8	Expiry date	35	No show history
9	Registration of any vehicle used to travel	36	Bag tag numbers
10	Place of birth	37	Details of whether travel arrangements are 'flexible'
11	Issue date of travel	38	Names of any infants or staff in travelling party
12	UK visa or entry clearance expiry date	39	Is traveller an unaccompanied minor?
13	Booking reference number	40	Details of who made the booking
14	Date of reservation	41	All historical changes to travel arrangements
15	Date(s) of intended travel	42	Number of travellers in party
16	Passenger name (if different to full name)	43	Seat information, including whether first class
17	Other passengers on same booking	44	Is the ticket one-way only?
18	Passenger's address	45	Any other biographical information
19	Form of payment, including any credit card number	46	Cost of fare
20	Billing address	47	Check-in time
21	Contract numbers, including hotel or relative being visited	48	Actual seat number
22	Travel itinerary and route	49	How much luggage checked-in
23	Frequent flyer information (miles flown and addresses)	50	Check-in agents initials
24	Travel agency	51	Out-bound travel indicator
25	Person at travel agent who made booking	52	Where did journey begin, if not first leg of trip
26	Reference number of any shared booking	53	Group indicator of whether a party is a family or friends etc.
27	Status of booking e.g. confirmed, wait-listed		

The 53 pieces of information required, at point of reservation, from 2007 for anyone entering or leaving the UK as part of the UK's 2007 e-borders strategy. The main contractor is the U.S. defense corporation, Raytheon, maker of Tomahawk cruise missiles.

A shift to biometrically organized international borders, structured according to U.S. stipulations, centers on the preemptive separation of "mobile bodies into kinetic elites and kinetic underclasses."[34] A process of "punitive preemption" profiles those deemed risky in advance and seeks to immobilize these populations before they are able to travel to the United States. Such a process "incorporates a range of disciplinary, punitive and militaristic technologies aimed at preempting arrival at the physical border."[35] In the process, border crossers who do not go through the myriad of screening systems and passage points are criminalized. While kinetic elites can increasingly bypass immigration controls altogether by opting into biometrically controlled schemes like Amsterdam airport's Privium system or the SmartGate system in Australia. This preemptively clears them as "safe," legitimate bodies.

Automated risk profiling of passengers, starting when they initially book, allow those deemed malign or improper to be highlighted and intercepted before embarkation to the United States.[36] In the United Kingdom's new "smart border" initiative, a range of fifty-three variables are constantly scanned by association rules that search for signals of "risky" or "abnormal" within the mass of data.[37] The screened appearance of a security threat," writes Louise Amoore, "is always already calculated by the algorithmic performance of association rules." These highlight data deemed to signify risk – "was the ticket paid in cash?; What is the past pattern of travel?; Is this a frequent flier?; What in-flight meal was ordered?" – shape the treatment of the passenger as he or she attempts to board the plane.[38]

The United States–Canada border is a particularly good case study of how multiple circuits are being constructed to process kinetic elites and kinetic underclasses in radically different ways. Long-standing ideas of E-Z Pass "fast lanes" on urban highways are being translated into the architectures of what we might call the E-Z Pass nation – but for a privileged minority. The experimental NEXUS program, for example, allows regular business travelers between

E-Z pass automated tollbooth, Buffalo, New York, which allows pre-registered drivers to enter premium "fast lanes" without stopping.

Canada and the U.S. to submit for profiling and pre-clearing, gain a special wireless biometric ID card and go through a priority lane, bypassing the congestion and delays of the border in the process. Cameras take iris-scans to verify the connection of driver and card. For such privileged and purportedly risk-free travelers, even the crossing of increasingly militarized borders becomes "a mere technical formality."[39]

While this business class or frequent-flyer travelers lucky enough to be enrolled into what Matthew Sparke has called a kind of "transnational para-citizenship"[40] become the vaunted, risk-free subjects operating smoothly across transnational space, those "kinetic underclasses" who cannot so enroll, or are deemed risky within the new systems, face greater problems of harassment, targeting, incarceration, and diminished legal and human rights. Such status thus has "altogether more oppressive and more unpredictable outcomes"[41] including the ultimate threat and immobility of incarceration or torture. "It should be noted," Matthew Sparke writes,"that as well as representing ever more appalling exclusions from the privileges of citizenship and civil rights, those surviving on this bleak underside of privilege also sometimes ironically experience very rapid movement too: rapid movement into detention centers, rapid movement between detention centers, and, ultimately, rapid transnational movement out of America, sometimes into incarceration elsewhere."

The mobilization of biometrics as a supposedly immutable measure of "true" identity, in both the urban warzones and broader rearticulations of nation, citizenship and circulation, work to reinforce each other. In both overlapping domains, the parallel deployment of biometric systems means that the field of politics is narrowed as all subjects are rendered as suspects and targets who can be managed in a way that allows them to be "legitimately subjected to such disciplinary technologies"[42] as (real or potential criminalized) others. The result of this convergence between war-zone and home-zone is another powerful example of what John Measor and Benjamin Muller call an "evolving global norm of securitized identity" which works to further destabilize conventional separations between domestic and foreign policy.

Cyber Passage-Point

The final "global homeland" of concern here centers on the U.S. efforts to observe global Internet traffic, even when it neither originates nor ends up within the U.S. itself. A large proportion of global Internet traffic is routed through switches in the United States – a legacy of the system's history. Because of cheaper international phone tariffs, and the invention of the Internet in the U.S., global traffic now overwhelmingly works through "a handful of key telephone switches and perhaps a dozen [Internet Exchange Points] in coastal cities near undersea fiber-optic cable landings, particularly Miami, Los Angeles, New York and the San Francisco Bay Area."[43] This means "the NSA could scoop up an astounding amount of telephone calls by simply choosing the right facilities."[44]

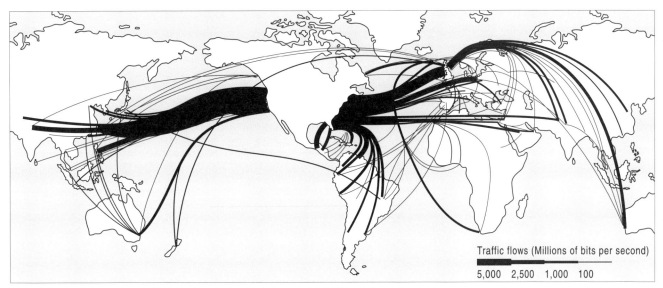

Much of the globe's international traffic flows through a few key 'telecom hotel' buildings in the United States, dramatically simplifying the NSA's attempts at global Internet surveillance.

In urban terms, these facilities amount to a few crucial buildings known as "telecom hotels" that house the key internet and telephone switching centers of the entire planet. "There are about three or four buildings you need to tap," Stephen Becker of the consultants Telegeography reveals. "In L.A. there is 1 Wilshire; in New York, 60 Hudson, and in Miami, the NAP of the Americas."[45] This situation provides the U.S. with a huge opportunity to build up extensive data mining, data fusion and other surveillance systems centered on these key urban and global architectures and passage points of global electronic communication. U.S. security institutions have not been slow to exploit this potential. In October 2007, the so-called Restore Act[46] ruled that the U.S. National Security Agency was free to tap this traffic at will, even when both its origin and destination lay outside of U.S. borders.[47]

Spurred on by fears of the use of the Internet to coordinate and finance terrorist actions, as well as its appropriation as a weapon of "cyberterror" to destroy of disrupt the electronic systems sustaining advanced capitalist nations, the U.S. National Security Agency has launched globe-spanning efforts to try and observe every packet of Internet traffic. Other initiatives are attempting to monitor global financial transactions, as a means to preemptively identify "unusual" or "threatening" patterns of activity.[48]

Conclusion

> The virtual border, whether it faces outward or inward to foreignness, is no longer a barrier structure but a shifting net, a flexible spatial pathogenesis that shifts round the globe and can move from the exteriority of the transnational frontier into the core of the securocratic state.[49]

The shift towards global "homelands," organized through the kinds of transnational surveillance and tracking, is an important part of a broader shift in the nature and experience of borders in our world. Such a shift involves nation-states moving away from their roles as guarantors of a community of citizens within a territorial unit, policing links between "inside" and "outside." Instead, they morph into international organized systems geared towards attempts at separating people and circulations deemed risky and malign from those deemed risk-free or worthy of protection. Crucially, this increasingly occurs on both the insides and outsides of territorial boundaries. In the process, international borders blur into urban and local ones. Indeed, the two increasingly seem to meld to constitute a "multiplicity of control points,"[50] distributed transnationally across urban space. These new urban passage-points become distributed along key lines of circulation and key geographies of wealth and power, crossing territorial lines between states as well as those within and beyond these boundaries. In the process they forge dynamic new architectures that must be understood by anyone attempting to get to grips with the geography of power in the contemporary world.

NOTES

1. Paul Andreu, "Borders and Borderers," *Architecture of the Borderlands*, (London : Wiley/ Architectural Design 1997), 57-61.

2. See Bülent Diken and Carsten Bagge Laustsen, *The Culture Of Exception: Sociology Facing The Camp*, (London: Routledge 2005), 64.

3. James Sheptycki, "The Global Cops Cometh: Reflections on Transationalization, Knowledge Work, and Policing Subculture," *British Journal of Sociology*, 49:1, 1998: 57-74. 70.

4. Marieke de Goede, "Beyond Risk: Pre-mediation and the Post-9/11 Security Imagination Marieke de Goede," *Security Dialogue*, July 2007;

5. Didier Bigo, "Globalized-in-security: The Field and the Ban-opticon," in John Solomon, Naoki Sakai, eds., *Translation, Philosophy and Colonial Difference* (Hong Kong 2005), at http://www.wmin.ac.uk/sshl/pdf/CSDBigo170106.pdf, 1

6. Deborah Cowan, "Securing systems: Struggles over supply chains and the social." Unpublished paper, 2006, 3.

7. Ibid.

8. Ed Soja, "Borders Unbound: Globalization, Regionalism, and the Postmetropolitan Transition," in Henk van Houtum, Olivier Framsch and Wolfgang Zierhofer, eds., *B/Ordering Space* (London: Ashgate 2005), 40.

9. Laurent Gutierrez and Valérie Portefaix, *Mapping HK* (Hong Kong: Map Books 2000).

10. Stephen Graham, *Cities Under Siege: The New Military Urbanism*, (London: Verso 2010).

11. Deborah Cowan, "Securing Systems," 2.

12. Antulio Echevarria and Bert Tussing, From "Defending Forward" to a "Global Defense-In-Depth": Globalization and Homeland Security, Strategic Studies Institute, 2003, at www.strategicstudiesinstitute.army.mil/ Pubs/Display. Cfm?pubID=210

13. Deborah Cowan and Neil Smith "After Geopolitics? Geoeconomics and the Territorial Politics of Security," unpublished paper, 2007, 18, 20.

14. Donna Miles, 'With Ongoing Terror Fight Overseas, NORTHCOM Focuses on Homeland,' *Security Innovator*, November 17, 2006 at http://www.securityinnovator.com/index.php?articleID=8403&sectionID=31

15. Ibid.

16. Cowan and Smith "After Geopolitics?" 18, 20.

17. Stephen Flynn, "The False Conundrum: Continental Integration versus Homeland security," in Peter Andreas and Thomas JBiersteker (eds) *The Rebordering of North America* (New York Routledge 2003) 110-127, 11.

18. Echevarria and Bert Tussing, From "Defending Forward" To A "Global Defense-In-Depth": Globalization And Homeland Security, Strategic Studies Institute, 2003, at http://www.strategicstudiesinstitute.army.mil/ Pubs/Display. Cfm?pubID=210

19. See, for example, Leslie Lebl, "Security Beyond Borders," Policy Review, April & May 2005 at http://www.hoover.org/publications/policyreview/2938761.html

20. See Keller Easterling, *Enduring Innocence* (Cambridge MA: MIT Press 2006).

21. This system organizes 90 percent of global trade through global supply chains and advanced logistics and delivers 95 percent of the overseas trade entering the U.S.

22. *The Economist*, "When Trade and Security Clash," April 4, 2002 reprinted at http://findarticles.com/p/articles/mi_hb5037/is_200204/ai_n18267885

23. Jon Haveman and Howard Shatz, Protecting the Nation's Seaports: Balancing Security and Cost, (San Francisco: Public Policy Institute of California), at www.ppic.org/content/pubs/report/R_606JHR.pd

24. IBM, Expanded Borders, Integrated Controls, marketing brochure, no date, at www-935.ibm.com/services/U.S./ imc/pdf/g510-6218-expanded-borders.pdf

25. Cowan and Smith "After Geopolitics?" 20.

26. Deborah Cowen and Susannah Bunce, "Competitive Cities and Secure Nations: Conflict and Convergence in Urban Waterfront Agendas after 911," *International Journal of Urban and Regional Research*, 2006; 30:2, 427-439, 30 (2)

27. Deborah Cowan, Securing systems," 7

28. Homi Bhabha, "The Third Space: Interview with Homi Bhabha," in J. Rutherford ed., *Identity: Community, Culture, Difference* (London: Routledge 1990), 208-224.

29. Accenture Digital Forum, U.S. DHS to Develop and Implement U.S. VISIT Program, 2004, available at www.digitalforum.accenture.com, 4. Cited in Louize Amoore, "Algorithmic War: Everyday Geographies of the War on Terror," *Antipode* (forthcoming).

30. Ben Hayes and Roche Tasse, "Control Freaks: Homeland Security and Interoperability" *Different Takes*, no. 45, Spring 2007, 1–4, 2.

31. Mark Salter, "The Global Visa Regime and the Political Technologies of the International Self: Borders, Bodies, Biopolitics," *Alternatives* 31, 2006, 167–189.

32. Richard Pruett and Michael Longarzo, *Identification Friend Or Foe? The Strategic Uses And Future Implications Of The Revolutionary New ID Technologies*, U.S. Army War College, Strategy Research Project, U.S. Army War College Carlisle Barracks, Pennsylvania, 2006, at www.strategicstudiesinstitute.army.mil/ pdffiles/ksil468.pdf, 8.

33. Ibid.

34. Dean Wilson and Leanne Weber, "Risk and Pre-emption on the Australian Border," *Surveillance & Society* 5:2, 2008: 124-141,125.

35. Ibid.

36. Karine Côté-Boucher notes that such "remote control border" strategies, that is, the pU.S.hing of border functions into foreign countries, have a long history. They were "already in use in the U.S. management of Chinese immigration as early as the beginning of the 20th century" Karine Côté-Boucher, "The Diffuse Border: Intelligence-Sharing, Control and Confinement along Canada's Smart Border,' *Surveillance & Society* 5:2, 2008: 142-165, 142.

37. Louize Amoore, "Algorithmic War," Antipode (forthcoming). Among the 34 items of passenger data required under the EU-U.S. passenger name record (PNR) or Advance passenger information system (APIS) agreement, legally challenged by the European Court of Justice in 2006, are credit card details, criminal records and in-flight meal choices. The data is sent to the U.S. within 15 minutes of flight departures from Europe.

38. Ibid.

39. Karine Côté-Boucher, "The Diffuse Border," 157.

40. Matthew Sparke , "A Neoliberal Nexus: Economy, Security and the Biopolitics of Citizenship on the Border," *Political Geography*, 25:2, 2006, 151-180, 167.

41. Ibid.

42. John Measor and Benjamin Muller, "Securitizing the Global Norm of Identity: Biometric Technologies in Domestic and Foreign Policy," Dahrjamailiraq.com, September 17, 2005, at http://www.dahrjamailiraq.com/covering_iraq/archives//000277.php#more

43. Ryan Singel, "NSA's Lucky Break: How the U.S. Became Switchboard to the World" *Wired*, October 10, 2007, at http://www.wired.com/politics/security/news/2007/10/domestic_taps

44. Stephan Beckert, the research director at Telegeography, cited in Singel, "NSA's Lucky Break."

45. Singel, 'NSA's Lucky Break: How the U.S. Became Switchboard to the World' *Wired*, 10th October, 2007 at http://www.wired.com/politics/security/news/2007/10/domestic_taps

46. "Restore" stands for Responsible Electronic Surveillance That is Overseen Reviewed and Effective, 2007.

47. Ryan Singel, "NSA's Lucky Break"

48. See Louize Amoore and Marieke de Goede, "Transactions after 9/11: The Banal Face of the Preemptive Strike," *Transactions of the Institute of British Geographers*, 33:2, April, 173-185.

49. Allen Feldman , 'Securocratic wars of public safety,' *Interventions: International Journal of Postcolonial Studies*, 6; 3, 330-350.

50. Karine Côté-Boucher, "The Diffuse Border,"153.

035. *Blow Up*, 1967. Courtesy Warner Brothers Entertainment.
036. photolib.noaa.gov/bigs/nssl0020.jpg
037. courtesy El Bee, New York
038. nasa.gov/images/content/124415main_image_feature_380a_ys_full.jpg

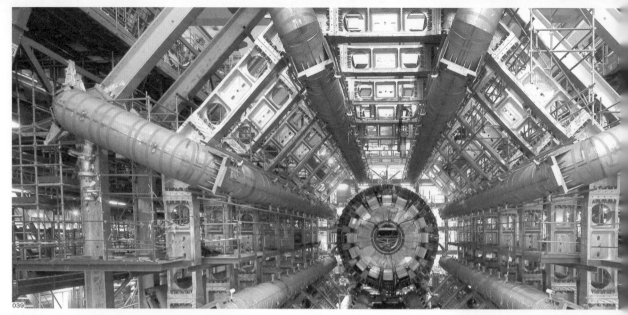

039. riseofthetechnologyclass.files.wordpress.com/2009/06/lhc.jpg

040. courtesy El Bee, Belize

041. nasaimages.org/download.php?mid=nasaNAS~20~20~120295~226994&file=
    GPN-2002-000166.jpg&src=http%3A%2F%2Fmm04.nasaimages.org%2FMediaManager
    %2Fsrvr%3Fmediafile%3D%2FSize3%2FnasaNAS20NA%2F121533%2F
    GPN-2002-000166.jpg

042. nasaimages.org/download.php?mid=nasaNAS~2~2~348~101427&file=PIA04232.
    jpg&src=http%3A%2F%2Fmm04.nasaimages.org%2FMediaManager%2Fsrvr%3Fmediafil
    e%3D%2FJP2K%2FnasaNAS-2-NA%2F1897%2FPIA04232.jp2%26x%3D0%26y%3D0%
    26height%3D1752%26width%3D2617%26level%3D0

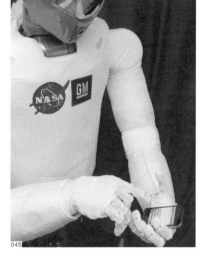

043. nasa.gov/images/content/471146main_jsc2010e089924_hi.jpg

044. nasa.gov/centers/ames/images/content/107315main_ACD04-0241-007.JPG

045. nasa.gov/images/content/471173main_jsc2010e110183_hi.jpg

046. grin.hq.nasa.gov/IMAGES/LARGE/GPN-2000-001635.jpg

047. courtesy El Bee, Hong Kong

048. courtesy El Bee, Hong Kong

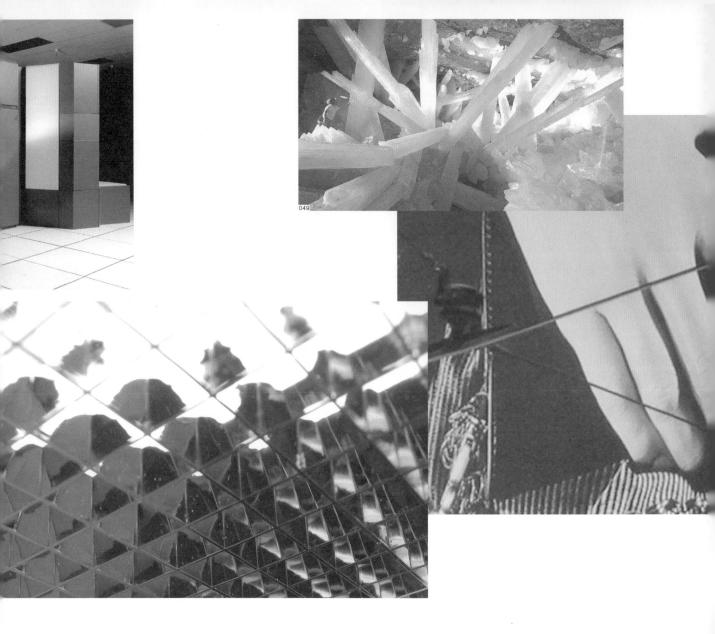

049. wohba.com/pages/images/caveC0307.jpg
050. drutang.files.wordpress.com/2009/08/img_4402.jpg

NATHALIE ROSEAU IS AN ARCHITECT–ENGINEER. SHE IS AN ASSOCIATE PROFESSOR IN THE ECOLE DES PONTS AT THE PARIS INSTITUTE OF TECHNOLOGY AND THE HEAD OF THE URBAN PLANNING PROGRAM. HER RESEARCH ACTIVITIES FOCUS ON THE CONTEMPORARY DYNAMICS OF THE METROPOLIS. SHE DEFENDED HER PH.D. ON THE URBAN IMAGINARY, DRAWING HER INSPIRATION FROM THE AERIAL CULTURE AND THE WAY IT SHAPES THE CULTURAL HISTORY OF AIRPORTS.

RESCALING URBAN MATTER

THE CITY VIEWED FROM THE AIR

When Nadar succeeded in taking the first aerostatic photograph in 1858, aerial views were already relatively common, as either perspective-based compositions in a tradition going back to the Renaissance or panorama views taken from towers and belfries. But it was the experience of going up and actually discovering "the immense, limitless carpet without beginning or end (that is the earth),"[1] that opened up new perspectives and possibilities. From the first Parisian images taken by Nadar on the Champs Elysées and the Place de l'Etoile, to the satellite images of megapolitan corridors circulated by NASA, these new visual perspectives allowed the aerial observer to rediscover the object constantly being lost: the city he thought he knew so well, in which he is now able to discover new forms from above.[2] "It is as though, at the moment when the great city, the metropolis, the *Grosstadt*, was beginning to call for an image of agglomeration other than a strictly architectural one, it seemed indispensable to preserve its visibility or, to evoke a Freudian problematic, its *representability*."[3] Hubert Damisch reminds us of the fundamentally narcissistic structure of the urban milieu, constantly on the lookout for means of representing its whole.

The city viewed from the air is not restricted to the vision of the "admirable spectacle" deployed beneath the gaze of aerial photographers; for those who manage to get up into the air, the horizon becomes so much bigger and clearer. As Yevgeny Zamyatin stressed in 1922, there is something very utopian about aerial perspectives:

> The word airplane is so Wellsian. The airplane lunges and kingdoms, kings, laws and faith slip out of view. And way, way above, lie the glittering domes of a fantastic tomorrow. Many of us who have crossed this new horizon over the past few years are now able to share in it and see with the new 'eyes' of the aviator. Wells has long possessed these eyes. Thence his anticipation of the future and these vast horizons in space and time.[4]

In *Air and Dreams: An Essay on the Imagination of Movement*, first published in French in 1943,[5] Gaston Bachelard pointed up the "vectorial" aspect of the aerial imagination that appears in the desire for clarification and transcendence that spurs on the aerial dream. Seen from the air, the spectacle of totality rediscovered gives rise to the projection of a global fiction. The aerial metaphor of a "new horizon" is projected onto the urban space as it grapples with physical and terrestrial congestion. It is within this context of broader possibilities that the first contours of the aerial infrastructure were sketched out: a place of mediation between the urban milieu and the aerial ocean, henceforth open to the movement of humankind, that will be projected like an engine of urban renewal. The following essay will attempt to explore these aspects of the city seen from the air – discovered and projected, imagined and practiced – by focusing especially on specific devices that have influenced the representation and production of the contemporary city.

Broadening Visual Horizons

Having been commissioned to cover the aeronautical meeting at Bétheny near Reims in late August 1909, the photographer Léon Gimpel discovered in situ the full impact of an air spectacle staged to enthrall huge crowds. The great and the good turned out in force to see Henri Farman beat the world record for both distance travelled and length of time in the air. Glenn Curtiss won the speed contest. Louis Blériot broke the world record when he won the Prix du tour de piste, while the prize for altitude was taken by Hubert Latham. Aerial mobility was finally real and had acquired a spectacular dimension reflected in speed, altitude, and endurance.[6]

Jacques-Henri Lartigue, only fifteen, was already crazy about aviation and provided the following account:

> Yesterday an airplane flew over me, right over my head! And I saw a man inside! Sitting on his seat with his legs spread... and suddenly something mysterious happened inside of me, a bit like vertigo in reverse! It was as though I was seeing out of the eyes of another... as if I was seeing what he saw!... The first thrill of excitement is often so intense that afterwards we seek in vain to rediscover the same sensation.[7]

In this inversion of perspectives, the aerial exploit triggers the photographic one. And while most scenes were snapped on the ground, on the final day of the Bétheny meeting, Gimpel went up in an airship to photograph both the airplanes in flight and the crowd from above. Both the instantaneousness and the radical newness of these photos added still further to the aerial prowess. With its customary "first with the news" pitch, *L'Illustration* magazine published Gimpel's photos at once. "After showing airplanes as they appear to spectators, we wanted to turn things around and get the same view as the aviators themselves."[8]

The structure of this article also heralded a reversal of the roles of text and image: photos were now accompanied by the text. The mass media was still in its infancy; yet the graphic design of pages devoted to air exploits was already transforming page layout, visuals, and perspectives. Photographs were splashed over double pages, or placed one over the other, collage-style, thus illustrating either the simultaneous or discontinuous nature of airplane flights.[9]

Representing/Projecting

Photography was not the only domain to latch onto this new visual universe, which was also taken up in cinematographic and pictorial developments. The tracking shots used in *Metropolis*[10] transfigured reality and enlivened space; the collages of the Russian suprematists assembled the unthinkable; and the aerial dive views depicted in the Italian *Aeropittura* movement both pierce and accuse.[11] Aerial perspectives revealed a different reality and triggered new ways of conveying images that compressed space, distended perspectives, condensed images, and broadened the range of sensations.

They also changed formal and conceptual perceptions of urban space. By experiencing the city from above, city designers used this new capacity to analyze and interpret the new scales and dimensions of the urban phenomenon. They superimposed a new fiction on this newly perceptible whole, as if being able to see again had triggered an almost immediate desire to remodel the object revealed. These vantage points ushered in a new reforming spirit, and the representation of urban totality acted like a reflexive mechanism that needed to be projected. Hugh Ferriss, analyzed New York and then rendered it from an aerial panoramic perspective as a city of skyscrapers – giant stalagmites – marked by passing air and land traffic.[12] Frank Lloyd Wright presented aerial views and projected an extension of the city-territory in his future Broadacre City project.[13] And Marcel Lods, an experienced pilot, denounced the Parisian smog as he overflew the new extensions to the capital on his way to his building projects.[14]

Le Corbusier used the power of the airplane as a weapon to challenge the existing urban environment and harnessed the same visual inspiration to recast or even create entire new cities. He visited South America in 1929 during a memorable trip, which included flights over Brazil with the help of the aviators Jean Mermoz and Antoine de Saint-Exupéry. He was so taken with these aerial views that he designed the plans for Montevideo, Sao Paulo, and Rio de Janeiro from the

Hugh Ferriss, "Hangars in the sky," *American Architect*, January 1931. Source Archives of Hugh Ferriss, Box 2, Drawings and Archives, Avery Architectural and Fine Arts Library, Columbia University of New York.

air, based on the "theorem of the meander," which first came to him in a plane:

> Following the outlines of a meander from above, I understood the problems encountered by human things, the dead ends in which they get stuck and the apparently miraculous solutions that suddenly resolve apparently inextricable situations. For my own use, I have christened this phenomenon the 'law of the meander.'[15]

And in *Aircraft* (1935), Le Corbusier went on to observe that:

> The airplane gives us a bird's-eye view. When the eye sees clearly, the mind can decide in more lucid fashion.[16]

The airplane turned land-bound powerlessness into air-borne lucidity. Architectural visionaries clarified their thinking and simultaneously rediscovered their powers of transformation.

Aerial views were used by regional planning as a tool for measuring and projecting. First, they began to be used systematically for cadastral surveys of the city and its environs. As New York's city limits swelled to include most of the metropolitan area, a huge project to photograph the city's urban fabric known as the Aerial Survey was initiated in the early 1920s; by 1921, the Fairchild Aerial Camera Corporation had produced a giant photo mosaic depicting the urbanized street-grid pattern of greater Manhattan. But it was In 1924 that the sheer visual power of the medium was revealed in an aerial map of Greater New York showing its five boroughs in a single image.[17]

This newfound perspective on metropolitan reality also pointed up regional imperatives. The Regional Plan of New York and its Environs, undertaken at the same time, projected a systemic scale. Infrastructure and parks were deployed within a new network that marshaled and organized the urban fabric and reestablished links of interdependence between the center and the periphery.[18] In France, aerial perspectives were also used extensively in planning, developing and sprucing up cities under the Cornudet Law from 1919, and from 1934 on within the scope of the Prost Plan for the future of the Paris region.[19] The aerial view facilitated a grand plan that aspired to reassert control over the capital: it was first used to trace out the new frontiers of the metropolis. It presented the metropolis on a regional scale in all its beauty and disorder; then, in mapping out the future of the region, using wide in-flight views, it laid out the future of the vast landscape of the Greater Paris region that would subsequently be criss-crossed by highways.

Dynamics of Elevation

After seeing the world from an airplane, Paul-Henry Chombart de Lauwe developed a new approach to the city. After the war, he conducted surveys of urbanized space based on aerial views: *La découverte aérienne du monde* [discovery of the world from the air] contained a new way of mapping the world.[20] Details and globality could now be assessed simultaneously to take in what could not be seen below, to forge links between dimensions such as lifestyles and territorial location, for example. He stressed that the traces left upon the earth by any human group can be discerned more clearly from the air. "More recent forms of social organization stand out more clearly in forms of habitation and how these are grouped together." He echoed the views of Patrick Geddes, who was also taken by the clarifying dimension of seeing things from above. The sociologist-urbanist felt that those who viewed the world from a plane could get a clearer, more detailed overall perspective.[21]

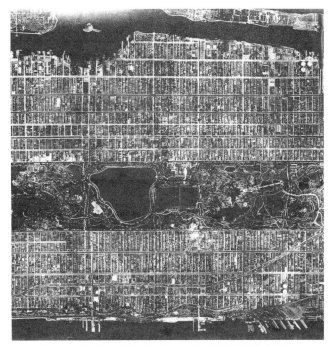

"Aerial Survey of Manhattan Island", 4 August 1921, Fairchild Aerial Camera Corporation, Library of Congress, Washington, DC

Frank Lloyd Wright, "Today, Tomorrow, America Tomorrow", *American Architect*, May 1932, Ill Ernest Born

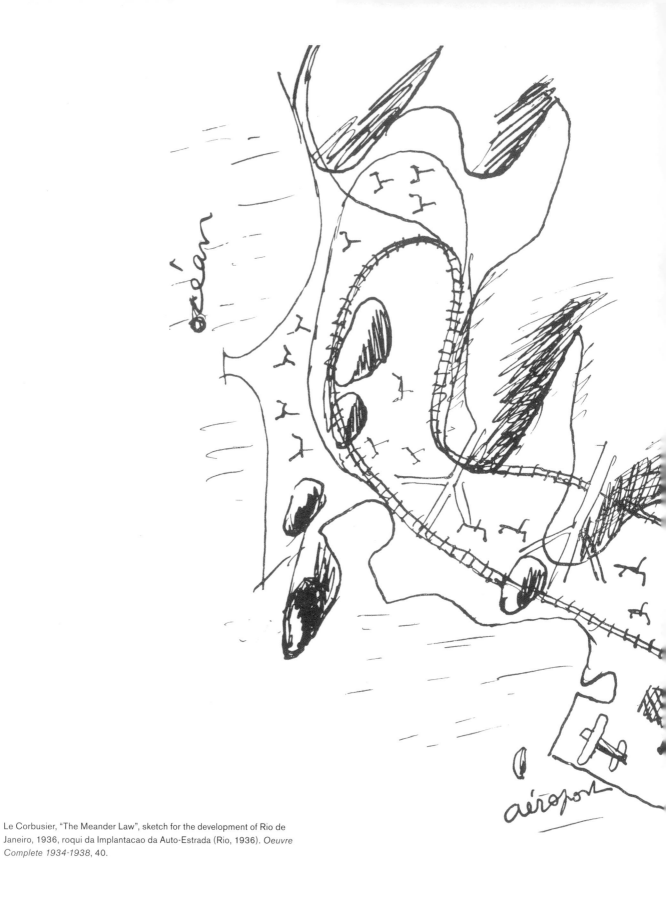

Le Corbusier, "The Meander Law", sketch for the development of Rio de Janeiro, 1936, roqui da Implantacao da Auto-Estrada (Rio, 1936). *Oeuvre Complete 1934-1938*, 40.

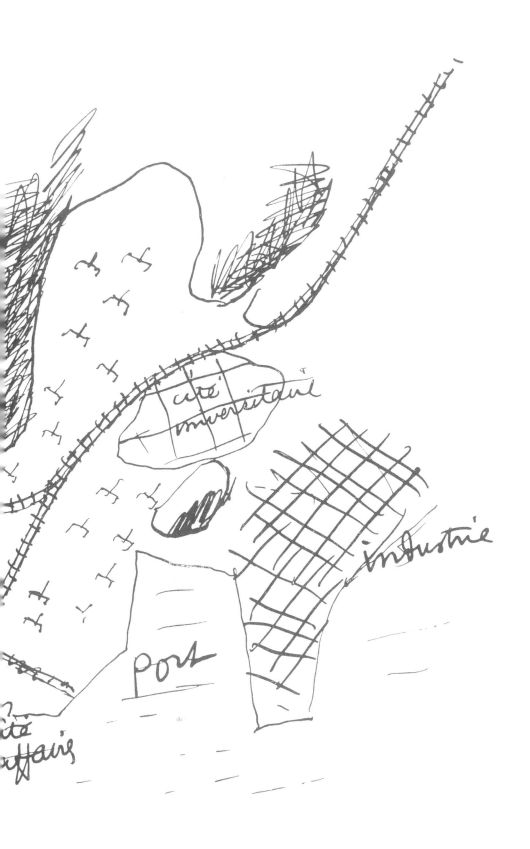

cité universitaire

industrie

Port

cité
affaire

In this long sequence of aerial takes on the world, vertical perspectives appeared to keep up with the uninterrupted progression of urban and metropolitan boundaries. Time and again, they made it possible to regain a global perspective on an urban cityscape that had been rendered illegible by repeated extensions. The verticality of the aerial dream involves a principle of order and lineage, and a narcissistic perspective that reveals the subject to the dreamer in condensed, transparent, and simplified form. It spurred Hugh Ferriss to develop a cartographic vision of the city and its territory:

> How do buildings look? It depends considerably on the elevation of your view-point. From the lowest view-point, you are in the world of Architectural detail. But suppose you look at things from a helicopter, one that is flying slow and low, say at plus 250'. You are now in a world of architectural masses. …Now suppose you are in a plane, one that is flying fairly low, say at plus 1200'. You still see buildings clearly but what you see even more clearly is their relations with their immediate surroundings- with the street system, the roads, the waterways, greenbelts, etc… You have entered the world of site planning, of neighborhood planning. …When the plane flies faster and higher, you enter—say, at plus 5000'…, you now feel like a town-planner, a city-planner. At plus five miles you turn into a regional planner! For right down there below you is a whole region plain to see, and you can't help wanting to design it, or redesign it. Try, someday, a series of thumbnail sketches in color showing how everything changes and simplifies as you go up.[22]

"Design it, or redesign it": first, the architect makes no distinction between vision and projection, as if they have become intertwined thanks to aerial clarification. Moreover, Ferriss simultaneously ranks and links relative elevations of viewpoints and scales of projection, further enhancing the powers of the architect who can now draw everything thanks to the aerial perspective. From ornament to planning tool, the relations between detail and outline, between architecture and landscape, and between city and region are expressed in verticality. Ferriss goes on to show us how he actually used aerial views in practice to study and draw the outline (more than the actual volumes) of the future location of the United Nations or to plot the landscape of the east coast, for example.[23]

Flight from the City: A Vectorial Imagination
The experience of aerial elevation helped shift boundaries. It was ground-breaking heroism that explored – sometimes nervously – what lay elsewhere. Frank Lloyd Wright stressed the eminently utopian aspect of aerial perspectives that allow us to break free of physical and terrestrial constraints: "It takes some time for [man] to know that he can fly… But when he realizes he is free, and learns, he's gone. And after all, *he* is the city."[24] Here, "flight from the city" takes on a literal as well as a metaphorical meaning, allowing for physical emancipation from the city and utopian freedom from its reality.

This reforming vision was to define the contours of the aerial infrastructure for a long time to come. Its history begins just when aviation was being revealed to the masses at huge aeronautical events for which Gimpel ensured photographic coverage in France. And a handful of visionary city planners were to use the exploits of the airmen to renew contemporary urban imagery. A look at the work of the architect/planner Eugène Hénard, who worked extensively for the City of Paris and was one of the founders of the Musée Social, gives a good indication of how aviation and urban developments were shaping the work of planners.[25] By catalyzing a certain number

of key models in Hénard's reflections, the aerial vector becomes the backbone of his approach to the city of the future. "The profound revolution in thought generated by aviation is so powerful and opens such enormous perspectives that all manner of dream is possible. Air conquest will usher in an era of peace and wealth. The cities of tomorrow will be easier to transform and to embellish: their magnificent towers will welcome giant birds from all points on the horizon and perhaps, in time, the major capitals will build their beacons closer and closer to the stars."[26]

A transnational debate rapidly emerged around the city as a space that was likely to be completely recast by the introduction of aerial mobility. From Eugène Hénard to Harvey Corbett, from Le Corbusier to Hugh Ferriss, and from the futurists to the suprematists, architects began designing the means for bringing aircraft into the city: landing pads on buildings and skyscrapers, and concrete slabs and platforms were the most commonly conceived solutions for accommodating airplanes and taxi-planes. The entire city would be turned into aerial infrastructure and spatial projection of the values promoted by the invention of controlled flight: ubiquity, transcendence, elevation, and immateriality. As planes spread into the city, they would give free rein to the most audacious ideas: bigger scales, new ways of dealing with urban functions, dematerialized buildings, and exploration of the possibilities of the third dimension.[27]

This perception of infrastructure as a vehicle for urban renewal was similar to the thinking that would guide the design of international airports later on. Such links were to be all the more marked insofar as some of the "aerial city" visionaries became key players in the construction of pre- and post-war airports. Hugh Ferriss, for example, was involved in the design of the airports at LaGuardia and Idlewild (the future John F. Kennedy airport).

Obviously the transition from the ideal to the real was not problem-free. World War II produced both the emergence of a formidable aviation industry and a realization that aircraft could constitute a weapon of mass destruction. It also ended the dream of individualized transport, and signaled fairly clearly that the future lay in increasingly cumbersome collective transport with more constraints attached. At the same time, there was a shift from the ideal city recast around aerial mobility to a quest for the airport as urban alternative. The current period has been marked by a gradual emancipation of the airport from the urban. The physical and institutional extraterritoriality of airports was embodied in the emergence of autonomous structures such as Aéroport de Paris (the Paris airport authority) or the Port Authority of New York, which wrested the concessions to run four major airports from the cities of New York and Newark following a fierce struggle. It also reflected this striving to create a parallel and global universe, functioning as an autonomous place over which perfect control could be exercised precisely because it was completely circumscribed. The isolation that is characteristic of contemporary airports was compounded by the use of architectural forms or functional processes that reinforced their introversion. The megastructure predominantly used for terminal buildings underpinned this wish to create a world apart. The "Terminal City"[28] metaphor employed for the new Idlewild Airport built in New York in the early 1950s or that of a "pump" for the first terminal of Paris Roissy Airport harked back to this idea of an independent body whose operations were condensed into a single system.

Learning from the Airport
Locating airport complexes away from their urban environment by no means erases urban issues: each time the airport is removed outside

of the city, the intention is to reconfigure it as a new alternative milestone or showcase project. This territorial distancing makes it possible to assess reality differently and facilitates construction of a pioneering object that transcends the constraints of the "host city" while regularly addressing the related urban debates and recreating a separate universe by redesigning the contours of the contemporary city. This magnetic role gives rise to a specific process that we may compare to the aerial view.

The possibility of emancipation from the urban – through high-speed transport links or the colonization or even reclamation of land[29] – goes hand in hand with the reconstitution of a city apart, a sort of utopian bubble that brings together and intensifies all of the latest urban amenities: shops, leisure, travel facilities, etc. In return, physical distancing and the sheer size of airports have resulted in the wish to bring airport-type features back into "the center." These have crystallized in the form of downtown "terminals" that offer all of the attributes you would expect to find in an airport, apart from planes. In such attempts to match the city with the airport and erase this physical distance, the urbanization of the airport through a host of signs and urban codes is closely bound up with what we would term the "airportization" of the urban sphere, reflected in the emergence and influence of these airports without planes that are creeping into urban hypercenters.

This hybridization built around mutual attraction and repulsion is a two-way process: the airport as an urban fiction come true has become one of the favored observation platforms for theoreticians of urban questions, who analyze them as a prism of live issues for the contemporary city.[30] Airports conjure up fascination and bitter criticism in equal measure – they are even described as counter-utopian, technicist or societal. They embody a sort of critical lesson whereby, like a deforming mirror, they illustrate the confusion of scales increasingly present in our contemporary environment: hybridization of the global and the local, of gigantism and detail, of intensity and dissemination, of ubiquity and expectation, of power and failure, and of future and "anteriority."

This singular position along the urban frontier is reflected in the capacity of such spaces to transcend limits. The virtually ceaseless exploits that we have witnessed since the advent of air conquest, space travel, breaking of the sound barrier, the sheer gigantism of airport facilities and the related technical prowess, have their immediate corollary in the latent risk so bluntly expressed in the myth of Icarus. Catastrophism is never far away where airports are concerned, as illustrated by the recurring articles, photographs, and other information related to breakdowns, accidents, and crashes, couched in spectacular language and imagery. Similarly, the hypermobility provided by aerial ubiquity makes the long moments of inactivity that precede and last for most of the trip all the more acute as we become mere passive spectators.

It is not only physical, spatial or technical limits that are exceeded but temporal limits as well. The airport as a futurist spectacle runs headlong into "anteriority" given that the future too has its own history. The phenomenon of chronic airport obsolescence, already identified as early as 1962 by Reyner Banham, is all the more acute as it is compounded by the prototypal dimension of airports in general.[31] Dealing with an airports' various project-specific temporalities when developing it within a context of increasing uncertainty and heavy investment also raises heritage-type questions concerning the value of monuments that are dedicated first and foremost to the future.

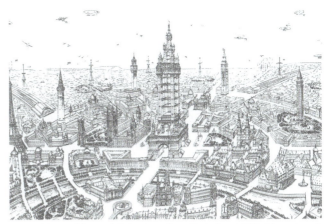

Eugène Hénard, "Vue à vol d'aéroplane d'une ville de l'avenir" [Birds'-eye view of the city of the future], in "Les villes de l'avenir", *L'Architecture*, 13 November 1910

Roissy 1 Terminal, Source Photothèque Aéroports de Paris

The "megastructure" of Orly Sud Terminal, circa 1963, Source Photothèque Aéroports de Paris

Aerial View of Roissy 2, 2005, Source Photothèque Aéroports de Paris.

Orly Sud Terminal, View of the general control room, 1961, Source Photothèque Aéroports de Paris.

Office for Metropolitan Architecture, Project for the new international airport of Jeddah, Terminal for the royal family, 2005, Source OMA

Scales of Invisibility

There is an ongoing conflict in this blend of the ideal and the real, of mirror and subject: the spectacle of the city viewed from the air; the reality of urban globality finally made whole once again; the spectacle of the airport, which both imitates and outdoes the city without being able to fully embody it; the reality of an artifact that heightens expectations in our contemporary societies. Standing apart from the city all the better to observe and redesign it, moving closer to the same city so as to understand and outdo it all the more effectively, the city *viewed* from the air can be defined vis-à-vis the existing city in a sort of a game that devices such as clarification, rationalization, panoptics, transcendence, and spectacularization. This conclusion finesses the all too frequent description of airports as non-places inasmuch as they define themselves first and foremost in relation to the city that they look toward.

Photographers specialized in aerial photography continue this aerial exploration by scrutinizing "artificialized" territory on a continental scale. For the past thirty years, Alex MacLean has been striving for ecological reform through in-depth studies of changes in the American way of life.[32] From planes to satellites, the aerial view prism has continually expanded, simultaneously rolling out the immense scope of the "urbanized" carpet and setting in motion a constant reconfiguration of landscape and territory. From the American megalopolis mapped out in the early 1960s by the geographer Jean Gottmann[33] to that of Osaka-Kobe or the Pearl River in South China observed by analysts of planetary urbanization, aerial views now focus on megapolitan phenomena. And they have recently moved into the next phase as Google Earth allows users to interact with the Earth's panoramas, thus creating new bases of perception and projection.

But by offering such apparent mastery over a situation that seems beyond our control, the aerial view reveals its own limits. This vision, which had such objective and universal pretensions, can go from being all-encompassing to totalitarian. It points up, by default, the relative absence of tools for representing and clearly depicting the confused reality surrounding all things urban and this unsettling of spatial dimensions, and the need to come up with another way of rendering intelligible the urban phenomenon together with all its *exteriority*.

– Translated from the French by Neil O'Brien.

NOTES

1. Felix Nadar, *Quand j'étais photographe* (originally published 1900), (Paris, Editions du Seuil, 1994), 97.

2. Albert Garcia Espuche, "La ville comme objet trouvé", in Jean Dethier and Alain Guiheux, eds, *La ville, art et architecture en Europe, 1870-1993*, (Paris, Editions du Centre Pompidou, 1994), 108-111.

3. Hubert Damisch, *Skyline: The Narcissistic City* (Palo Alto: Stanford University Press, 2001), 12.

4. Eugène Ivanovitch Zamiatine, "Herbert Wells," *Le métier littéraire*, (Lausanne: L'âge d'homme, 1990), 87-8; Zamyatin was the first counter-utopian author of the twentieth century: Yevgeny Zamyatin [1924], *We*, Penguin Books, 1993.

5. By eds. José Corti, Paris.

6. "La grande semaine de Champagne", *L'Illustration*, no. 3471, September 4, 1909, 153-164.

7. Jacques-Henri Lartigue, *Instants de ma vie* (Paris: Editions du Chêne, 1973), no pagination.

8. "La grande semaine de Champagne," 163; see also Léon Gimpel, "Mes grands reportages" [1944], extract published in *Etudes photographiques*, no. 19, Décember 2006, 120-39.

9. Thierry Gervais, "L'exploit mis en page, la médiatisation de la conquête de l'air à la Belle Epoque" in Musée du Jeu de Paume, *L'événement, les images comme acteurs de l'histoire* (Paris, Editions Hazan, 2007) 60-83.

10. Directed by Fritz Lang in 1926, the futuristic film set was designed by Otto Hunte and Erich Kettelhut.

11. Christoph Asendorf, *Superconstellation, Flugzeug und Raumrevolution* (Berlin, Springer, 1997) 119-122.

12. Hugh Ferriss, *Metropolis of Tomorrow*, (Ives Washburn Publishers, 1929).

13. Frank Lloyd Wright, *The Disappearing City* (New York, William Farquhar Payson, 1932).

14. Marcel Lods, "La crasse de Paris ou les hommes enfumés", *Architecture d'Aujourd'hui*, Juin 1938, 82-89.

15. Le Corbusier, "American Prologue " and "Brazilian Corollary," in *Precisions on the current state of architecture and city planning* [1930], (Cambridge, The MIT Press, 1991).

16. Le Corbusier, *Aircraft* (London, The Studio Publications, 1935).

17. "Aerial Survey of Manhattan Island", 4 August 1921, Fairchild Aerial Camera Corporation, Library of Congress, Washington DC; See Paul E. Cohen and Robert T. Augustyn, *Manhattan in maps, 1527-1995*, (New York, Rizzoli, 1997), 156-157.

18. Thomas Adams along with Harold M. Lewis and Laurence M. Orton, "The Making of the City", *The building of the City, Regional Plan of New York and Its Environs, vol. 2*, New York, 1931.

19. Pierre Remaury et Jean Royer, "Région parisienne" in *L'œuvre de Henri Prost* (Paris: Architecture et urbanisme, Académie d'architecture, 1960), 143-181.

20. Paul-Henry Chombart De Lauwe, *La découverte aérienne du monde* (Paris, Horizons de France, 1948), 325-326.

21. Ibid., 51 and, concerning Patrick Geddes, see Armand Mattelart, *Histoire de l'utopie planétaire, De la cité prophétique à la société globale*, (Paris, La Découverte, 2000), 223.

22. Hugh Ferriss, "Random Thoughts of Hugh Ferriss," (undated text, but probably from the late 1940s) from the archives of Hugh Ferriss, Box 7, Second file, Avery Drawings and Archives, Columbia University, New York.

23. Ibid.

24. Frank Lloyd Wright, "Today, Tomorrow, America Tomorrow", *American Architect*, May 1932, 17. This extract also features in *The Disappearing City* (1932).

25. Nathalie Roseau, "Reach for the skies, Aviation and urban visions circa 1910", *The Journal of Transport History*, vol. 30, n. 2, 2010.

26. Eugène Henard, "Les villes de l'Avenir", Town Planning Conference, Royal Institute of British Architects, 14 October 1910, Published in *L'Architecture*, 13 November 1910, 387.

27. Nathalie Roseau, *L'imaginaire de la ville aérienne*; doctoral thesis, University of Paris-Est, 2008, 2 vol. Forthcoming from Editions Parenthèses (2011). It retraces the history of the relationship between urbanism and developments in aerial mobility as seen from Paris and New York.

28. Read the text by Wallace K. Harrison presenting the concept of *Terminal City* for the Port Authority, 16 February 1955, Archives of Wallace K. Harrison, Box 3, Drawings and Archives, Avery Architectural and Fine Arts Library, Columbia University, New York.

29. See the example of Kansai Airport in Osaka which was built on water.

30. Read, for example, Marc Auge, "Non-lieux et espace public", *Quaderns*, n. 231, 2001, 11; Rem Koolhaas, *Mutations, Harvard project on the city* (Bordeaux: Arc en rêve Centre d'architecture, ACTAR, 2001), 721-42; Manuel Castells, The rise of the network society, *The Information Age: Economy, Society and Culture*, vol. 1, Wiley-Blackwell, 2000 (second edition).

31. Reyner Banham, "The Obsolescent Airport", *Architectural Record*, December 1962, See also, Nathalie Roseau, "The Obsolescence of the Monument, the Future of Airport Icons", in *The Challenge of Change, Dealing with the Legacy of the Modern Movement*, D.Van Den Heuvel, M. Mesman, W. Quist, B. Lemmens, eds. (Amsterdam: IOS Press, 2008), 87-92.

32. Alex MacLean, *Over*, (Paris: Editions Dominique Carré, 2008).

33. Jean Gottmann, *Megalopolis: The Urbanized Northeastern Seaboard of the United States* (New York, The Twentieth Century Fund, 1961).

FRÉDÉRIC POUSIN IS AN ARCHITECT AND A RESEARCH DIRECTOR AT CNRS, THE FRENCH NATIONAL CENTRE FOR SCIENTIFIC RESEARCH. HE SUPERVISES RESEARCH AND CURRENTLY TEACHES HISTORY AND THEORY OF LANDSCAPE AT THE UNIVERSITY OF PARIS 1. HE CARRIES OUT RESEARCH WORK ON URBAN LANDSCAPE AND THE EPISTEMOLOGICAL VALUE OF VISUALITY IN ARCHITECTURE AND URBANISM.

AERIAL VIEWS AND THE FUTURE
OF METROPOLITAN PARIS

Launched in 2008 by the Ministry of Culture and Communication at the request of the President of the Republic, the international consultation on the future of metropolitan Paris gathered ten teams led by renowned architects who developed proposals in two main fields. The first one, entitled "The 21st century post-Kyoto metropolis," consisted of a theoretical reflection on the consequences of the Kyoto conference on metropolitan development. The second theme, "prospective diagnosis of the Parisian agglomeration," was conceived as an application of the first on the extended and complex territory of Île-de-France, that is the region around Paris.

Unlike a competition, this international consultation in research and development in architecture required from its teams the ability to combine designers, research labs, and experts. This was necessary to lead the theoretical reflection on the post-Kyoto metropolis, but also because intervention on a large territory implies the mobilization and even the production of different types of knowledge. Historically, there has always been an important production of knowledge about the region around Paris. The Institute for development in the Île-de-France region (IAURIF) and the Paris development workshop (APUR) have gathered a lot of knowledge and know-how, and so they were consulted by the teams. Moreover, the IAURIF presided over the production of the new urbanistic scheme for the Île-de-France region (SDRIF) that was approved by all actors in 2008.

As a result of the nine-month consultation, the teams produced important reports, totaling more than 7,000 pages and including theoretical views, methodological elements, and a great variety of projects, even though several proposals converge in certain respects. The general impression is one of a seminal, stimulating ferment of ideas. This material led to an exhibition for the general public that took place at the Cité de l'architecture et du patrimoine in Paris between the spring and the fall of 2009.

Large Scale and its Representations

Large-scale architecture diverges from both planning and urban design because of its aims and methods. The main difference is that it cannot rely on a clearly identified area of intervention. In fact, large scale implies multiple areas and the notion of a continuum. The ten teams involved had to take a stand on the issue of the *limit* of the metropolitan territory, which each did in different ways. The Atelier Castro Deniss of Casi suggests that the limit of the Paris agglomeration should be based on its various landscape entities. The Rogers Stirk Harbour + Partners team defines the metropolitan limit through the proposal of a green belt. The idea of a green belt is at the core of an original landscape project suggested by landscape architect Michel Desvignes with the Ateliers Jean Nouvel/Michel Cantal Dupart/Jean Marie Duthilleul. In contrast, the Atelier Portzamparc avoids the issue by using fractals. The porous city imagined by Studio 09 does not really raise this question but considers instead the limit between urban and green areas. The Grumbach & Associés team answers the question with the notion of a linear city. The Descartes Group does not really suggest any strategy, while AUC relies on local situations to consider the global nature of the territory. This is why no specific visualization is offered. Even more radically, the metropolitan phenomenon is not considered as a spatial fact but as the *metropolitan condition*. Several teams refuse to give an a priori global point of view and suggest that we need to start from what exists: such is the case of the Jean Nouvel team, Studio 09, and AUC, who outlined the methodological consequences of this stance:

To bypass the representation crisis in the Parisian metropolis, we suggest the *Greater Paris matrix* as a means to reveal the concrete dynamics of a 'metropolitan know-how' from a selection of 18 territories that are very different from each other.[1]

All the projects fall into two major groups: those who see the historical city as the core of a high-performance urban and functional archipelago; and those who favor a less hierarchical organization whose ordinary components would be the basis of an important transformation. Such a duality in the projects under scrutiny seems to reveal the double standard of a commission that is both interested in a great project for today and a research for the city's future evolution.

Urban Planning and Aerial Photography

To better understand the importance of satellite images in the projects produced by the consultation, I will briefly revisit the history of aerial photography, because satellite images raise issues that have been emerging since the birth of aerial photography. In France, the use of aerial photography in urbanism developed after World War I. Photography, as we know, was a weapon of war. With film, it became an instrument to measure destruction.[2] Later still, the needs for urban reconstruction and development encouraged better performance and technological innovation.

In 1919, the Cornudet law decreed that cities with more than 10,000 inhabitants should have a planning, improvement, and expansion scheme. Deadlines were very tight: three months for stricken cities and three years for the others, even though records were not accurate. In this context, analysis techniques for photographic images such as metrophotography and stereophotography emerged. Such techniques gave birth to new jobs and new businesses, even though their use was limited since planning schemes required field surveys that were too expensive.[3] The urbanists' photomaps were then mainly used as negotiation tools, in the tradition of vertical city views. It was only later that the full application of aerial photography developed.

In urbanism as in geography, it was after World War II that the aerial view became a means of representation that was widely publicized and therefore used. This was a key moment for geography, because numerous expeditions were undertaken. They were echoed by enthusiastic comments on the renewal of knowledge, in the wake of discourses on the aerial view put forth by Modernist architects.[4] Chombart de Lawe's first texts see in the aerial view a metaphor of knowledge.[5] Later developments expressed a doubt concerning the exact nature of the knowledge gathered."[6]

With the reconstruction, the national territory changed thanks to the new equipments, infrastructures, and towns. The aerial view then appeared as a privileged medium to show transformations on a territorial scale. It allowed a synoptic and strategic view of the territory. The view from a plane, and then from a helicopter, was part of a visual culture that favored a dominant, strategic look, finding its roots in a military vision of space. The aerial view was often opposed to terrestrial photography or the "pedestrian" view, which also played a role in the visual practices of reconstruction. Dominique Gauthey shows that all the iconographic documents are interrelated according to different cartographic scales, from the local to the national. "In this post-war reconquest of the towns, the photographic image became a tactical weapon serving a strategic aim. The aerial view drew the maps of the operations, while the detail maps worked as biopsies in the urban network and served as evidence to convince everyone to lead this fair war."[7]

The Interpretation of Aerial Views

In the 1945-1951 period, urban aerial photographs played an important role (more than 5.7 million acres were covered by 46,300 pictures, counting only the 1/5,000 views). Reconstruction could never have been achieved without this gigantic effort in urban topography, led by the Department for Topographic Works at the Ministry of Construction.[8] Aerial views were taken and interpreted (stereoscopically or not), and very large-scale maps were established thanks to metrophotographic techniques. These rigorous maps were widely disseminated in urbanism and architecture agencies. Aerial photogrammetric methods have continually been redesigned and adapted, since the validity of urban schemes depends on constant updating.[9] The way urban schemes were established evolved with the urbanism they were supposed to represent, as the basis of any land development. As for oblique aerial views taken at low altitude, they have usually been considered an "unbiased" take on reality, as opposed to the selective point of view of architects' perspectives. However, different interpretations coexist to describe what best qualifies as a reality effect.[10]

Finally, aerial flight took on an undeniable symbolic value. As early as the end of the 1950s and throughout the following decades, technocrats considered that urban planning required gaining height, literally and metaphorically. Therefore, the creation of new towns implied numerous flights over the territory. In the 1960s and 1970s, photographic missions were launched to develop touristic projects on the waterfront. In the 1980s, the famous DATAR photographic mission broke with the practice of aerial views and entrusted artistic photographers with a survey of the territory based on pedestrian views.[11] Implementing touristic urbanism on the waterfront, for example, a sensitive space, both geographically and environmentally (erosion, large forests) strongly revealed the necessity of integrating varied scales – that of the global planning scheme, that of the implantation of buildings in the environment, and that of the integration of circulation in a given area.

At the end of the 1970s, two aerial photography campaigns were launched as part of the inventory of the waterfront, which from then on replaced the research and monitoring missions for territory planning. These campaigns, in 1977 and 1982, allowed for the establishment of a precise cartography of ground use. A national database was created to monitor the evolution of uses over time.[12]

Aerial photographs and satellite images have become not only tools for territory planning but also major instruments for analysis and action. In this case, the image constitutes the starting point of the survey, providing the first clues and the first questions. Images or pictures thus become a research technique in their own right.

Satellite and Aerial Images and the Future of Metropolitan Paris

The international consultation on the future of metropolitan Paris led to no flight over the territory. However, an important documentary corpus was handed out to the teams. It comprised several cartographic and topographic databases as well as local orthophotographic databases (IGN source). The first workshop inviting teams to develop theoretical reflections on the twenty-first century post-Kyoto metropolis did not particularly lead to the use of satellite or aerial views, except for one case. Indeed, the teams that worked on this theme (Atelier Portzamparc, Atelier Castro, Denissof, Casi, Grumbach & Associés, MVRDV) mainly used maps, schemes, and photographs that were not taken from the sky. Is this an effect of the commission, or can we find here a deliberate avoidance of the tool? Developing an analytical and prospective discourse, as well as an educational one, the Rogers team is the only one that strongly relies on aerial views. These views are always composed (framing the geometrical components of the image, highlighting the relationship between the item represented and the background). They carry an aesthetic content and are often published on a full page. Here, whether oblique or vertical, the use of these views is mainly rhetorical. They back up the discursive elements thanks to an emblematic illustration of the phenomenon under scrutiny, in a way that pedestrian views would not. For example, an aerial image of Sao Paulo (figure 1) fails to reveal what it is meant to express: the social performance that is at the core of the proposal. Such a rhetorical use of aerial views, based on aesthetic values, tends to become a cliché able to fit different discourses, for example the general-public-oriented discourse expressed by Yann Arthus-Bertrand[13] or the more specialized, critical discourse of Alex MacLean, who reflects on the state of territories and on their social and environmental uses.[14] Presenting MacLean's work, Gilles Tiberghien evokes his debt to geographer John Brinckerhoff Jackson:

> MacLean has the same talent for observation and the same passion for investigation, so that an image, as beautiful and as surprising as it may be, is always at the same time a question. For him, landscape is a construction of reality whose history can be deciphered by going backwards, as it were, from the sky to the earth. As if, paradoxically, the landscape held, in an inverted way, the material and human values of reality.[15]

Some teams showed a concern for grounding their theoretical reflection on the territory of Île-de-France made a more important use of satellite images as well as aerial photographs. Because they support the discursive analysis of urbanization, we could consider that these pictures also have a rhetorical function. However, they are also useful in describing a territory inasmuch as they make characteristic features explicit, just as discourse does. The image represents a phenomenon, in the full meaning of the word, and the questions derive from the image. Thus with the Descartes group, aerial views show how villages and towns are divided into sectors (figure 2). Aerial views (IGN) and satellite views (Google Earth) are used without distinction. For example, satellite views are used to represent farming enclaves or asymmetrical landscapes.

We could wonder, however, if items represented thanks to aerial views – infrastructures, highways and interchanges, or urban networks in their morphological diversity – do not constitute canonical items that would appear as such on aerial views.[16]

Vertical satellite views are widely used to build thematic cartographies that help to visualize various human, economic, and urbanistic phenomena (buildings and infrastructures.) As such, they are part of the mobilization and even construction of knowledge that a project can trigger, as Bernardo Secchi underlines. If thematic cartography appears in the Jean Nouvel team (maps of forest-covered and farming lands, and hydrologic maps), vertical, aerial, and satellite views appear in the first workshop only to back up the discourse on large territory, through topics such as river links. Using the notion of existing territory as their starting point, the Jean Nouvel team favors, methodologically, the surveying of land as an instrument of knowledge – hence photographs taken at human eye level, as well as a great quantity of details that capture the eye. Studio 09 uses the same approach with a "step by step" walk through the metropolis, in contrast to the bird's flight over the city. This approach suggests a new canon – the description from the ground as an alternative or a complement to the description from above – that the LIN and AUC teams do not claim. Indeed, to define the identities of the scattered city, LIN uses oblique aerial views as well as pedestrian views used in surveying, integrating them within a visual device: a table. The chart is also used to represent the stages of an evolutional phenomenon such

1. Rogers Stirk Harbour + Partners. The Paraisapolis favela in Sao Paulo and private housing with a pool on each terrace. Copyright: Tuca Vieira

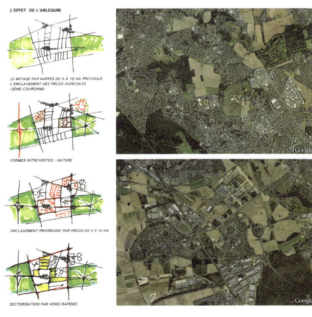

2. The Descartes Group. The Harlequin strategy. The growth of the agglomeration further isolates rural areas. Copyright: Groupe Descartes

as the pre-programmed transformation of a business park (figure 3). In the study of international metropolises, the chart is also used for comparisons (study of limits between low and high densities). In this case, pictures have no symbolic value, in opposition to those used by AUC in its matrix for a polyphonic and polymorphic metropolis.

LIN sets the frame of the study by featuring a satellite view of Metropolitan Paris. Some aerial photographs, such as those of the purification of water, anticipate development proposals and allow us to visualize spatially the territorial reality of a development device not yet embodied in a specific territory. This embodiment takes place during the second part of the consultation, and the vertical satellite view is used to represent the pools located along the Seine that allow the river to widen.

In the projects for the Parisian metropolis, the satellite image plays a crucial role when it represents a walk through or a flight over the territories. The metropolitan territory can be crossed by a green path on its eastern part, from south to north, as Studio 09 describes (figure 4); it can be included in the path of the Seine Valley from Paris to Le Havre, as Antoine Grumbach suggests (figure 5); it can also be spread between polarities and the light city (LIN) (figure 6). The oblique satellite view offers a geographical representation of a large territorial project, apprehended from a set aerial point of view that remains an abstraction, just as the views of built cities were when it was not yet possible to travel in the sky. Such a synoptic point of view, which used to present similarities with God's point of view, makes us believe in the possibility of a perceptive experience publicized by the technological tool. Oblique views present themselves as a theater of operations for the unfolding of a project concerning a large territory (perhaps even the globe) expressing itself through its strategic aims. The satellite view on which the Grumbach project inscribes itself is so striking that it becomes its symbol. Does it not suggest that, from Paris to Le Havre, only one city is possible, as Bonaparte suggested in the nineteenth century? In the case of Studio 09, the green path would be an updating of the project already designed at the beginning of the twentieth century by the first French urbanists (Léon Jaussely, Jean Claude Nicolas Forestier). The satellite view allows for the inscription of this project on the concrete territory of the Parisian metropolis. The satellite view casts a close look on the space across which we move. Following the example of environmental corridors that ensure a continuity of organic spaces, moving across urban spaces would give them a continuity based on open spaces, often green areas located by the water. Satellite views are also a means for the team to question the limits and margins of the compact city. The Rogers Stirk Harbour +Partners team uses the satellite image to represent the green thoroughfares (figure 7), when schemes of green belts and networks are represented on a map. The satellite view seems to work as an image of a globe on which evolutionary phenomena are inscribed, revealing a certain form of organicity.

The Grumbach team uses satellite views to support the geopolitical argumentation of its project; this shows that satellite views play the political role once played by globe images and atlases. "The plane is a sort of atlas in action," writes Jean-Marc Besse. "Its movement above the landscape allows one to measure at a glance the territorial shapes and the limits of these forms, the spatial discontinuities, the differentiated uses of space that coexist in the world. The plane and aerial photography are the engines of a comparative intelligence that gathers and opposes."[17] Satellite views on a large territory direct our minds to strategies on a global scale, beyond what the image visualizes. At the same time, they allow us to apprehend and therefore to appropriate a line of thought that could otherwise seem too abstract. Nevertheless, the very visualization of this scale already supposes

Green intensification **Urban diversification** **Climatic envelope**

3. LIN. The preprogrammed transformation of a business park. Copyright: LIN Finn Geipel + Giulia Andi

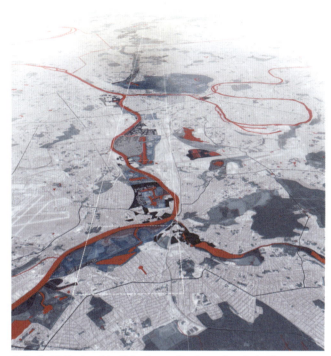

4. Studio 09. Region of the Seine Amont, South-east from Paris. The green path. Copyright : équipe Studio 09. Secchi-Vigano

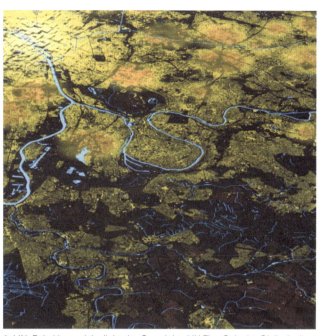

6. LIN. Polarities and the light city. Copyright : LIN Finn Geipel + Giulia Andi

7. Rogers Stirk Harbour + Partners. Green thoroughfares linking town and country. Copyright : Rogers Stirk Harbour + Partners/ London School of Economics / Arup

5. Grumbach & associés. "Paris, Rouen, Le Havre, one city whose main street is the Seine" Bonaparte. Aerial view. IGN. Copyright : Antoine Grumbach et Associés

the ability to cut oneself off from the world, to put it at a distance. Here lies a paradox that is nevertheless the key to the use of satellite images. Moreover, as with Grumbach, aerial views can be used for the analysis and argumentation of the landscape dimension of the project. Thus an oblique aerial view is associated with a perspective-section of the Mantois (figure 8).

Vertical aerial views allow the LIN team to represent multifunctional landscapes (figure 9). A clever framing underlining the articulation of two different types of space can highlight a heterogeneity ready to be rearticulated thanks to the network of local circulations activating the territory. Moreover, vertical aerial views reveal that space can be used in many different ways, and diversity is the principle of multifunctional landscapes. A building structured around a main road can also play a role in a readjustment and symbiosis between agricultural spaces and housing sites; in their turn, these spaces will be induced to de-densify thanks to a reconquest of planted or cultivated spaces. Aerial photography then becomes a means to define the project.

It is mainly for this reason that the Jean Nouvel team uses aerial photographs. Oblique aerial views are articulated to a vertical view, according to a canonical device: the topographic map. Let us take the example of the "limits, margins, verges" theme (figure 10). Whereas the vertical view allows us to see the "theater of operations" – to extend the military metaphor – oblique aerial views allow us to assess the spatial impact of the interventions suggested on the landscape. But unlike the perspective image that allows control over the impact of the neighborhood, the oblique aerial view does not permit any selection, and therefore requires a greater inscription into a given context (a quality already mentioned). Moreover, inscribing the transformations of a project into a perceived space, thanks to photography, is a militant gesture made popular by the 1970s debates on urban landscape.[18] Let us add that oblique aerial views are also inserted into the photographic tables offering a list of occurrences, at the beginning of each series (figure 11). Surveying territories, as claimed by the team, does not exclude an aerial discovery of the phenomena in the great tradition of territory planning. However, because photographs are reframed and cut as if they were samples, the aerial view does not allow any synoptic vision of space, and this is an important difference.

Reflecting on the uses of aerial views, whether photographic or satellite images, requires replacing the images within the traditions to which they belong. Thus if oblique views tend to lend themselves to a rhetorical use, it is because they are more readable, but also because bird's-eye views are part of a political tradition, well updated by the first urbanists of the twentieth century.[19] As for the technical uses of aerial views, they also emerged with time, from an operational purpose in the drawing of plans and maps, to the diachronic analysis allowed by the repetition of recordings in resource or use inventories, to the contribution to notions such as densification, that usually expresses itself symbolically, and that vertical aerial views make plausible thanks to a comparative corpus of images. It is also necessary to pay attention to the devices in which images appear, such as tables, series, and montages. For the meaning of images proceeds from these manipulations, that far from being gratuitous or aesthetic games, are full cognitive acts, as anthropologists specialized in writing and images showed.[20] I will add that such devices fully participate in the representation through which the project takes shape, communicates, and embodies itself. This is what this international consultation reveals.

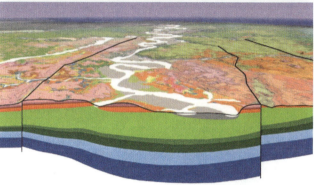

8. Grumbach & associés. The oblique aerial view and perspective-section of the Mantois (Region around Mantes-la-Jolie, North-west from Paris). Copyright: Google

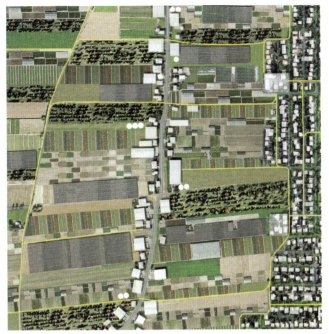

9. LIN. Multifunctional landscape. Copyright : LIN Finn Geipel + Giulia Andi

10. Jean Nouvel/Michel Cantal Dupart/Jean Marie Duthilleul Team. The Paris rebirths. Limits, margins, verges, interferences. Copyright : Proposition du Grand Paris de l'équipe: Jean Nouvel, Jean-Marie Duthilleul, Michel Cantal-Dupart

11. Jean Nouvel/Michel Cantal Dupart/Jean Marie Duthilleul Team. Photographic table. Copyright : Proposition du Grand Paris de l'équipe: Jean Nouvel, Jean-Marie Duthilleul, Michel Cantal-Dupart

NOTES

1. L'AUC, in AMC Le Moniteur Architecture, le Grand Pari(s). International consultation on the future of metropolitan Paris, 94.

2. See Teresa Castro, "Vues aériennes et cinématisme (1898-1938)," in Mark Dorrian, Frédéric Pousin (eds.), *Vues aériennes. Fragments d'une histoire culturelle*, Paris, CNRS-Éditions, forthcoming.

3. See Catherine Bruant, "la vue aérienne et l'urbanisme dans l'entre deux guerre," lecture delivered at the conference *La vue aérienne: enjeu pour les savoirs et les pratiques de l'espace*, Paris, Institut de Géographie, 07 juin 2007.

4. For Le Corbusier the aircraft embodies the look of an eagle, a searching gaze that penetrates the stark reality and creates a condition of modern consciousness, see Le Corbusier, *Aircraft*, (London: The Studio, 1935). For architect Jose Luis Sert, the aerial view exposes a new urban façade, it reveals the large scale and chaos of the industrial metropolis and thus motivates large scale interpretations, see Jose Luis Sert, *Can Our Cities Survive?* (Cambridge, MA: Harvard University Press, 1942).

5. Paul-Henry Chombart de Lawe, *La découverte aérienne du monde* (Paris, Horizons de France, 1948).

6. See Philippe Bonnin, "Pour une eth(n)ologie sociale de l'espace", *Espaces et Sociétés 103, Paul-Henry Chombart de Lawe et l'histoire des études urbaines en France*, 2000, 113-139.

7. Dominique Gauthey, "les archives de la reconstruction (1945-1979), *Etudes Photographiques* 3, November 1997, 114-115, quoted by Vincent Guigueno, La France vue du sol. Une histoire de la Mission photographique de la DATAR (1983-1989), *Etudes photographiques* no.18, May 2006, 101.

8. See Bernard Dubuisson, "La photographie aérienne au service de l'urbanisme", *Urbanisme* no. 1-2, 1952, 44-46.

9. See Bernard Dubuisson, "Nouvelles applications françaises de l'aérophotogrammétrie au Ministère de la Construction", *Urbanisme* no. 87, 1965, 71-80

10. On the challenges raised by oblique and vertical aerial views, see Mark Dorrrian, "The aerial view: notes for a cultural history", *STRATES-Matériaux pour la recherche en sciences sociales* no. 13 , 105-118; strates.revues.org/

11. See Vincent Guigueno, "La France vue du sol. Une histoire de la Mission photographique de la DATAR (1983-1989)"

12. See www.geolittoral.equipement.gouv.fr/rubrique.php3?

13. Yann Arthus-Bertrand, *La terre vue du ciel : un portrait aérien de la planète* (Paris, La Martinière, 2002).

14. Alex Mac Lean, *Over, Visions aériennes de l'American Way of life: une absurdité écologique*, Paris, ed. Dominique carré (Paris, La Découverte, 2008).

15. Gilles Tiberghien, "La leçon de MacLean", in Alex S. MacLean, *L'arpenteur du ciel* (Paris, Editions Textuel, 2003), 84.

16. By "canonical items", I mean here a form of representation widely used by a disciplinary or professional milieu, taking on a legitimacy value, and whose origin is not questioned, see Marie-Claire Robic, "Rendre visible la ville", in *Figures de ville et construction des savoirs. Architecture, urbanisme géographie,* (Frédéric Pousin ed.) (Paris, CNRS Editions, 2005), 205-208.

17. J.M. Besse, *Le goût du monde. Exercices de paysage*, Paris, Actes sud/ENSP, 2009, p.95. See also également *Les grandeurs de la terre. Aspects du savoir géographique à la Renaissance.* (Paris-Lyon, ENS éditions, 2003).

18. See Frédéric Pousin, "Du townscape au "paysage urbain", circulation d'un modèle rhétorique mobilisateur", *STRATES-Matériaux pour la recherche en sciences sociales* n. 13, 25-50; strates.revues.org/

19. See "The bird's-eye view as a rhetorical tool in democratic decision-making" in Erik de Jong, Michel Lafaille, Christian Bertram, *Landscapes of the Imagination* (Rotterdam, NAI Publishers, 2008), 102.

20. See Jack Goody, *The Domestication of the Savage Mind*, Cambridge, New York (Cambridge University Press, 1977). See also Philippe Descola, *Par delà nature et culture* (Paris, Gallimard, 2005).

KELLY SHANNON TEACHES LANDSCAPE URBANISM AT THE UNIVERSITY OF LEUVEN AND IS A MEMBER OF OSA (THE RESEARCH GROUP OF URBANISM AND ARCHITECTURE). HER RESEARCH IS AT THE INTERSECTION OF ANALYSIS, MAPPING, AND NEW CARTOGRAPHIES AND DESIGN. MOST OF HER WORK FOCUSES ON THE EVOLVING RELATION OF LANDSCAPE, INFRASTRUCTURE, AND URBANIZATION IN ASIA.

BRUNO DE MEULDER TEACHES URBANISM AT THE UNIVERSITY OF LEUVEN (BELGIUM) AND AT THE TECHNICAL UNIVERSITY OF EINDHOVEN (THE NETHERLANDS) AND IS AFFILIATED WITH OSA, THE RESEARCH GROUP URBANISM AND ARCHITECTURE OF THE UNIVERSITY OF LEUVEN. HE COMBINES RESEARCH ON COLONIAL AND POSTCOLONIAL URBANISM WITH CONTEMPORARY URBAN DESIGN EXPLORATIONS IN DYNAMIC CONTEXTS OF CHANGE.

ANNELIES DE NIJS IS A PHD RESEARCHER AT OSA (THE RESEARCH GROUP OF URBANISM AND ARCHITECTURE), UNIVERSITY OF LEUVEN (BELGIUM). HER RESEARCH FOCUSES ON WATER URBANISM IN THE CONTEXT OF CLIMATE CHANGE. VIETNAM IS HER CASE STUDY, AND DESIGN IS AN IMPORTANT ASPECT OF THE WORK.

FROM ABOVE, FROM BELOW THE CASE OF CANTHO

The constructive and complex interplays of infrastructure, landscape, and urbanism – and the systems value of combing different logics (engineering, ecology, and occupation) – remain evident in the numerous networks that criss-cross Cantho, a Vietnamese city in the heart of the Mekong Delta. The impressive transformation of a regional landscape "from above" – from a colonized urban nature (via waterworks) by the French to a modernization of colonization (via industrial and military installations) by the Americans to impositions of socialist urbanism and culminating in projects of today's era of *doi moi* (market-driven) – is tempered 'from below' – by the unavoidable (yet changing) interactions between landscape, modernization processes, and the perversions and subversions caused by everyday life. The spiral of increasing growth, development, and modern intervention has come to a point where a more rationalized continuation of the dialectic practices of hybridization might become a necessity. For more than three centuries, the Vietnamese landscape in Nam Bo (the frontier region of south Vietnam, where Cantho is located) and cultural practices in the territory have been defined by the region's water dynamics and inherent contradictions between liquidity and stability.

Inscription in the Landscape

The Mekong Delta has been called "modern by nature" with a geography amenable to the commodity economy and that easily accommodated cultural hybridization.[1] In pre-colonial times, the delta was a thriving hub of regional commerce, a major exporter of rice, and a place where merchant ships clustered in search of profitable cargo.[2] From the feudal era through colonial times and until the present day, there has been a strictly governed policy of public works and land reclamation to both increase land productivity and to organize safe settlement – as "agricultural colonies" (*dinh dien*) and "military colonies" (*don dien*). Cantho and other Mekong Delta cities represent what Karl Wittfogel, the renowned Frankfurt School sinologist, referred to as a "hydraulic civilizations" – a particular type of urban/rural social formation founded on centralized state water engineering and control. The comprehensive system of the hydraulic civilization (which employed extensive *corvée* labour) created productive water works (for irrigation and drainage) and protective waterworks (for flood control), and also provided drinking water and communication conduits. Wet-rice cultivation requires a relatively equitable distribution of water and necessitates a system of canals, dikes, irrigation canals, terraces, and locks to regulate water levels. Strong and well-organized power structures that coordinated and imposed public works were the answer at the time. This despotic "traditional" way of managing the region appears impossible today in a regime with a more decentralized organizational system that sometimes seems primarily driven by the woes of the market economy.

In the early feudal era, the swampy, half-liquid, half-stable area of Nam Bo was transformed into fertile plains for wet paddy cultivation. Settlements developed linearly, following the alluvial, nonsalted highland banks of rivers and canals formed by sedimentation. Villages advanced following the incremental construction of the pre-colonial canal system. Unlike other parts of Vietnam (where feudal urbanization regulations were strict) and as an incentive for the cultivation of new lands, the population of the south was allowed to freely occupy land, incubating an entrepreneurial spirit. Markets were established along the natural waterways, and prosperous floating markets burgeoned. Stilt houses occupied thresholds between water and land. A network of market places, transient stations for traders, service stations for the repair and maintenance of boats and supply of fresh water, and areas for rice processing (oriented toward export) was established. A particular water-based civilization took hold with

Inscription in the Landscape: The rich liquid geomorphology of the Mekong River Delta was originally a largely waterlogged world of black muddy sponge and mangrove trees, 'bordered by thick tropical forests where the land rose away from the flooded plain. Drainage canals had only slowly begun to ensure that some areas were protected from the annual floods that came with the rainy season and the steady rise of the Mekong's level, its volume swollen both by the rains and by the melting of snows in faraway Tibet' (Osborne 2000:21).

society living from the water and on the water. As cultivation and settlements find a balance in the world of water dynamics, entrepreneurship appears condemned to surf on the waves of successive political regimes, being overwhelmed one moment and then catching up with the next state-initiated (social) engineering work.[3]

Engineered Interplays of Rivers and Canals

Cantho is strategically located at the confluence of the Hau (lower branch of the mighty Mekong) and Cantho rivers (and a multitude of other tributaries of the Hau). At 100 kilometers from the East Sea, it was far enough away from the vagaries of coastal habitation, yet close enough to function as a competitive entrepôt city of regional importance. Cantho was established in the mid-eighteenth century as Tay Do (the "western capital") and was an important crossroads between areas deep in the delta and Saigon (now Ho Chi Minh City). During the colonial era (1876–1954), massive programs of modern infrastructure were implemented: railways, port facilities, roadways, bridges (known as *ponts* Eiffel) and, most importantly, the massive irrigation and transport canal system of the Mekong Delta specifically directed at the promotion of commercial agriculture.

While development of railways, port facilities and the like essentially "integrated" Vietnam with the exterior (or at least the French imperial) world, the canal system internally restructured the specific condition of the Mekong Delta. As these canal/infrastructural interventions made more land suitable for cultivation (and consequently habitable), colonization and intensification of occupation rapidly took hold. Cantho was reaffirmed by French imperialist expansion as a node and was equipped with a port, ferry system, military camp, market, town hall, treasury, and prison. Other social "equipment" followed. The French radically transformed Vietnam's lower Mekong Delta from a scarcely populated swamp into the granary of Vietnam and a bustling heartland of commercial export agriculture. From 1890 to 1936, 1,360 kilometers of main canals and 2,500 kilometers of auxiliary canals were dug by a combined effort of machines and manual labor, in addition to 3,000 kilometers of interprovincial land routes between 1880 and 1913.[4] Prior to 1880, the total cultivated area in Cochin China was estimated at 552,000 hectares; between 1880-1937, irrigation increased this to 2,200,000 hectares.[5] The Mekong Delta became a highly engineered landscape of agricultural productivity without precedent. The region harvests two to three crops of rice per

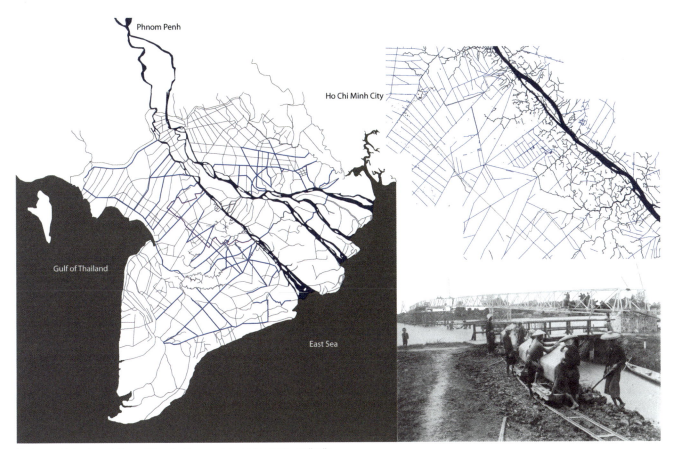

Engineered Interplays of Rivers & Canals: The massive canal system – radically changing the nature of the swamp landscape – parasites on the river system. The taming of the organic geometry of the 'original' landscape was made by the induction of the Cartesian order (that made the land cultivatable) that was greatly expanded during the French colonial era.

year and remains the country's "rice basket". The river-canal dialectic thrives upon the engineering logics that exploit the force of the natural system – with an inherent fertility of the land (due to the flooding of the Mekong and replenishing of the land with rich nutrients) – and the region's abundant labor force.

Urbanizing and Cultivating the Territory

The resettlement schemes and fundamental reengineering of the nature/ culture dialectic coincides with the imposed and often conflicting notion of "state visions." For Scott, the "from above and from the center" engineering projects and planned social order were not possible without "some elements of the practical knowledge they tend to dismiss" – the "below" here being through the notion of *metis*. This was rearticulated in the next major transformation of the territory that came with the American occupation of South Vietnam (following French defeat in 1954). Cantho and its surroundings fell within the "Fourth Tactical Zone." From the 1960s onward, the population of Cantho steadily increased due to migration from North Vietnam and those fleeing extensive carpet bombing in the countryside during the Second Indochine War and finally the Strategic Hamlet Program

– intended for "rural pacification," but in reality leading to mass migration toward the cities. The city was turned into the industrial center, commercial liaison, and naval base of the entire delta. As a new scale of infrastructure (including an airfield and military quays) were plugged in on the fine-mazed water structure and scarce road network of the territory. Some relabeled Cantho as a "barrack city." Two territorial armatures emerged: a linear structure along the Hau River, which connects Cantho to Long Xuyen (52 kilometers to the northwest), and the other bringing Cantho into relation with the inland city of Soc Trang (52 kilometers to the southeast). Cantho became the center for "supplying, storing and redistributing goods" from Saigon to the extensive rural areas of the delta. To make its first industrial zones operational (in 1968), low lands were filled. Large tarmac surfaces became a new integral component of the urban landscape. The waterways (natural and man-made) and the roadways operated as complementary networks – new hybrid systems in a dialectic process of reordering the landscape Plugged into the water/ road network were industrial zones, airports, quays – all elements operating at the larger scale, be it in connection with the exterior, being it in the internal organization of the territory. Settlements took on a

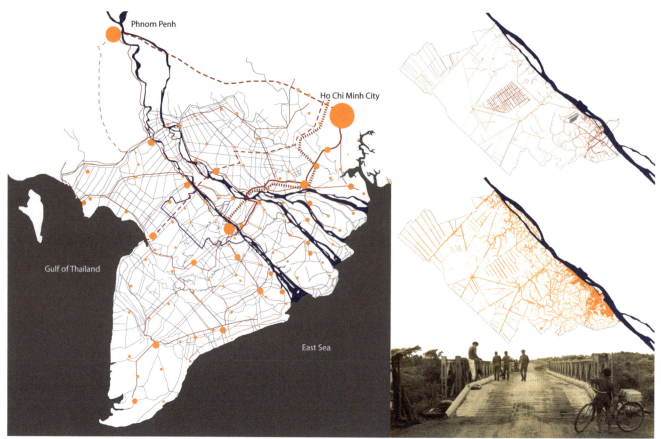

Urbanizing the Territory: The original settlement structures, strung along the delta's many waterways, are complemented by small parallel road infrastructures. Larger towns and cities were 60 km apart, due to rhythms of nature (flow velocity and sedimentation load of the water causality). While canals are infills, anchored on the larger river system, the regional road system framed the fine-meshed tissues of parallel water- road-settlement bundles.

hierarchy (hamlets, villages, cities) in a diffuse field. The organized dispersal of the territory is obviously tied to the intricate balance and interdependent structure of water and land, permeable and impermeable surfaces – all organized by the necessary hydraulic systems for water management and soil stabilization – and capitalized upon by productive lowland paddy and high-land orchards atop dikes. The landscape is one of minute yet important topographical differences and levels of inundation determine distinct land uses (productive/inhabited, safe/unsafe, etc.).

New Challenges

Over time, Cantho's population witnessed a near continuous swelling – except for a dip between 1975 and 1986 when harsh post-war deurbanizing policies sent a portion of its population to reeducation camps or forced them to resettle in new economic zones.[6] Today's burgeoning population of approximately 1.2 million is within a large area (1,402 square kilometers) and the city has a special status (along with Hanoi, Ho Chi Minh City, Danang, Hai Phong, and Hue) in that it is considered of national importance and under direct control of the state in Hanoi. The population continues to rise; restrictions on residence permits have been abolished since 1993, and there is

massive rural-to-urban migration. The 2006 approved master plan for Cantho marked the city again as the region's premier industrial center. In the imagery of a Singapore-like super city, the large Hung Phu EPZ (938 ha) on the southeast bank of the Cantho River is to be a state-of-the-art port facility and Nam Song Hau (1722 ha) a new living and housing district. Construction is well under way and an instant city is emerging on platforms of 2-3 meters of fill, while the port is shaped by monumental concrete platforms on stilts. It is as if the majestic bridge over the Hau River (opened in April 2010) prompted for a new scale of operation in the city and region, repositioning Cantho in terms of new economies, proximities, and hierarchies. The Hau River Bridge is representative of massive investments in infrastructure, including highways that connect Cantho in a manner befitting a city of national importance.

The present-day city-building processes raise crucial ecological questions. The repercussions of increased flooding will surely be felt in the city extension area, but also in the existing city, as the absorptive capacity of the land is severely compromised. Compounding this are the predicted effects of climate change. The sea-level rise is expected to subject millions of people to flooding and cause damage in the Mekong Delta. A rise in seawater level will worsen saline water

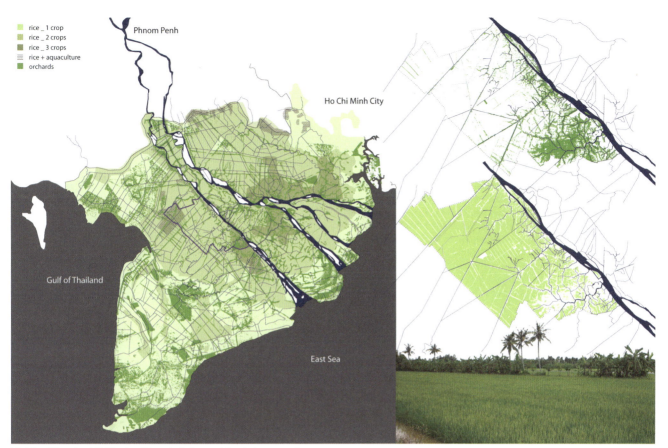

High-land/ Low-land Cultivation: The spindly figure of Cantho's surrounding mesh of high-land orchards in the southwest is anchored on the natural waterways while the low-land paddy is cultivated in the vast open and marshy landscape in between. The productive landscape of Cantho exploits the topographical differences of the territory.

intrusion in coastal zones (and partly effect the northwest agricultural area of Cantho), already a problem in some areas due to fresh water extraction for irrigation and drinking. The construction of canals in the deltas and upstream dams exacerbates the problems. Water resource management has become a central concern for Cantho, the Mekong Delta, and Vietnam more generally.

New Tools
The further development of Cantho can be guided by new interplays of landscape, infrastructure, and urbanization. A "civic spine" could be created as a new armature to operate at the citywide scale. Morphological cohesion between infrastructure and urbanity would then be deliberate and opportunistic — vehicular movement and public transport intelligently married to a hierarchy of public programs and developed as an instrument to guide urbanization. Sectional richness is explicitly designed and the landscape, infrastructural design, building edges and utilities below surface are to be built concurrently and thereby form a new system of transport, promenade, utilities, and power. The civic spine intertwines transportation infrastructure, recreational areas, platforms for regional and city-scaled public programs, flood and drainage engineering, and the creation of a scenic

landscape. It traverses scales; it is simultaneously particular and comprehensive in scope and local and metropolitan in impact. Urban planning, civil and sanitary engineering, and landscape architecture are folded into one another, as are concerns for mobility, health, recreation and scenery. The spine of the emerging new Cantho, crosses blue spaces, rationalized orchards and other green spaces, and the various districts that compose the new linearly organized metropolis in the making. The enormous scale of the geometrical and monumental spine gives concrete shape to the backbone of the city as giant platform along the majestic Hau River, marking rhythms and defining new higher lands for building.

A new layer of multifunctional waterworks could be developed for Cantho. A system of water purification (constructed wetlands and aerated lagoons) and water retention systems could double as recreational parks and form the public core of various new housing neighborhoods. In such parks, spaces could be created to accommodate certain programs in the dry season, which are then flooded in the rainy season. Each park could be designed to have a different identity, with a mix of local and regional programs. New orchards could be cultivated near the public space, providing shade while strengthening the agricultural economy; they could also work as obstacles to urban sprawl. Water transportation could be developed for the major river, connecting the rural productive areas of the south to the linear city/chain of centers along the Hau River. Transfer stations and stops could correspond with the intensification of public programs.

Finally, in a country where the difference of a few centimeters is already significant, the precise manipulation of topography becomes a powerful urban design tool. The high-land network of roads (existing and planned) can be offset by the lower-land waterways/plains and medium-land level vegetation meshes, in a system of organized decentralization. The expanding city and its periphery can be intentionally planned as a juxtaposition of centers with different characters and scales, resulting from the specific interplays they orchestrate through the infrastructural net and the natural (green and blue) systems, topographical differences, and related soil conditions, and with the programmatic destinations allocated to them. This will allow urbanization to occur where infrastructure (including high-land platforms for structures) is organized. An intermingling of urban and rural activities across the territory's networks of water and roads can not only maintain the region's productivity but also keep the ecological balance in check. By aligning public functions and civic amenities along the spine, the city potentially creates unity while simultaneously decentralizing and specializing. Through context responsiveness and scale control of each center, a middle ground is offered in which structuring from above and substantiating from below can, in the best tradition of the region, weave an additional layer into the landscape. The new interplays from "above" can then be appropriated from "below" to take Cantho into the twenty first century.

NOTES

1. Philippe Taylor, *Fragments of the Present: Searching for Modernity in Vietnam's South* (Honolulu: University of Hawaii Press, 2001).
2. Tana Li, and Anthony Reid, *Southern Vietnam Under the Nguyen: Documents on the Economic History of Cochinchina 1602-1777* (Singapore: Institute of Southeast Asian Studies, 1993).
3. James Scott, *Seeing Like a State: How Certain Schemes to Improve the Human Condition Have Failed* (New Haven: Yale University Press, 1998).
4. QV Nguyen, "Urbanization in the Mekong Delta," in *Vietnam's Socio-Economic Development 5*, 1996, 44-55.
5. Gerald Hickey, *Village in Vietnam* (London and New Haven: Yale University Press, 1964).
6. Nigel Thrift and Dean Forbes, *The Price of War: Urbanization in Vietnam 1945-1985* (London: Allen and Unwin, 1986).

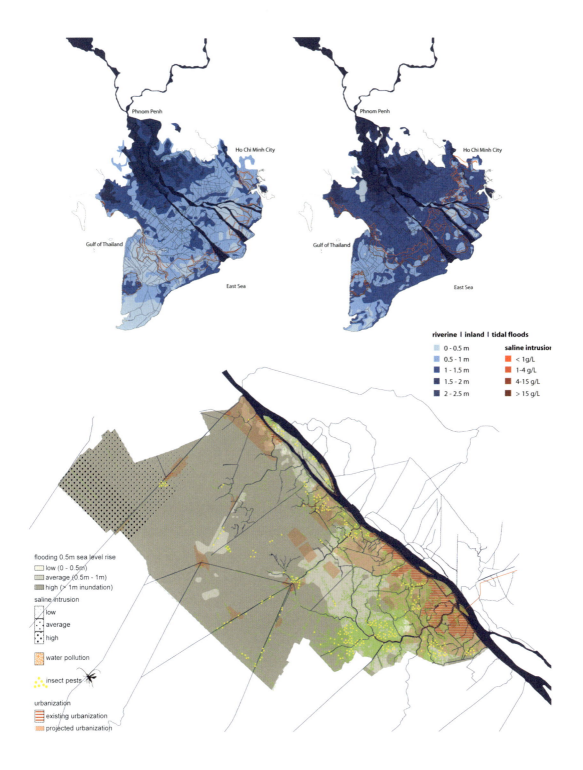

riverine | inland | tidal floods

0 - 0.5 m
0.5 - 1 m
1 - 1.5 m
1.5 - 2 m
2 - 2.5 m

saline intrusion
< 1g/L
1-4 g/L
4-15 g/L
> 15 g/L

flooding 0.5m sea level rise
low (0 - 0.5m)
average (0.5m - 1m)
high (> 1m inundation)

saline intrusion
low
average
high

water pollution

insect pests

urbanization
existing urbanization
projected urbanization

Implications of Climate Change: The Mekong Delta will be severely effected
by climate change. The coast and the Plain of Reeds will be most effected by
flooding. The whole territory of Cantho will be exposed to severe flooding with
50cm sea-level rise. Saline intrusion, although a smaller threat, will inevitably
deteriorate the conditions for agriculture.

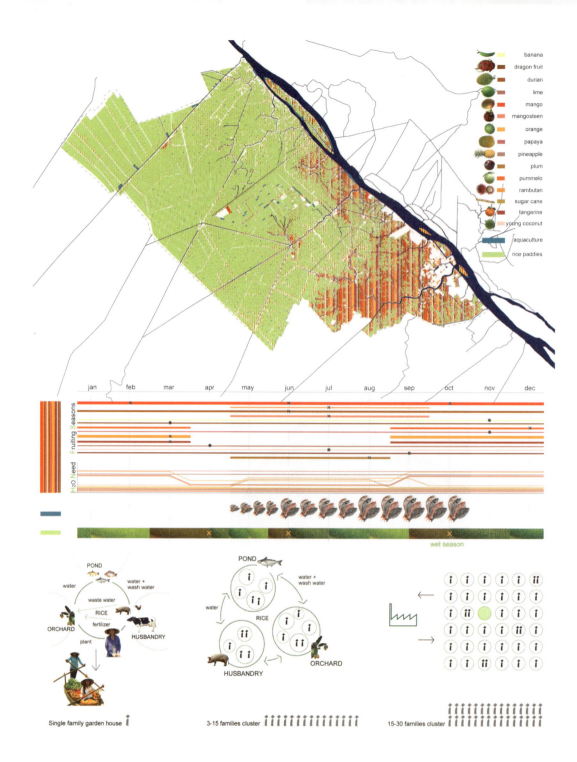

banana		
dragon fruit		
durian		
lime		
mango		
mangosteen		
orange		
papaya		
pineapple		
plum		
pummelo		
rambutan		
sugar cane		
tangerine		
young coconut		
aquaculture		
rice paddies		

jan   feb   mar   apr   may   jun   jul   aug   sep   oct   nov   dec

Fruiting Seasons

H_2O Need

wet season

POND

water   water + wash water

waste water

RICE

fertilizer

ORCHARD

plant

HUSBANDRY

Single family garden house

POND

water + wash water

water

RICE

ORCHARD

HUSBANDRY

3-15 families cluster

15-30 families cluster

Shifts in Logics of Production: Today, most of Cantho's productive land consists of paddy, orchards (with a large variety and mixture of fruit types) and aquaculture. At the same time, there is a pressure to shift towards a more diverse agri-aquaculture system (in order to decrease risks and increase eco-logical biodiversity) and to up-scale in order to take advantage of economies of scale.

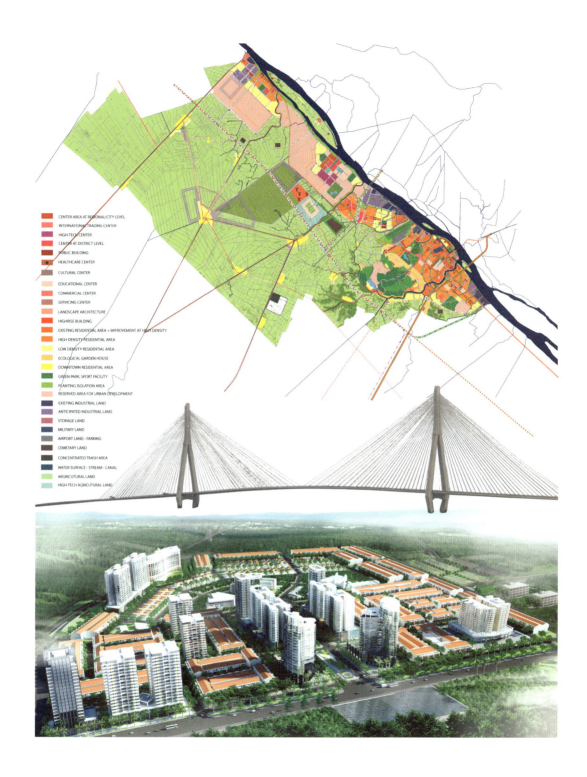

CENTER AREA AT REGIONAL/CITY LEVEL
INTERNATIONAL TRADING CENTER
HIGH-TECH CENTER
CENTER AT DISTRICT LEVEL
PUBLIC BUILDING
HEALTHCARE CENTER
CULTURAL CENTER
EDUCATIONAL CENTER
COMMERCIAL CENTER
SERVICING CENTER
LANDSCAPE ARCHITECTURE
HIGHRISE BUILDING
EXISTING RESIDENTIAL AREA + IMPROVEMENT AT HIGH DENSITY
HIGH DENSITY RESIDENTIAL AREA
LOW DENSITY RESIDENTIAL AREA
ECOLOGICAL GARDEN HOUSE
DOWNTOWN RESIDENTIAL AREA
GREEN PARK, SPORT FACILITY
PLANTING ISOLATION AREA
RESERVED AREA FOR URBAN DEVELOPMENT
EXISTING INDUSTRIAL LAND
ANTICIPATED INDUSTRIAL LAND
STORAGE LAND
MILITARY LAND
AIRPORT LAND - PARKING
CEMETARY LAND
CONCENTRATED TRASH AREA
WATER SURFACE - STREAM - CANAL
ARGRICUTURAL LAND
HIGH-TECH AGRICULTURAL LAND

State-of-the-Art:The masterplan of Cantho to 2020 has been developed in a manner similar to those used throughout Vietnam – whereby figures from socio-economic scenarios are directly transferred to mono-functional land use zoning. With a nod towards the specificity of the place, Cantho's development is to be (theoretically) oriented towards the northwest and south and the existing city center is to be de-densified – for hygienic reasons.

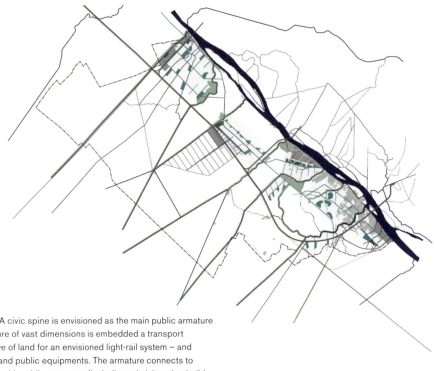

New Tools: Civic Spine: A civic spine is envisioned as the main public armature for Cantho. In this armature of vast dimensions is embedded a transport boulevard – with a reserve of land for an envisioned light-rail system – and embedded waterbodies and public equipments. The armature connects to elevated urban platforms with public programs (including administration buildings, hospitals, universities) as well commercial and office spaces.

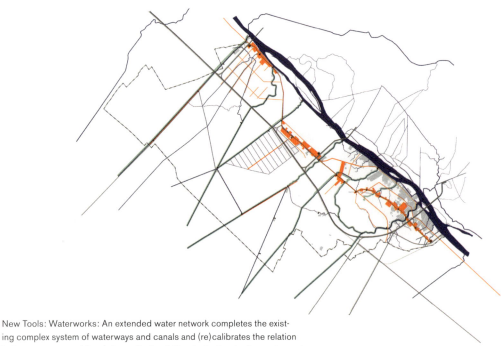

New Tools: Waterworks: An extended water network completes the existing complex system of waterways and canals and (re)calibrates the relation between porous and (non)absorptive land. Flood retention basins, water purification and storm-water drainage swales and channels are the main elements plugged into and complementing the already complex system.

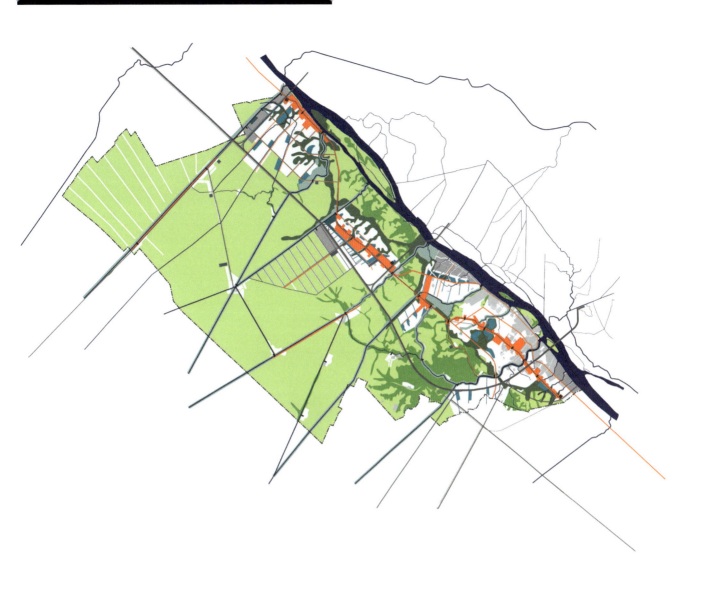

Landscape Urbanism Structure: New urbanization is to be built on high-
land platforms in both the rural and urban areas of Cantho. The platforms
are developed as various heights of fill (from 2-3 meters) and correspond to
desired levels of safety (from flooding). Their geometry is partially informed by
the pre-existing conditions of the landscape, while simultaneously accommodating and shaping tissues that rationalize and modernize the rich native
building traditions.

Landscape Urbanism Fabric: As part of a strategy to counter ad-hoc development, infrastructure (including roads and high-land platforms for buildings) is explicitly phased and builds upon the existing conditions. As much as is possible, water-based and road-based urbanism is married through new infrastructural works.

051. courtesy El Bee, Hong Kong
052. anonymous camera capture
053. New York Building Survey, 1933
054. courtesy El Bee, Hong Kong
055. barco.com/projection_systems/images/DubaiPolice_2_l.jpg
056. anonymous surveillance camera capture

057. anonymous surveillance camera capture
058. anonymous camera capture
059. courtesy El Bee, New York
060. courtesy El Bee, Houston

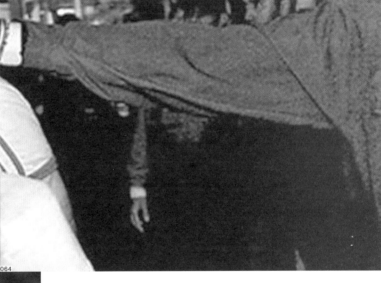

061. anonymous surveillance camera capture
062. anonymous surveillance camera capture
063. courtesy El Bee, Hong Kong
064. anonymous surveillance camera capture
065. courtesy El Bee, Hong Kong
066. anonymous surveillance camera capture

067. anonymous surveillance camera capture
068. anonymous surveillance camera capture
069. grin.hq.nasa.gov/IMAGES/LARGE/GPN-2000-000484.jpg
070. courtesy El Bee, New York

NINA EDWARDS ANKER RECEIVED HER MASTER IN
ARCHITECTURE FROM THE HARVARD GRADUATE SCHOOL OF
DESIGN. SHE IS CURRENTLY A RESEARCH FELLOW AND PH.D.
CANDIDATE AT THE OSLO SCHOOL OF ARCHITECTURE AND
DESIGN. HER DOCTORAL RESEARCH BRIDGES PHENOMENO-
LOGICAL THEORY AND SOLAR DESIGN. SHE IS PRINCIPAL OF
NEA STUDIO, AN ARCHITECTURE AND DESIGN OFFICE.

PEDER ANKER IS ASSOCIATE PROFESSOR AT
THE GALLATIN SCHOOL OF INDIVIDUALIZED STUDY AND
THE ENVIRONMENTAL STUDIES PROGRAM AT NEW YORK
UNIVERSITY. HIS WORKS INCLUDE *IMPERIAL ECOLOGY:
ENVIRONMENTAL ORDER IN THE BRITISH EMPIRE, 1895-
1945* AND *FROM BAUHAUS TO ECO-HOUSE: A HISTORY OF
ECOLOGICAL DESIGN.*

VIEWING THE EARTH FROM WITHOUT OR FROM WITHIN

Global warming poses new challenges to the architectural community. The immediate response has been a turn toward a host of energy-saving technologies. What has rarely been addressed, however, is the problem of scale. How can the designer make sure that global solutions do not come at the expense of local traditions, cultures, and environments? There is a top-down and also a bottom-up answer to this question. The first takes a Google-Earth view from without and zooms in on the local, while the second begins within the human condition and zooms out toward the horizon. These two ways of viewing the Earth, we argue, represent two different modes of design in which the first reinforces a narrow objectifying rationality while the second embraces a richer understanding of human experience. The view from without has its own history, reaching back to the age of outer-space explorations during which the Earth and its environmental problems were seen by astronauts from above. The view from within, on the other hand, can be found in some of the Modernist designers of the Bauhaus heritage who placed human rational, emotional, technological, and social needs at the center in answering global environmental concerns. In our discussion of these different historical trajectories, we propose a design in keeping with Edmund Husserl's horizontal perspective: "The earth is a spherical body, certainly not perceivable in its wholeness all at once and by one person; rather it is perceived in a primordial synthesis as a unity of mutually connected single experiences."[1] Geography thus conceived is not about mapping and planning the landscape from without, but a "condition of flux"[2] in which the individual understands the surrounding world from within.

The View from Without

Viewing the Earth from above is a dominating trend in current understandings of geography and space. It allows an elevated and privileged perspective that, when enforced by tools such as geographic information systems (GIS), reduces nature to an abstract visual database. The growing use of environmental planning programs based on GIS allows its users to zoom in on particular places from points of view in outer space, as if they were rapidly descending astronauts. Though such mapping programs may look innocent at first, it is worth contemplating what this view represents both historically and methodologically for the design community. As we will argue, the view from without empowers a type of planning and design that is insensitive to local conditions and cultures and alienates humans from themselves. It mobilizes narrow managerial rationalities at the expense of a more widely defined human condition.

The landscape designer Ian McHarg may serve as a suitable starting point in tracing the importance of the problematic Google-Earth perspective. His *Design with Nature* (1969), which became a phenomenal success (more than 350,000 copies sold over thirty years), came to define the field for a generation of landscape designers. McHarg advised readers to adopt the perspective of an astronaut when trying to design with nature on the ground. "We can use the astronaut as our instructor," he argued, as he (they were all men at the time) saw the Earth from above, allowing a managerial overview of the landscape.[3]

McHarg was inspired by the sciences that, since the late 1950s, were working toward sending humans into outer space. The chief method was to try to build spaceships in which water, air, and food would circulate within what was called "space ecological systems."[4] In the following decades ecologists, space enthusiasts, and NASA would pour considerable resources into researching how to build closed ecological systems in outer space. A NASA report from 1977, for example, was adorned with somewhat fantastic images

Drawing by Don Davis from 1975. From *Space Settlements*, (1977). Courtesy of NASA.

of future landscapes inside a giant turning wheel that would create artificial gravity in outer space. Its enclosed ecosystem included human-made rivers, beaches, forest, and hills, with humans living in modernist buildings.[5]

McHarg found inspiration in these unworldly ecosystems for astronauts in outer space. He saw them as a model for how humans should live in harmony with nature on Earth. To him, these ecologically construed spaceships and settlements came to represent the rational, orderly, and wisely managed in contrast with the irrational, disorderly, and ill-managed environments on Earth. Technology, terminology, and methodology developed for outer space became his tools for designing with nature on the ground. In his subsequent writings, environmental ethics often became an issue of trying to live like astronauts by adapting space technologies such as bio-toilets, solar cells, recycling, and energy-saving devices, along with a utilitarian philosophy.

McHarg was not the only environmental designer enthused by the life of the astronaut and the managerial view from without. "We are all astronauts," Richard Buckminster Fuller explained in his famous book *Operating Manual for Spaceship Earth* (1969), which basically postulates using space ecological engineering manuals for astronauts to solve environmental problems on Earth.[6]

The astronaut, it is worth noting, was a great hero across political spectrums at the time, including the counterculture. His home

in outer space became a model for architects shaping the future of green buildings equipped with the spaceship's water and air recycling technologies. The astronaut's photos of "Spaceship Earth" evoked an elevated perspective that significantly influenced our conceptions of space.

This view from without was reinforced by technological innovations from the space industry that enabled self-sufficient buildings. From the vertical perspective of the astronaut, they could be seen as closed objects shut off from the surrounding environment. With the slump in the space industry in the early 1970s, key movers of its technology began marketing know-how to the architectural community. The result was a surge in ecological remedies such as new waste-disposal systems prompted by space recirculation technology, a sewage system prompted by the astronaut's toilet, and an energy-efficiency system for homes that became known as "autonomous" buildings.

Key "autonomous" designers include early British ecological architects such as Alexander Pike and John Frazer, and their students such as Kenneth Yeang and Brenda Vale. Similar projects came along under names such as "bio-shelter" and "integral house" in the United States by Sean Wellesley-Miller and Day Chahroudi, the co-directors of the Solar Energy Laboratory at MIT, Sim van der Ryn, Phil Hawes, and perhaps most prominently, John and Nancy Todd and the so-called New Alchemists at Cape Cod.

These designers had in common the fact that the buildings they designed were detached from the environment they were meant to save. Paradoxically, they came to regard the surrounding social and natural environment as irrelevant. Just as a spaceship was detached from the surrounding environment in outer space, a building designed as a self-sustained microcosm was, at least in theory, detached from the Earth. As a consequence, some of today's ecological buildings tend to resemble spaceships by incorporating closed ecosystems, and space technologies such as solar cells, and by often being isolated from the local landscape they are supposed to protect.

For all its good intentions, the problem with such ecological designs is an overemphasis on technology and a narrow understanding of rationality. Juhani Pallasmaa points out a similar problem in the use of technology in architecture today: "the tendency of technological culture to standardize environmental conditions and make the environment entirely predictable is causing a serious sensory impoverishment. Our buildings have lost their opacity and depth, sensory invitation and discovery, mystery and shadow."[7] Current ecological design tends to suffer from the same tendency to neutralize architectural spaces. "Autonomous" ecosystems representing a microcosm of the global often dismiss local realities, cultures, environments, and traditions. To avoid this loss of humanism in ecological architecture, we suggest turning to a different tradition in designing with nature as experienced from within.

The View from Within

There are "unmistakable signs that the climate of the North Atlantic region is growing warmer," Herbert Bayer pointed out in 1953, in a surprisingly early reference to what is now known as global warming.[8] Bayer, also an architect and earth artist, was at the time a leading graphic designer and former head of the printing and advertising workshop at the Bauhaus. His statement came in his *Geo-Graphic Atlas*, published to attract readers to the environmental cause. On its frontispiece, he placed an image of a human being encircled by related scientific fields, with carefully defined colors that recalled Goethe's chromatology. The Atlas was to mobilize a human-centered view from within in reading the spatial geography of a landscape. He tried to develop a visual language of communication that could create proximity between individual responsibility and global environmental crisis.

Yet unlike ecologists preoccupied with building closed ecosystems, Bayer believed that the best way to address the issue was to begin with the human condition and our ways of sensing the world. The eco-crisis was to him a crisis of human alienation from the natural world, and like his friend and compatriot Richard Neutra, he fashioned his own role as architect and designer in the image of a Freudian therapist healing the unfortunate separation.[9]

Bayer was not the only former member of the Bauhaus faculty who became deeply concerned with environmental issues. At Harvard, for example, Walter Gropius would address suburban sprawl, telling his students, "until we love and respect the land almost religiously, its fatal deterioration will go on."[10] Similarly, Lázló Moholy-Nagy in Chicago formulated his own "biological 'bill of rights'" by incorporating the environment.[11] To simplify the Bauhaus program as design for the "machine age" where nature serves the role of ornamental background is misleading.[12]

Bayer believed that graphic design would be functional if its form followed human conscious and subconscious reactions to light and structure. He sought a simplified graphic that could better human functioning in a dramatically changing social and natural world. His call for designing according to people's environmental, rational, emotional, and social needs was, in effect, also a plea for proximity between the individual and the global.

Maxwell Fry and Jane Drew also serve as examples of designers who embraced the International Style while insisting on placing human experiences at the center of environmental and climatic conditions. For that reason they disliked incorporating air-conditioning systems and even electrical fans in their buildings for the tropics, as they believed that these devices created closed and claustrophobic environments. Instead, the human body should be shaded and in contact with the breezes created by climatic filters of the building threshold: "Tropical air conditioning should be done as much as possible using the building fabric itself," they argued in *Tropical Architecture* (1956). Air conditioning was "pleasant enough," but it had the unfortunate consequence of creating "a shock, both physical and psychological" when one left the building.[13] Thus the issue was not a matter of saving energy but of opening the building from within to the world outside.

The brothers Aladar and Victor Olgyay also came to pursue architectural design with nature in which human experience becomes the point of departure. Both graduates in architectural engineering, they developed a design program that prioritized a structure's environmental setting. When they came to New York in 1947, they immediately began to promote a design program that took the proximity of human being and earthly climatic forces into account, where bodily sensation of thermal qualities were included at the inception and all phases of the design process.

A similar line of reasoning can be found in Lisa Heschong's *Thermal Delight in Architecture* of 1979. According to her, architects often neglect thermal pleasure and variation: "thermal conditions are commonly standardized with the use of modern mechanical systems that can be specified, installed, and left to function independently of the overall design concept."[14] Because shadow can provide relief from solar heat or glare, the use and distribution of materials

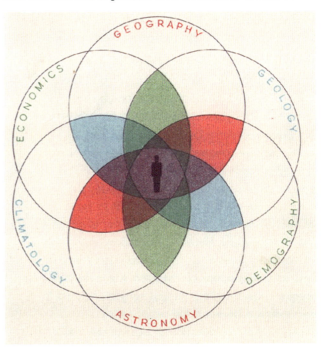

Herbert Bayer, World Geo-graphic Atlas (1953), 1. ©2010 Artists Rights Society (ARS), New York /VG Bild-Kunst, Bonn.

corresponds partly to the amount of shade needed in a particular place and time. The building's representation is an outcome of this logical process, not its initial conception.[15]

To the Olgyays, "architectural expression," had to be "organic" in order to behave "in a manner somewhat similar to the great coordinator, nature."[16] The shading devices they describe were designed according to their belief that architecture was subjugated to natural forces. The constancy of the sun contrasts with the variety of outcome of its laws: "The motifs vary, but are subordinate to the sun, whose strength and angles, according to orientation and location, prescribe the regional patterns."[17] They encouraged a type of breathing structure that contrasts with sealed, controlled environments.

Fry, Drew, and the Olgyays' porous building skin's subtle mediations of external forces find their opposite in the enclosed interiors found in many ecological designs. They encouraged the passage of sun and air, and they used the wind to cool their buildings. Their geographic approach to design prefigured the words of architect Linda Pollak: "Architecture is construed not as object but as device that can transform an urban landscape yet at the same time is not in complete control of the relationships between its constitutive elements."[18] Architectural designs thus conceived are as open as possible to local geographic circumstances.

In Victor Olgyay's classic *Design with Climate* (1963), he developed a design program in which local weather and climate were the main determinants in the sheltering of humans. Detailed analyses of a place with respect to directions of wind and sun, as well as seasonal fluctuations of temperature, were the basis of design suggestions and served as key tools in the design of effective environmental structures and devices on a global scale. We believe the solar-control principles, diagrams, and climatic charts outlined by the Olgyays in 1957 in their *Solar Control and Shading Devices* are as relevant today in our efforts to address global warming as they were then: "Today, as the view of architectural problems approaches a global scale and as our buildings become more vulnerable to heat exchange, a rediscovery of solar control principles arises and the pursuit of solutions becomes an important matter."[19] Olgyay sought to develop a language of shadows based on shading devices and forms adjusted to varying climatic conditions.[20] The great variety of screens they presented, categorized into vertical, horizontal, and egg-crate types, were fine-tuned to respond to the subtleties of individual climates and local conditions.

A shared belief in bringing the full human being in proximity with the global environment by means of engaging local cultural and climatic conditions through systematic design methods brings together the work of Bayer, Fry, Drew, and the Olgyays. Fry and Drew, for example, were so concerned about not creating enclosed spaces that they were reluctant to use mosquito screens in the tropics. "[T]he night is cool, the stars are brilliant" without them, they noted in their plea for proximity between the human and the universe.[21]

With the help of a type of architecture that promotes tactile experience through passive heating and cooling methods, we may touch the presence of the things we see in a visceral way. In the words of Maurice Merleau-Ponty:

> The painter accepts with all its difficulties the myth of the windows of the souls: one has to take that which vision teaches one literally: only through her do we touch the sun, the stars, we are at the same time everywhere, as close to the beyond as to things near, and the same our power to imagine ourselves elsewhere.[22]

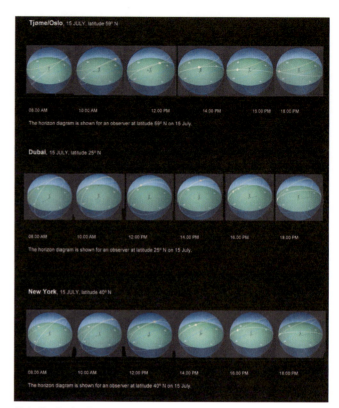

Solar Declination Arcs, source: Motions of the Sun Simulator

A View from Within a Shelter

An unbuilt project from nea studio may serve to outline an approach to design in which perception of the site's geographic constituents drives the outcome. In our proposal, we do not suggest a naive return to the wisdom of the designers discussed above but offer instead a reinterpretation suited to our time. Our point of departure has been to explore what type of design the view from within would generate. With the support of local institutions, we propose a shelter to be placed in New York's Red Hook, Brooklyn waterfront.[23] Shaped by the site's geographical world, it will shelter from extreme weather conditions, including winds, hot summer sun, rainfalls, cold winter winds, and perhaps even dramatic waves hammering a pier on which it could stand. At the same time, it will underline and intensify the presence of cyclical and unpredictable environmental rhythms, thereby stimulating perception through multisensory experience. By responding to the surrounding climatic and cultural conditions, we also aim to create an architectural space that embraces layered notions of time and scale.

We used the reasoning of the Olgyays to generate its S-shaped structure. The form is the result of a digital model based on their climatic statistical calculations for ideal shading conditions for the New York City region. It is derived from an analysis of the minimization of shadows behind the shelter in the morning and the maximization of shadows during the overheated afternoon. Fry, Drew, and the Olgyays' use of climatic charts that operate on a "glocal" scale helped us to design in subtle dialogue with nature. When the body senses temperature changes within the thermal comfort zones outlined by the Olgyays, thermal pleasure is felt more intensely. By pinpointing a comfort zone, we address the sensitivity of perception.

The structure's surfaces and shadows, which move according to wind, sun and tidal forces, mediate between human and global scale.

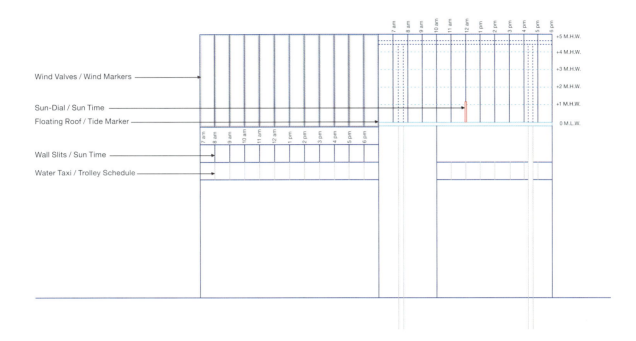

Wind Valves / Wind Markers

Sun-Dial / Sun Time

Floating Roof / Tide Marker

Wall Slits / Sun Time

Water Taxi / Trolley Schedule

Elevational diagram of a shelter as a register of time through light and shadow

By adapting to the vast forces of the natural surroundings, the responsive skin of the structure incorporates the concept of the extra-large scale and the infinite. Both visible and invisible forces acting at multiple scales influence visitors' perceptions. Global scale is brought to the bodily scale of its users by paying attention to sun, wind, tide, and ground and how they can be registered in multisensory experience. The combination of auditory and visual sensations, for example, leads to a heightened awareness of scale where the flickering sound of the wind valves evokes the vastness of the horizon. Different conditions of shading for Oslo, Dubai, and New York are illustrated in the "solar declination arcs" diagram that makes visible this dialectic between horizontal and vertical perspectives. Since these sun paths are based on human perspectives at different latitudes, it is the human scale that defines the global.

Referring to this diagram, the shelter adopts an adaptable global language that enables a rule-based design process following the parameters set out by Fry, Drew, and the Olgyays. By changing the geographic conditions to a different location, the shelter can take on a different shape. Adaptable geometry is facilitated by the use of digital parametric modeling techniques. We decided to let the shelter's location generate environmental data through digital measuring devices, which also helped us to understand local climatic conditions. Using recycled wood and steel from nearby building demolitions, the shelter will reflect local construction techniques.

Cultural rituals are often rooted in environmental factors, such as the afternoon siesta in hot climates. In the case of New York, the daily rhythm of travel to and from work starts and ends later than in Oslo, for example. Therefore the positioning of the sun slits and ferry schedule markers, as well as the shape, materials, and degree of openness of the structure's skin, will adjust according to location, physiological, and cultural criteria.

We organized the shelter to register both scheduled and unscheduled time. It will become a type of architectural clock and light modulator, with its various moving elements and light slits generating shifting spaces of gray and light. It will have the capacity to produce a constantly changing temporal experience of waiting through the overlapping of rhythmic and unexpected movements. The moving elements will interact with changes in local climate and weather conditions. The steel columns supporting the roof will, if placed on a pier, move up and down with the rhythm of the tide and waves. Twelve metal wind-valves graphically aligned with the marked hours will open and close to relieve wind pressure. A curved transparent glass wall toward the harbor will allow views while protecting against rain and wind. A horizontal stripe at eyelevel will provide bus or ferry schedules. The wall will consist of thin vertical perforations marking the day's scheduled hours through the sun's daily travel. The sun shining through slits in the east section of the wall will mark the hours by creating light strips on the shaded floor behind it. A sundial on top of the glass roof will also indicate solar time. The marking of overlapping times in the structure will give the user the recognition of departure and arrival, diurnal, annual, and tidal rhythms through direct sensory experience.

Contrary to a design strategy that reinforces the eye and a sense of distant control, we allow geographic parameters to control the design. The shelter will oscillate between open and closed, both protecting from the environment and capturing its vitality in an attempt to reconcile the human with the climatic condition. This structure will act as a transitory threshold that provides a pleasurable space for immersion in the flow of time.

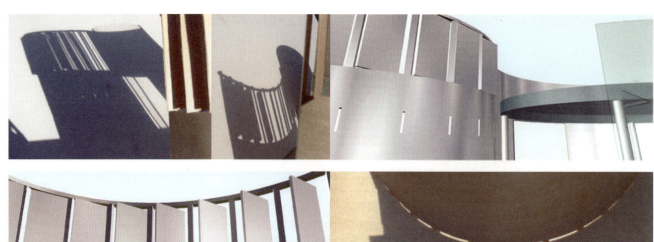

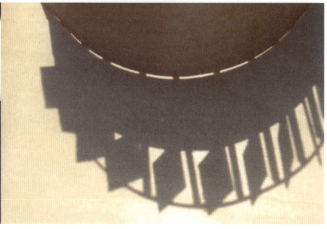

Shelter Light and Shadow Rendering

NOTES

1. Edmund Husserl, "Foundational Investigations of the Phenomenological Origin of the Spatiality of Nature: The Originary Ark, the Earth, Does Not Move," in *Husserl at the Limits of Phenomenology*, edited by Leonard Lawlor with Bettina Bergo, translated Fred Kersten, revised by Leonard Lawlor, (Evanston: Northwestern University, 2002), 117-131, quote on 118.
2. Hashim Sarkis, "New Geographies: Notes on an Emerging Aesthetics," *New Geographies 0* (Cambridge: Harvard University Press, 2008), 98-109.
3. Ian L. McHarg, *Design with Nature* (Garden City, NY: Doubleday, 1969), 95.
4. Eugene B. Konecci, "Space ecological systems," *Bioastronautics*, edited by Karl E. Schaefer, (New York: Macmillan, 1964), 274-304.
5. *Space Settlements: A Design Study*, edited by Richard D. Johnson and Charles Holbrow (Washington, DC: National Aeronautics and Space Administration, 1977).
6. Richard Buckminster Fuller, *Operating Manual for Spaceship Earth* (Edwardsville: Southern Illinois University Press, 1969), 46.
7. Juhani Pallasmaa, "Hapticity and Time' – Notes on Fragile Architecture," *The Architectural Review* 5 (1) (/2000), 1.
8. Herbert Bayer, *World Geo-Graphic Atlas: A Composite of Man's Environment* (Chicago: Container Corporation of America, 1953), 27. Spencer R. Weart, *The Discovery of Global Warming* (Cambridge: Harvard University Press, 2008).
9. Sylvia Lavin, *Form Follows Libido: Architecture and Richard Neutra in a Psychoanalytic Culture* (Cambridge: The MIT Press, 2004). Christine Macy and Sarah Bonnemaison, *Architecture and Nature: Creating the American Landscape* (New York: Routledge, 2003).
10. Walter Gropius, *Scope of Total Architecture* (New York: Harper & Brothers, [1943] 1955), 184. Gropius' emphasis.
11. László Moholy-Nagy, *Vision in Motion* (Chicago: Paul Theobald & Comp., 1947), 5. Moholy-Nagy's emphasis.
12. Reyner Banham, *Theory and Design in the First Machine Age* (New York: Frederick A. Praeger, 1960).
13. Maxwell Fry and Jane Drew, *Tropical Architecture in the Dry and Humid Zones* (New York, Reinhold,1956), 236, 49.
14. Lisa Heschong, *Thermal Delight in Architecture* (Cambridge: MIT Press, 1979), vii.
15. David Leatherbarrow and Mohsen Mostafavi, *Surface Architecture* (Cambridge: MIT Press, 2002), 183.
16. Aladar Olgyay and Victor Olgyay, *Solar Control and Shading Devices* (Princeton: Princeton University Press, 1957), 6.
17. Ibid., 15.
18. Linda Pollak, "Constructed Ground: Questions of Scale," in *The Landscape Urbanism Reader*, edited by Charles Waldheim, (Princeton: Princeton Architectural Press, 2006), 126-139.
19. Olgyay and Olgyay, *Solar Control and Shading Devices*, 10.
20. Victor Olgyay, *Design with Climate: Bioclimatic Approach to Architectural Regionalism* (Princeton: Princeton University Press, 1963). See also Alberto Pérez-Gómez and Louise Pelletier, *Architectural Representation and the Perspective Hinge* (Cambridge: MIT Press, 1997). Junichiro Tanizaki, *In Praise of Shadows* (New Haven: Leete's Island Books, 1977).
21. Fry and Drew, *Tropical Architecture*, 54.
22. Maurice Merleau-Ponty, *L'Oeil et l'Esprit* (Paris: Gallimard, 1964), 83. Our translation.
23. Nina Edwards Anker and Peder Anker, "Red Hook Shelter," winning entry New York State Council on the Arts award, 2002. Shown at "Going Public" at the Center for Architecture, New York, 2003.

ALEX MACLEAN PILOT AND PHOTOGRAPHER, HAS FLOWN HIS PLANE OVER MUCH OF THE UNITED STATES DOCUMENTING THE LANDSCAPE THROUGH PHOTOGRAPHY. TRAINED AS AN ARCHITECT, HE HAS PORTRAYED THE HISTORY AND EVOLUTION OF THE LAND FROM VAST AGRICULTURAL PATTERNS TO CITY GRIDS, RECORDING CHANGES BROUGHT ABOUT BY HUMAN INTERVENTION AND NATURAL PROCESSES.

A SOUTHWEST PERSPECTIVE

Flying is an off-earth way of experiencing landscapes that is mostly visual. There is no sound to be heard beside the engine noise. In my thousands of hours of flying, I can remember hearing sound only once, and that was the thunder of accelerating engines over an auto drag strip in north-central Florida at 3,000 feet. But now that I mention it, I do remember hearing real thunder as well. Smell is noticeable, once in awhile, as when flying over industrial areas, or preferably over rose fields in the Central Valley. Temperature varies with flight altitude, and topography is sometimes sensed by wind currents and turbulence. Aerial photography and motion picture is the best way to record and share a landscape that you see at a scale and angle like none seen from the ground.

There is adventure and freedom in flying as you move through a three-dimensional space to record the natural and built environment. There is a continuum of spatial relationships as you move in and out, and the lighting on the ground will change dramatically with the view angle in relation to the sun. Controlling these variables is the true pleasure of flying and photographing as you try to understand, explain, and share some of the wonders you see on the ground as you are swooping around.

I remember well first coming to the Southwest to photograph the Grand Canyon and Las Vegas in the mid-1970s. The Strip was just that, with mid-rise buildings extending out into the desert from a downtown node. Today the downtown is visually secondary to the new high-rise hotels and casinos that line the Strip. But most remarkable now is the new sea of dense suburban housing built in a relatively short time that stretches more than ten miles out to Red Rock Canyon to the northwest.

Since that first visit, I have come back to the Southwest on various assignments. In 2005, I was photographing for a project called "Visualizing Density," and in 2009 for a project comparing the landscape of Las Vegas with that of Venice, Italy. What you see and photograph is shaped by what is going through your mind, as well as by present issues such as climate change.

A key to image making is enticing viewers and having them return to the image for a second look and to create an image that they hold and revisualize in their minds. Much of this is done by the photographer in a combination of ways, including the graphic representation of content, the use of light and color, the placement of elements within the frame, and often the elimination of the larger context that surrounds the picture. The composition is driven by the desire to communicate thoughts and feelings to the viewer.

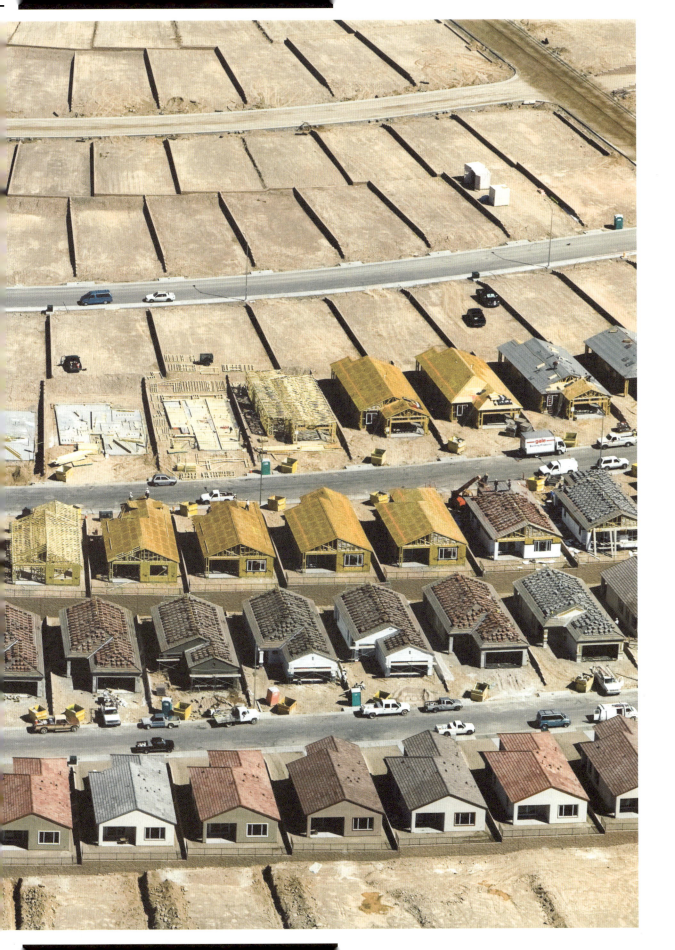

HASHIM SARKIS IS THE AGA KHAN PROFESSOR OF LANDSCAPE ARCHITECTURE AND URBANISM AT THE HARVARD GRADUATE SCHOOL OF DESIGN AND DIRECTOR OF ITS AGA KHAN PROGRAM. HE IS ALSO CURRENTLY LEADING AN INITIATIVE TO ADVANCE RESEARCH AT THE GSD. SARKIS IS A PRACTICING ARCHITECT AND URBAN DESIGNER WITH OFFICES IN CAMBRIDGE AND BEIRUT. HIS WORK HAS RECEIVED SEVERAL AWARDS AND HAS BEEN PUBLISHED AND EXHIBITED THROUGHOUT THE WORLD, INCLUDING MOST RECENTLY AT THE MUSEUM OF MODERN ART IN NEW YORK AND THE VENICE BIENNALE.

THE WORLD ACCORDING TO ARCHITECTURE

BEYOND COSMOPOLIS

Victor Pimstein, *Horizon 39*, 2009. Oil on wood, 54.5 x 78 cm.

Why should the city be considered the ultimate spatial manifestation of globalization?[1]

Much of the literature about urban development today presents the global city or cosmopolis as the spatial outcome of globalization with which we have to contend. World migration patterns, ecological and other collective risks, and unfathomable flows of capital are generating new patterns of social, economic, and political organization that specialists are still trying to identify and understand. They are all unprecedented, we are told, and if they could only be carefully modeled and well analyzed, and if some of their undesirable impact could be addressed, they could lead to more effective individual emancipation and better forms of collective life. When it comes to their spatial modeling, however, we are generally noticing the recurrence of centralized metropolitan patterns of urbanization.

Granted, these settlements are rising at an unprecedented scale and pace and in new settings. We have also no doubt benefited enormously from two decades of rigorous documentation and analysis of new settlement conditions across the world, but this literature persists in describing the new phenomena through established gradients of density and centrality such as urban-suburban-rural, with conventional land-use categories and within the confines of nation-states. Many radically different morphologies and typologies are being recorded but their collective impact remains the city, as big or fast-paced as it may have become.

To be sure, and whether coming from within the disciplines of urbanism, landscape, geography, or ecology, we are witnessing an increasing number of new positions that try to respond to the complexity of the problem by proposing more complex interdisciplinary approaches, but these positions, as analytically rigorous as they may be, are ultimately so pre-occupied with the nature of their interdisciplinarity that they tend to forget the object of their inquiry. No matter how novel the combination of tools, these interdisciplinary propositions do not seem to offer better insight into the way that global economic and social changes have transformed the built environment.

If one of the ambitions of architecture and urbanism is to make visible emerging social conditions, why are we not seeing the world as a possible scale of operation? If financial and demographic flows are challenging national boundaries, why is our imagination about space still bound to the city and city-region-state order? Can we find an equivalent to the scope of globalization in the space of the world, as one spatial entity?

The City-World: A Brief History

An age, Gilles Deleuze repeats after Michel Foucault, does not precede the visibilities that fill it. The image of a city-world predates the advent of globalization, but it has yet to come into consciousness as a representative visibility. The representation may be too literal, but the world conceived as one spatial entity corresponds to the scope of globalization, where national and natural borders do not set limits to the physical environment and to its perception.

Early science-fiction writers such as H.G.Wells foretold of the whole world at war with itself ahead of a period of peace in which the unified conception acquired during wartime is maintained. Led by technocrats, the world operates as one entity, as a city-world. Science fiction has continued to re-imagine the world as a single entity, whether in the Asimov's Trantor or in more popular renditions such as Star Wars' Coruscant and Death Star. Admittedly, these worlds differ considerably in their governance, social and spatial organization, density, and degree of urbanization, but they do anticipate and rehearse the yearning for a spatial totality at the scale of the world.

Discerning such a yearning from a totalizing project such as that of empire or colonialism is as necessary as it is difficult. In the context of imagining the world as one entity, we cannot overlook the grounds that such political aspirations cleared; as emphasized by the likes of Fredric Jameson and Bruno Latour, the necessity of the separation between the pursuit of totalities and of totalizing projects is important if we are to persist in developing clearer mappings or representations of the world. Jameson's reference to Kevin Lynch's cognitive mapping parallels Latour's to the phenomenon of the nineteenth century panorama.[2]

In architecture, the classical project, and, in related, ways that of the early Modernist universalism culminating in the International Style, have aspired to a certain sameness across national boundaries. This aspiration was driven more by a temporal understanding of the world than a spatial one. The world it imagined wanted to move in sync. Not that a spatial conception was lacking, but it was lagging. The aspiration for sameness of high Modernism emulated and expressed the aspiration for equality among human beings and states. The criticisms of this project are all too familiar and they have helped us discern the indelible ties between formal and political projects. Here again, however, we should not miss out on the outlooks of connectedness and continuity that Modern architecture effected across the world. As visibilities, they should be able to live past their political associations.

From the 1930s onward, the qualities of connectedness, continuity, and sameness move from wish images to become projected outcomes of development. Jean Gottman's premonition featured a Megalopolis where cities grow and connect to create regional bands of urbanization enabled by increasing creation of communication and transport. This premonition was magnified to the scale of the world and turned into an inevitability by Constantinos Doxiadis in his proposition for an Ecumenopolis, a city-world formed out of settlements around major routes of transportation. Slowly, all development is drawn to this infrastructural grid while clearing the rest of the planet for agriculture and preservation. Speed of movement and proximity of people to each other guided Doxiadis' anticipatory and remedial approach to urban planning. His contemporaries and fellow world-warriors, such as Yona Friedman, Superstudio, Constant Nieuwenhuis, and Buckminster Fuller, all aspired to a worldly conception of their domain of operation that transcended locality and city.

Friedman scaffolded a parallel city on top of the ground-bound and sequestered one we inhabit. In doing so, he accelerated spatial mobility and generated a new topography that diffused boundaries and multiplied uses and connections. For Superstudio, the connectivity of the world's citizens to each other depended on the establishment of a fictive, smooth infrastructure that provided continuity and connectivity against the earth's geographic hurdles and minimized the superstructure that is architecture to almost nothing. Fuller's obsession with mapping the world in ways that could make its finitude and fragility visible led him to invent such representational devices as his famous maps as well as the geoscope. Even though the scope of Unitary Urbanism continued to be the metropolis, the degree of diffusion of activities and land uses proposed by Nieuwenhuis clearly transgressed the centrist models of development toward more fluid continuities that heralded the global space of New Babylon.

Not all of these attempts at representing and imagining the world stemmed from a need to shape the larger totality, but they all shared a dissatisfaction with the urban models of high Modernism. The overwhelming revocation of these models by postmodernist urban theories has in many ways consolidated the Modernist centralized understanding of the city. It has also ratified it as the largest scope of the inhabited environment while detracting from the radical attributes of these late Modernist experiments in which the world as one entity was articulated in architectural terms.

The renewed interest in this cast of renegade characters and creations has primarily stressed the systemic versus object-oriented approach to urbanism. Their environmental and democratic motivations no doubt make them all the more attractive and current, but even in the present reiteration of these visions, their rendering of the world as one entity has not been stressed. The global city has somehow eclipsed the city-world. The difference between the two models is important to stress even though city-world should not be seen as the opposite of the world-city (or of the global city or cosmopolis or whatever name will be applied to it in the coming years). The city-world is the scope, spatial parameters, geometries, land-uses, and infrastructures that connect the world and make us actively take part in its description, its construction, and its perception as a totality.

"Worldliness"

Difficulties abound in thinking the world as one architectural entity, but these difficulties are being slowly, if inadvertently, overcome. We are venturing into a situation where the city-world becomes a necessity. The seeming immodesty of such a proposition and its imperial scope should be countered with the scale and scope of risks that contemporary society confronts, be they generated by environmental, nuclear, or public health concerns; the scope of action these risks generate requires a worldwide response, including the coordination of the world's spatial resources. The capacity to understand and map the lived environment beyond the scope of the city, corresponding to new patterns of global mobility and demographic shifts, is now greatly enhanced by new technologies and modes of representation and communication that make us constantly aware of the world as one entity. The lack of corresponding governing authority that can help coordinate shaping the world remains a major impediment to thinking the world but this may weaken the totalizing dimension and mobilizes architects to think of ways in which the qualities of the forms they produce – their sameness, repetitiveness, connectedness to larger geographic attributes like the horizon or trans-regional phenomena – can mobilize the physical and aesthetic dimensions of form in more effective ways than a servile association with a political project.

Most importantly, while the emancipatory dimensions of such a scope of imagination and operations, which predate the global city to as far back as Heraclites, have been unnecessarily bundled with the larger package of globalization, several social theorists and philosophers such as Jean Luc-Nancy, Kostas Axelos, and Michel Serres have recovered the project of being in the world from the suffocating impositions of globalization.[3]

Furthermore, and despite valid criticisms that have accompanied its resurgence, the discourse on cosmopolitanism has helped imagine the subject of the world as a positively nomadic stranger whose constant yearning for being here and there at the same time produces ways of describing and representing the world as the scope of individual imagination. The writings of Edward Said on worldiness and those of Anthony Appiah on strangeness are particularly poignant on this issue.

World history, as an established field of inquiry into the history of the world as a set of collective phenomena, has also helped generate historiographic and spatial models for this investigation. In this respect, the recent work on the history and historiography of the Mediterranean is compelling. The Mediterranean that is most relevant to the idea of the world is that of historian David Abulafia, who speaks of distant shores with a frequency of communication between them. Abulafia has argued that what most characterizes the Mediterranean is a geography of opposed but accessible shores with a frequency of exchange. In this conception, the edges of the Mediterranean consist of cities and towns that are loosely connected with their hinterland but are mostly connected via trading communities and businesses. The opposing shorelines could and should be taken at different and nested scale.

What is most pertinent in Abulafia's proposal is that the Mediterranean is a model that could be applied to the world. The increasing sameness within cities and between each city and the rest of the world points to the dissolution of place and to the acceleration of development to the point where we can anticipate a world moving in a real-estate development sync, especially after the last recession and the global risks it generated. These global risks include security and economic vulnerability that tie every city's patterns to those of the world and bring it sometimes to the point of brinkmanship and collapse, perhaps, as some argue, to speak to the world.

We ought to think again about whether the sameness in the world is a sign of poverty of form or of an untapped richness − a new source of inspiration for urbanism and architecture.

This sameness that I am anticipating is not dull. It points to the fact that we are all worldly, that we work to link to the world from where we are, to achieve a sense of the totality and to anticipate a city-world before and beyond globalization that flows with Heraclitus' River, where identities could be constantly constructed, and constructed in part by design.

The World as an Architectural Question

But will the world ever be placed at the doorstep of architects as an architectural question?

Increasingly, architects and planners are being compelled to address and transform larger contexts and to give these contexts more legible and expressive form. New problems are being placed on designers' agendas (e.g., infrastructure, urban systems, regional and rural questions). Problems that had been confined to the domains of engineering, ecology, or regional planning are now looking for articulation by design. This situation has opened up a range of technical and formal possibilities that had been out of reach for designers. The need to address these "geographic" aspects has also encouraged designers to reexamine their tools and develop means to link attributes that had been understood to be either separate or external to their disciplines. The importance of such questions as those of sustainability and risk are beginning to put measurable standards in front of architects so that they have to think about the world as a physical scope of impact, if not of operation.

Yet engaging the geographic does not only mean a shift in scale. This has also come to affect the formal repertoire of architecture, even at a smaller scale, with more architects becoming interested in forms that reflect the geographic connectedness of architecture, by its ability to bridge the very large and the very small (networks and frameworks) or to provide forms that embody geographic references (e.g., continuous surfaces, environmentally integrated buildings).

Curiously, while most of the research around these various attributes has tended to be quite intense, the parallel tracks of inquiry have remained disconnected. For example, the discussion about continuous surfaces in architecture ignores the importance of continuity of ground in landscape ecology. Even if there is not a common cause driving these different geographic tendencies, a synthesis is possible, even necessary, to expand on the formal possibilities of architecture and its social role. This makes the need to articulate the geographic paradigm all the more urgent, because the role of synthesis that geography aspired to play between the physical, the economic, and the social is now being increasingly delegated to design.

Even though the term geographic is used primarily in a metaphorical way to designate a connection to the physical context, the paradigm does overlap with the discipline of geography. Some clarification is necessary in this respect to benefit from the overlap while avoiding confusion. The history of geography is strongly linked to the history of discovery and colonization. The instruments for the discovery of territory were extended into its documentation and then, in turn, into its appropriation and transformation. And yet the discipline has evolved to become more diverse and broad, to become institutionalized around geographic societies; to split into human and physical geography producing very different approaches and even subject matters; then to disintegrate (as in the case of Harvard) and migrate into other disciplines (sociology, public health, information systems); and then to be revived around central contemporary issues such as globalization. The paradigmatic role of geography in our thinking about design in this proposition could be taken in the narrower sense of geographic as being an attempt to study the relationship between the social and the physical at a larger territorial scale, but also to attempt a synthesis along the lines of "high" geography by design. It may be an exaggeration to propose that something like a geographic attitude, in both method and content, is guiding different strands of design thinking today toward convergence, or that a geographic aesthetic dominates formal pursuits in the same way that the machine aesthetic inspired functionalism at the turn of the century, but it would be important to study the extent and potentials of such a tendency.

As a way of pushing these formal possibilities, the question of human settlements should be cast at the scale of the world. Within this scale, the marks of the urban centralities would be diffused and we can identify new spatial patterns that transcend the limitations of cosmopolis and help us imagine a better city-world.

"Worldmaking"

According to Nelson Goodman, "the way the world is" is not predetermined. Moreover, it is not useful to draw an exact distinction between what is given (out there) and what is represented (mental or cognitive). To speak of the world means to speak of one of its representations or constructions. If two equally rigorous representations seem incompatible, this implies two incompatible but nevertheless possible worlds. Truth or "rightness of rendering" can only be determined instrumentally, within a construction and around the purpose for which it is constructed. Goodman has always called on philosophers to examine the way artists construct worlds through their media and techniques. Art anticipates and elucidates the idea of world-making.

Goodman's proposition bridged between the logical and semiological approaches to the question of representation, but its emphasis on the world as the space in which a scope of operation is internally consistent (and therefore real) could be linked to the proposal of thinking the world as an entity. As per Latour's conceptualization of the totality in his *Reassembling the Social*, we ought to take these panoramic representations seriously because they provide the "only occasion to see the 'whole story' *as a whole*." He goes on:

> Their totalizing views should not be despised as an act of profes-
> sional megalomania, but they should be adding, like everything else,
> to the multiplicity of sites we want to deploy. Far from being the place
> where everything happens, as in their director's dreams, they are
> local sites to be added to as so many new places dotting the flattened
> landscape we try to map. But even after such a downsizing, their
> role may become central since they allow spectators, listeners, and
> readers to be equipped with a desire for wholeness and centrality. It is
> from those powerful stories that we get our metaphors for what 'binds
> us together,' the passions we are supposed to share, the general
> outline of society's architecture, the master narratives with which we
> are disciplined. It is inside their narrow boundaries that we get our
> commonsensical idea that interactions occur in a 'wider' context;
> that there is a 'up' and a 'down'; that there is a 'local' nested inside a
> 'global'; and that there might be a Zeitgeist the spirit of which has yet
> to be devised.[4]

Along these lines, we should think of the ability of architects to construct new worlds and to encourage new forms of inhabitation, or habits, in these worlds. This *constructionist* position in architecture could be expanded into the following main ideas:

– The idea that each building could be a world or part of a world, that it would start from an internal logic and that it would unwind outward to meet the edges of other worlds and transform them. That this transformation could also transgress the conventional boundaries between building and context so that a new spatial relationship could emerge, something like a new geography, to redescribe the terrain in which architecture operates.

– The idea that the functional dimension of architecture should remain important in this process, but that it should be addressed as habits of living, as inhabitation. In that sense, these habits of living should be interrogated and revised to allow for the formation and expression of new habits. This is the core of world-making à la Goodman.

– The idea that we should inhabit these new contexts with new eyes, that the new habits of living encourage new habits of representation and seeing, which in turn help in achieving another level of

significance to architecture. This significance is one that maintains a level of openness to the experiences of its inhabitants. They are acquired rather than imposed.

– The idea that the attributes of sameness, repetition, placelessness, scalelessness, and homogeneity that have so far been scaring us and compelling us to obsessively articulate and differentiate by architecture could be turned into a treasure of qualities waiting to be re-explored.

– The idea that architecture, by virtue of its ability to balance between internal worlds and external ones, should maintain a certain level of operative autonomy and behave more like an object than systemic thinkers (blinded by the utilitarian approaches of ecology or technology) would like. The possibility of a quasiobject, to borrow from Michel Serres, is also waiting to be explored.

These ideas are not foreign to our palette of moves or to the history of our formal pre-occupations. Every building by Mies van der Rohe alternated between constructing an internal world and inscribing part of the horizon that links it to the world. Every other building by Enric Miralles wrapped a belt around the world but bled into it. Elias Torres uses geometry as the means of mediating between the particularities of the setting and larger orders that tie a locality to the world. The practice of an exaggerated silhouetting of buildings flattens an object into constructing skylines rather than being fixed into grounds. The quasi-object-like character of much of contemporary architecture is latently pointing to this direction and impatiently waiting to become conscious.

NOTES
1. This essay is the outcome of research toward the course "New Geographies" that I have been teaching at the Graduate School of Design since 2006. I am grateful to the students who have participated in the class through its different iterations, particularly to those who took part in the last version on "Imagining a City-World Beyond Cosmopolis" and whose research and insights have helped clarify many arguments made here. Peder Anker, as usual, has helped in raising the bar on intellectual provocation. I am also very grateful to Neil Brenner for his insights and for pointing me in the direction of Stuart Elden and Kostas Axelos.

2. See, for example, Fredric Jameson's canonical essay on Ideology… See also Bruno Latour, *Reassembling the Social: An Introduction to Actor-Network-Theory* (Oxford and New York: Oxford University Press, 2005)
3. See the paper by Stuart Elden in this issue.
4. Bruno Latour, *Reassembling the Social*, 189.

ADNAN MORSHED RECEIVED HIS PH.D. FROM MIT ARCHITECTURE'S HISTORY, THEORY AND CRITICISM SECTION. HE IS CURRENTLY ASSOCIATE PROFESSOR OF ARCHITECTURE AT THE CATHOLIC UNIVERSITY OF AMERICA. HE HAS RECEIVED FELLOWSHIPS AND GRANTS FROM THE NATIONAL GALLERY OF ART, SMITHSONIAN INSTITUTION, GRAHAM FOUNDATION, AND THE NATIONAL ENDOWMENT FOR THE HUMANITIES. HIS ARTICLES HAVE APPEARED IN THE *JOURNAL OF THE SOCIETY OF ARCHITECTURAL HISTORIANS*, *JOURNAL OF ARCHITECTURAL EDUCATION*, AND *ARCHITECTURAL DESIGN*. HIS BOOK, *THE ARCHITECTURE OF ASCENSION*, IS FORTHCOMING FROM THE UNIVERSITY OF MINNESOTA PRESS.

ASCENDING WITH NINE CHAINS TO THE MOON

BUCKMINSTER FULLER'S IDEATION OF THE GENIUS

Long before satellite technologies enabled a galactic perspective on Earth, enlarging the scope of humanity's geospatial knowledge, Richard Buckminster Fuller (1895–1983) presciently argued in his first book, *Nine Chains to the Moon* (1938), that the optimization of the world's resources called for vertical thinking and holistic views of the universe.[1] An efficient civilization seemed tenable, he posited, when humanity could look back on itself from orbital heights, a planetary gaze inspiring both introspection and strategies for human progress. Edgy, loquacious, and fraught with typical "Fulleresque" intellectual pyrotechnic, the book elicited a wide range of reviews, from appreciative to lukewarm to dismissive.

Sinclair Lewis, America's first Nobel Prize winner in literature in 1930, encapsulated the book's promise and perils thus: "It is at once a guidebook and dream book of the future, a purge of the past, a debunker of architecture, economics, political science, and your pet preconceptions" written by "a philosophical whirling dervish."[2]

Sharing Fuller's iconoclastic futurism, Frank Lloyd Wright wrote, with an admiring personal touch: "Buckminster Fuller — you are the most sensible man in New York, truly sensitive. Nature gave you antennae, long-range finders you have learned to use. I find almost all your prognosticating nearly right — much of it dead right, and I love you for the way you prognosticate."[3]

Nine Chains gives the impression of a rambling manifesto of an oddball genius — 44 short chapters on a bewildering spectrum of topics keep the reader on a tightrope. Yet across the jumble of ideas, Fuller weaves together an ascending narrative, one that endeavors to demonstrate how space flight and the totalizing view of Earth that it affords could be a measure of humanity's mental evolution. If distilled from all of the metaphors, fables, and Fuller's linguistic follies, the book's core argument is that unorthodox viewpoints are necessary to effect a new beneficent civilization and that new thoughts would be possible only when humanity attained the ability to look back on itself and outward at the universe for new resources. The dual facility for the introspective and cosmic gaze would be the hallmark of a new human race and its cerebral prowess.

The *locus classicus* of *Nine Chains*, then, resides in the intertwined discourses of vertical thinking and mental development, proffered as a common gospel of human progress. They are, somewhat tautologically, the two sides of one "civilizational coin": Cerebral evolution is codified through the metaphorical act of ascending, while ascension is only possible when evolution's wheel keeps rolling with directed human agency. Architecture could play its role as a container of civilization insofar as it changes, accordingly, to internalize the ascensional dynamic of the human mind. The architecture of physical shelter parallels the architecture of thought that, according to Fuller, must now transcend the parochialism of narrow Earth-centric views of the universe. Fuller's justification for his book's title explains this thought:

> The title, Nine Chains to the Moon, was chosen to encourage and stimulate the broadest attitude toward thought. Simultaneously, it emphasizes the littleness of our universe from the mind viewpoint. A statistical cartoon would show that if, in imagination, all of the people of the world were to stand upon one another's shoulders, they would make nine complete chains between the earth and the moon. If it is not so far to the moon, then it is not so far to the limits—whatever, whenever or wherever they may be.[4]
>
> ...
>
> Man is, therefore, empowered to a sense of personal contact with all astronomical bodies of the universe in addition to his earth.[5]

By emphasizing the comprehensibility of the "littleness of our universe," Fuller seeks to magnify the power of the human mind. Nine complete human chains between the Earth and the moon represented, then, a coded advocacy to think outward and upward, a milestone in the growth of a cosmic consciousness that enables "*personal contact with all astronomical bodies.*" Fuller argues, "Scientific shelter design… is linked to the stars far more directly than to the earth. STAR-GAZING? Admittedly. But it is essential to accentuate the real source of energy and change in contrast to the emphasis that has always been placed on keeping man 'down to earth.'"[6]

Fuller was an avid reader of evolutionary philosophies, a genre that enjoyed wide currency in interwar America. He especially favored Franco-American scientist Alexis Carrel's mystical work on racial hierarchy.[7] Fuller believed, with a strong dose of meritocratic elitism, that a most effective way to gauge the advancement of human races was to consider their relative ability to rise above a telluric life system and the fractured vision that results from it. Fuller writes the

following in "We call it 'earth,'" a section of Nine Chains:

> By means of his harnessed inanimate servant, power, and his extended mechanisms, man has now explored, measured, and "set" under control much of his earth's crust and his once-"outside" universe, entirely despite the inertia of vanities, superstitions, exploitation, humpty dumpty moralities, laws and destructive selfishness. He has flown in his imagination-conceived, intelligence-wrought, de-selfed mechanisms at 72,000 feet above the earth's surface, almost three times the height of the earth's highest mountain, and sixty times higher than the Empire State Building. Yet this is an insignificant feat compared with flights and heights to be attained in the NOT FAR AHEAD "NOW," in new intelligence-to-be-wrought mechanisms of flight.[8]

What is the basis for Fuller's musing in the 1930s about extreme altitude or human chains to the moon? Although invested in a complex amalgam of subjective ruminations on human progress, Fuller's verbose depiction of a stratospheric airplane in the guise of an "imagination-conceived, intelligence-wrought, de-selfed mechanism" capable of flying at 72,000 feet and his fictional human chains to the moon were couched in the ongoing American romance with space as a new extraterrestrial frontier.[9] As the natural satellite of Earth, the moon had already been the object of much fantasy. Speculative fictions of lunar voyages captivated a future-minded American readership in the 1930s, especially when escapist fantasies fed on people's anxieties during the Great Depression. Books and magazines regularly published the most up-to-date research on astronomical phenomena and the future of space exploration. This American fascination evolved into a burgeoning pulp industry of science fiction and then a fledgling, if somewhat secretive, American science of rocketry.

A major influence on Fuller's intellectual development, H.G. Wells had written about the clash of galactic civilizations in War of the Worlds (1898) and The First Men in the Moon (1901). The latter was reprinted in installments, from December 1926 through February 1927, in issues of America's first science fiction magazine, Amazing Stories.[10] In having his Homo Sapiens protagonists embark on a lunar journey by means of a gravity-defying material, cavorite, Wells broadened the horizon of man's planetary thinking, while offering a self-reflexive gaze

on humanity from the vantage of Selenites, the so-called lunar population.

Five years before Nine Chains, Wells published his seminal The Shape of Things to Come, a work of science fiction in which he probed both the political future of the human race and the startling affiliation of aerial transportation with the advent of a utopian civilization ruled by a dubiously benevolent regime called the "Air Dictatorship."[11] In the summer of 1934, during a visit to America, Wells posed before Fuller's recently completed streamlined vehicle, the Dymaxion Car. The photograph appeared in The Saturday Review of Literature, with the following caption: "The Shape of Things to Come Confronts Mr. Wells."[12]

The convergence of Wells's and Fuller's futurism and their prognostications on humanity's progress evince their mutual interest in the real potential of the machines of mobility, as well as these machines' political symbolism. For Wells and Fuller, new modes of mobility articulated a measure of civilization's intellectual celerity. Wells's fantasy of lunar voyage and Fuller's human chains to the moon both stem from a core interest in the politics of human evolution.[13]

The dystopian undercurrent in Wells's postapocalyptic civilization in The Shape of Things to Come notwithstanding, his faith in the political righteousness of the Air Dictatorship in ordering a neat world history reverberates in Fuller's self-assured optimism in viewing the "house designed as an utterly prosaic scientific mechanical agglomeration for the protection, maintenance and abetment of life" as the product of the "ninth chain to the moon."[14] To be thinking about reaching the moon was a sure-fire indicator of where one was on the evolutionary scale. Thus, in Nine Chains, the moon was a symbolic peak in Fuller's fiction of the evolutionary ladder.

But the moon was not just a staple fare of the utopian genre during the interwar era. Reaching the moon by means of gravity-defying projectiles already had scientists salivating.[15] A group of science fiction writers founded the American Interplanetary Society in 1930 in New York City to promote space expeditions. During the interwar years, American physicist Robert H. Goddard, an admirer of Jules Verne and Wells, was obsessively but secretly seeking to figure out a method of reaching extreme altitudes.[16] With the support of the Smithsonian Institution, Goddard administered, in 1926, from a field near Auburn, Massachusetts, the "first successful launch of a liquid fuel rocket."[17]

The First Men in the Moon, cover

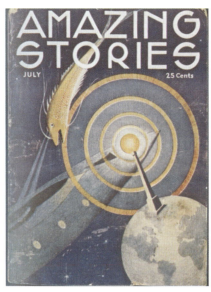

Amazing Stories, July 1933, cover

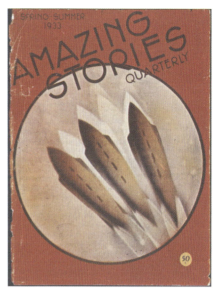

Amazing Stories Quarterly, Spring-Summer, 1933, cover

The media generally, if superficially, interpreted Goddard's effort in creating a gravity-defying projectile or a rocket able to reach the moon as far-fetched since the feasibility of lunar expedition still remained in the gray zone between fiction and reality. Not surprisingly, Goddard's research failed to garner adequate federal grants or corporate patronage. Yet, convinced of human benefits from the "future of rocket flight," aviator Charles Lindbergh, one of Fuller's early heroes, came to Goddard's aid in 1929 and secured funding from the Carnegie Institute and Guggenheim Foundation for America's fledgling science of rocketry.[18] Even when the American economy was making a perilous downturn as the Depression crippled the market, Lindbergh managed to keep the Guggenheim funding flowing for Goddard's rocket laboratory in Roswell, New Mexico.

Whether Fuller ever met Lindbergh or Goddard personally is unclear from archival sources. However, Fuller's fiction of lunar journey shows that he was eager to validate his self-image as an eccentric genius by delving into the contentious discourses of the era. As Howard McCurdy wrote, "The leaders of the rocket societies proclaimed a gospel of remarkable power. Humans, they said, would carry out expeditions of discovery in space as ambitious as those of earlier explorers on Earth, maintaining the spirit of adventure and discovery they had inspired."[19]

Fuller tapped into this ongoing American preoccupation with the new frontier of air and space – the twentieth-century counterpart of the nineteenth-century Wild West – and how the conquest of that frontier would be the sacred province of the American genius. Despite the allusion to the moon as a new frontier, his book was less concerned with the rocket that would carry humanity to the moon than with the visionary mind that conceives rocketry itself. In other words, Fuller negotiated the discourse of reaching the moon by human chains or rocketry as a prelude to his research proper that seeks to provide an understanding of, say, Goddard's intellect as a forum for a broader discussion on the development of an advanced human race.

In this context, Fuller's view of the machine merits elaboration. One of Fuller's arguments in his book is that the machine is ultimately a technological extension of the inventor or the genius, the hallowed protagonist of Nine Chains.[20] Along this line of argument, the engineering feat of the Spirit of St. Louis was already nascent in the genius of Lindbergh. The tool is a mechanical analog of the inventor, even if the tool begins to acquire a new social agency to effect change and eventually extend the latitude of the human mind. This view of technology suggests that man ultimately has the power to steer his own development by conscious maneuvering of the world of tools

and his environment. From early on, Fuller experimented with this idea, a worldview with which he wished to craft his own image: a man who shapes his own destiny.

In The Post-Industrial Prophets, William Kuhns calls it Fuller's "ecological pattern transformation," a sort of post-Darwinian mode of self-evolution in which man adapts to his environment with his own volition and programs.[21] When man creates the radio or the airplane, he ushers in new ways to adapt to, and transform, his environment. Kuhns writes: "Fuller sees the most recent major ecological pattern transformation in the revolution achieved by the automobile and the airplane… Fuller's ecological concept of evolution resembles Julian Huxley's 'social revolution' and Teilhard de Chardin's 'noosphere.' All three suggest that man can consciously pattern his own evolution and that technology represents the new nerve fibers of an emerging superorganism. This latter emphasis is especially strong in Fuller."[22]

In a somewhat tautological argument, within what Kuhns calls a "super-organism," technology is produced in a way so that it is eventually internalized within the man's mind/body network. In Nine Chains, Fuller calls this super-organism "Phantom Captain," which maintains or drives the techno-biological body, and "[w]ith the Phantom Captain's departure, the mechanism becomes inoperative and very quickly disintegrates into basic

Portrait of Robert H. Goddard, Credit: Courtesy NASA/Goddard Space Flight Center

chemical elements."[23] In other words, the Phantom Captain breathes creative life into the seemingly vegetative world of physical bodies. The body and other technologies, including architecture and means of transportation – two primary exemplars of creative endeavors, according to Fuller – are nothing but machinations of the Phantom Captain in its bid to harness the environment for optimum human growth. If architecture provides a kinesthetic metaphor of the Phantom Captain's ship, "the goal is not 'housing,' but the universal extension of the Phantom Captain's ship into new areas of environment control, possibly to continuity of survival without the necessity of intermittent 'abandoning ship.'"[24]

Fuller's esoteric argument boils down to this: It was with, and only with, the attainment of super-consciousness – the Phantom Captain – that the modern man could ensure an expedited self-development, while the architecture/technology network as an extension of the physical body proffered the means of environmental control. If the Phantom Captain meant a self-conscious cognitive leap across normative evolutionary cycles, then such irrationalities as reaching the moon enter the mental domain of possibilities, or "miracles, once irrational, will be continually rationalized and set under service to man by man."[25]

In the period following the lunar conquest in 1969, Fuller wrote the foreword to a book on space photography and included a quote by Scottish poet Robert Burns: "Oh wad some Power giftie gie us / To see oursels as ithers see us!"[26]

Human ingenuity and technology had finally simulated a reflected gaze on Earth by planting a mechanical eye on the moon and relying on an astronaut's eye. Decades earlier, however, Fuller had already articulated this possibility in *Nine Chains*, through the attainment of higher consciousness, the sacrosanct province of the genius.

NOTES

1. R. Buckminster Fuller, *Nine Chains to the Moon* (Philadelphia and New York: J.B. Lippincott Co., 1938). The manuscript is in the Buckminster Fuller Archive, Green Library, Stanford University, Series 2, Dymaxion Chronofile, Box 38, Vol. LIX, 1938. A decade earlier, Fuller self-published his mimeographed manifesto, *4D Time Lock*.

2. Sinclair Lewis, Newsweek (Sept. 12, 1938).

3. Frank Lloyd Wright, *The Saturday Review of Literature* (Sept. 17, 1938).

4. R. Buckminster Fuller, *Nine Chains to the Moon*, xiii.

5. Ibid., 66.

6. Ibid., 67.

7. Alexis Carrel, Man, *The Unknown* (New York and London: Harper and Brothers Publishers, 1935). Fuller read the book and quoted from it to justify many of his own ideas on human progress.

8. Fuller, *Nine Chains*, 68.

9. The science of rocketry was, by the 1930s, still primitive at best or mostly in the realm of fantasy. America would wait another twenty-five years for a realistic space vehicle or rocket able to carry even the smallest object into space. For American romance with space exploration, see, for example, Howard E. McCurdy, *Space and the American Imagination* (Washington and London: Smithsonian Institution Press, 1997) and Willy Ley, *Rockets, Missiles, and Men in Space* (New York: Viking Press, 1968).

10. David Kyle, *A Pictorial History of Science Fiction* (London: The Hamlyn Publishing Group Ltd., 1976), 38. Fuller understood aviation's potential to win wars from Wells' *The War in the Air* (1907); see *Nine Chains*, 293–294.

11. H.G. Wells, *The Shape of Things to Come* (New York: MacMillan Co., 1933), 348.

12. *The Saturday Review of Literature*, Henry Seidel Canby, ed. (New York, Saturday, June 2, 1934).

13. Wells was a student of Thomas Henry Huxley, Darwin's acolyte. In setting up the clash of civilizations, Wells endeavors to show that the more evolved or "fit" a race becomes, the better its chances of emerging victorious from the planetary battles of survival.

14. Fuller, *Nine Chains*, 325.

15. McCurdy, *Space and the American Imagination*, 16–20.

16. For biographical accounts of Goddard, see Milton Lehman, *This High Man: The Life of Robert H. Goddard* (New York: Farrar, Straus and Co., 1963).

17. McCurdy, *Space and the American Imagination*, 17.

18. A. Scott Berg, *Lindbergh* (New York: G.P. Putnam's Sons, 1998), 226.

19. McCurdy, *Space and the American Imagination*, 20.

20. For a similar explanation of Fuller's argument, see Betty Franks, "Futurists and the American Dream: A History of Contemporary Futurist Thought," Doctor of Arts Dissertation, Carnegie-Mellon University, 1985. Franks argues that Fuller expressed "faith in the individual whose genius would provide the knowledge necessary to alter the future."

21. William Kuhns, T*he Post-Industrial Prophets: Interpretations of Technology* (New York: Weybright and Talley, 1971), 232–233.

22. Kuhns, *The Post-Industrial Prophets*, 232–233.

23. Fuller, *Nine Chains*, 18–30.

24. Ibid., 41.

25. Ibid., 69.

26. Paul Dickson, *Out of This World: American Space Photography* (New York: Delacorte Press, 1977), 1.

OLA SÖDERSTRÖM IS PROFESSOR OF SOCIAL AND CULTURAL GEOGRAPHY AT THE UNIVERSITY OF NEUCHÂTEL, SWITZERLAND. HIS RESEARCH INTERESTS INCLUDE VISUAL CULTURES, URBAN GLOBALIZATIONS, COSMOPOLITAN-ISMS, AND THE MOBILITY OF URBAN POLICIES. HE HAS PUBLISHED A MONOGRAPH ON THE VISUAL IN URBAN PLAN-NING, *DES IMAGES POUR AGIR*, AND HE HAS RECENTLY PUBLISHED AN INQUIRY INTO URBAN CHANGE IN *PALERMO: URBAN COSMOGRAPHIES*. HE CO-EDITED (WITH MICHAEL GUGGENHEIM) *RE-SHAPING CITIES: HOW GLOBAL MOBILITY TRANSFORMS ARCHITECTURE AND URBAN FORM*.

HOW IMAGES ASSEMBLE THE URBAN WORLD

Is Scale Thinking Still Useful?

The scale of the world has in recent years come to coincide with the scale of the Earth.[1] In others words, a world society has come into being. It is constituted by a global interconnectedness in terms of economic and cultural flows and by the slow but certain emergence of global political institutions and agendas. One may question, however, to what extent that world society can be considered as a scale? And if there is something like a scale of the world, what are its constitutive elements?

Scale thinking and mapping is a favorite hobby of geographers, past and present. Recently, scale talk has been revivified in the discipline through calls to think about and practice human geography without using the concept of scale.[2] Unsurprisingly, other geographers have spoken in defense of scale.[3] Some even wish that such supposedly "dangerous" discussions (for the future of the discipline, not for you and me) would not reach the ears of non-geographers.[4] In a nutshell, the arguments of the authors proposing this radical erasure from our spatial vocabulary are the following: scale is not an ontological category but an epistemological one. There is no such thing as a nested hierarchy organizing the social world. Scale is rather a tool that pre-organizes the analysis and leads to scientifically fallacious and politically problematic interpretations. Scale thinking invites us to see global-local determinations between phenomena where in fact there are complex assemblages with emergent proper-ties. It is also politically disempowering because it portrays local life-worlds as dominated by placeless and largely uncontrollable global forces. We should therefore abandon scale and imagine a flat ontology where entities (spaces, objects, institutions, actors) are a priori given an equal status.

Non-geographers such as Bruno Latour and Arturo Escobar have developed broadly similar arguments.[5] Pursuing his associational socio-technical network theory of all things possible, Latour has called for abandoning the local-global distinction in favor of a flat vision of the world. This is the only route, he argues, if we want to understand the *production* of scales, dimensions, and localities, instead of attributing them a priori to the phenomena we investigate.

Like the deconstruction of other mega-categories such as culture and identity, the deconstruction of scale is both helpful and unsatis-factory. It is helpful because it alerts us to the possible confusions between things in the world and things in our heads, and because it opens up new and more complex ways of seeing the social and spatial organization of the world. Nevertheless, political institutions, administrative borders, ordinary thinking and talking are filled with scales, Russian doll hierarchies, "locals and globals," and the like. Scalar thinking has *produced* scales and relations of power between large spaces (such as national territories) and smaller ones (regions, communes, etc.). The International Criminal Court, for instance, thinks of its action and works at a global scale. We should therefore not avoid talking about scales, scaled institutions and territories, but do it while considering these elements as constitutive of complex assemblages.[6] Our task in the social sciences is to analyze the constitution of these assemblages without presupposing a scalar organization of the world. It also means trying to understand how the scale of the world *becomes* a relevant and efficient category for thought and action.

If we accept this stance, we must observe that the extent to which the tools, through which the world is becoming a relevant and efficient scale for thought and action, vary according to the social spheres considered. In other words, there is a differential timing and there are different (socially produced) substances to the world scale.[7] The advent of a substantial legal world scale is, for instance,

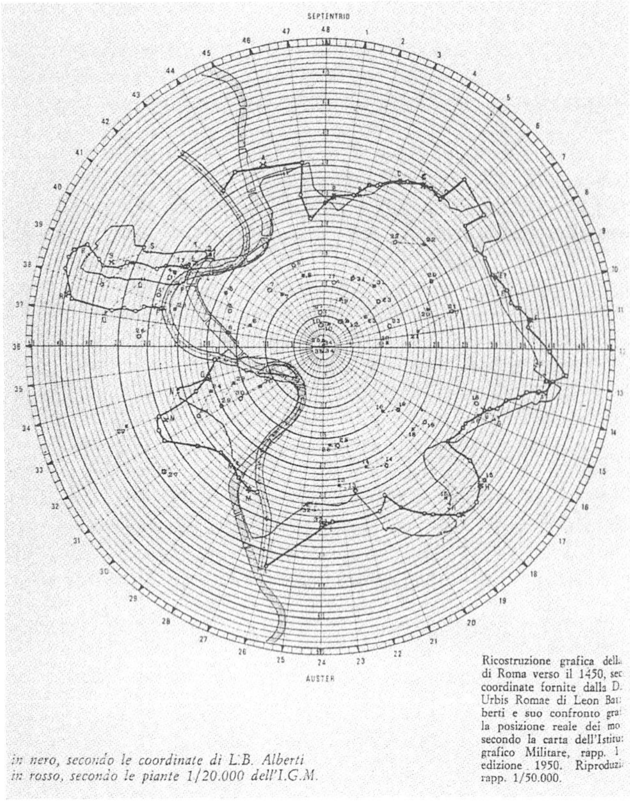
SEPTENTRIO
AUSTER
Ricostruzione grafica dell
di Roma verso il 1450, sec
coordinate fornite dalla D.
Urbis Romae di Leon Bat
berti e suo confronto gra
la posizione reale dei mo
secondo la carta dell'Istitu
grafico Militare, rapp. 1
edizione 1950. Riproduzi
rapp. 1/50.000.
in nero, secondo le coordinate di L.B. Alberti
in rosso, secondo le piante 1/20.000 dell'I.G.M.

1. Alberti's plan of Rome on the basis of his *Descriptio Urbis Romae* (ca. 1445) as reconstituted by Vagnetti.[18]

a very recent process based on a series of political events (such as genocides), political decisions, legal categories, etc. One of the basic preconditions for the creation of the International Criminal Court (ICC) in 2002 was the concept of "crime against humanity," in other words a legal category whose definition was based on a broad international consensus. Both that concept and the ICC can thus be considered as important building blocks of an emerging legal world scale.

What then are the building blocks of the urban world scale?

They are of course quite numerous, but I suggest considering five main types of entities: institutions, firms, networks, mobilities, and mediations.

Institutions are the most obvious ones. There is a long history of international exchange between architects and urban planners structured by international professional associations. The CIAM was, during the first half of the twentieth century, a powerful provider of thoughts and solutions for cities worldwide. The step from such international networks of exchange to global urban programmes was taken when state-funded international organizations began to develop strategies and actions to tackle problems of urban development on the basis of a world-scale diagnosis. The World Bank, with its first generation of urban projects aiming at an improvement of housing and urban services in the 1970s, and later UN-Habitat are central in this regard.[8]

Firms have a global reach in the fields of architecture, real estate, and civil engineering. They have developed specific expertise in grasping the urban as a world phenomenon and process.[9] A large number of transnational corporations and especially global producer service firms have also developed such an expertise even when their core business may have little connection with the construction industry, because it is functional to their development strategies.[10]

Networks relating professionals with similar activities (planners working in public administration, for instance) or common ideas (such as the creation of green cities) function as exchange platforms for global solutions to urban development issues. The network of "New Urbanists," for instance, is organized through elements such as a charter, regular congresses, newsletters, journals, etc.[11] In a broader sense, non-specialized web-based resources such as Google's visual arsenal (Google Earth/Google Maps/Streetview) are progressively giving visual access to all cities in the world and as a consequence to a form of urban globality.[12]

Mobilities, considered as the socially produced movements of entities (actors, images, ideas, information, capital)[13] across the globe, are also crucial to understand the interconnectedness of cities. Such connections cannot be seen as made of unhampered flows, but should instead be conceived as established by highly sorted movements using different sorts of vehicles. Finally, *mediations* are the vehicles through which these entities are mobilized. In other words, an urban world scale is also produced through the circulation of specific ideas (models of urban development, for instance), architectural types (like the office tower), urban types (like the waterfront development), architects and planners with an international career as well as texts, images and diagrams.[14]

Two observations concerning these 'global building blocks' should be made at once. First, it is not the simple addition of these elements that makes the urban world scale, but, again, the specific

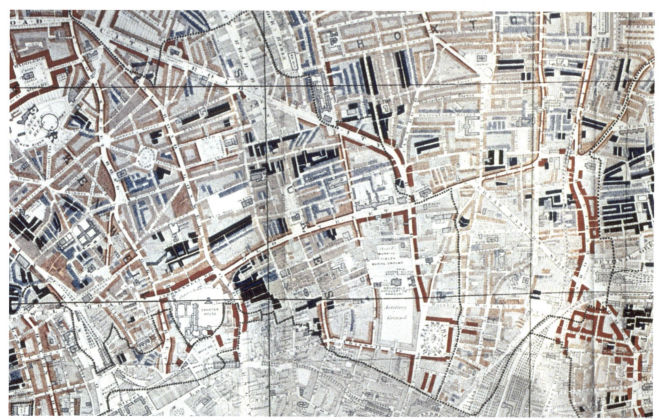

2. Booth's famous *Descriptive Map of London Poverty* (1889, detail).

assemblages of these elements for thinking and acting on cities globally. UN's much-discussed report on slums is, for instance, a global assemblage combining a worldwide institution, networks of mobile experts, texts, and images (UN-Habitat 2003). Second, different elements play different roles in the production of the global reach of these assemblages. In UN-Habitat's *The Challenge of Slums*, the institutional building block is of course of crucial importance: the same content published by a team of researchers not financed and diffused by the UN would not have had the same impact.

In the two following sections, I will focus on one specific type of mediation: images and their role in the production of a global urban ecumene.[15] To put the role of contemporary images in perspective, I will first briefly provide some general comments on the role of images in the history of urban planning.

The performance of images

Images are of decisive importance in the constitution of an urban world scale, because they are central for the thought and action of architects and planners. Graphic simulation, together with mathematics, are the means through which architecture emerged from the crafts of the building site and rose to the status of a Liberal art in the Italian Renaissance.[16] More relevant here, is the fact that the constitution of urban planning is premised on the production, a few years later, of a stable, totalizing image of cities.[17] Alberti's *Descriptio Urbis Romae* (figure 1) and Leonardo's plan of Imola gave the bases of the visual techniques allowing for efficient strategies and interventions on the scale of whole cities. The geometric city plan was, in other words, central in the creation of 'urbanity', defined as an awareness of the city as a specific space.

More generally, urban planning can be considered as created historically by a layering of different images. After the Renaissance, at later stages of the development of the discipline, other images of the city have provided planners with new means of action. Late nineteenth century zoning plans in Germany provided the means for modern functional planning; early twentieth century thematic urban cartography provided the possibility for targeted slum clearance interventions[19] (figure 2), major shifts in national traditions of urban planning, such as the Italian one, are related to the creation of new ways of representing the city.[20] Such traditional (i.e., non-digital) images can, however, hardly contain immaterial, mobile, and transient dimensions of urbanity. Because of their technological limitations, they tend to select material, immobile, and permanent features of the city. This does not entail that they have univocal functions and effects. Images are open signifiers allowing for different forms of meaningful associations and interpretations. To talk only about urban planning: images can reduce the complexity of its referent; they can persuade and manipulate their "audience," but they can also add complexity to common interpretations of the city and work as tools in collaborative planning processes.[21] This is even more the case with digital images in which the multiplicity, immateriality, and changeability of the city can be more easily inscribed than in analogical images.[22]

Different images of the city thus perform differently. This raises the question of the characteristics of those images that are efficient in the institution of an urban globality. I would suggest that those images

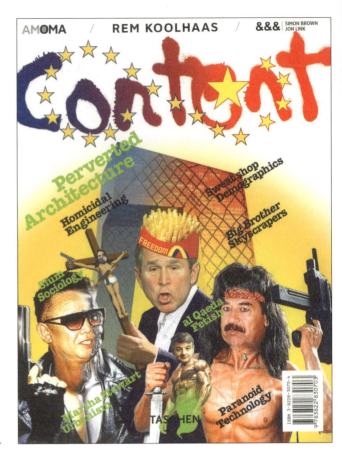

3–5. OMA/AMO, *Content*, 2004.

must have at least two features: they must refer to the global urban ecumene and circulate on a global scale.

In a recent paper on global architectural types, Monika Grubbauer provides an example of such images when she explores the role of photographs from the Getty image bank in the global diffusion of the high-rise office tower type.[23] She shows how these visual mediations contribute to the global uniformity of that specific building type and thus how architecture on a world scale is visually produced. Grubbauer analyzes "lay" images, but there are also more specialized ones. Here I will rather look at images in academic and professional circles. In the next section, I will therefore focus more specifically on world-scale urban images produced, on the one hand, by the Office for Metropolitan Architecture and by authors in world city literature, on the other hand.

Visually Performing the Global Urban Ecumene

Producing images of the world has been central to geography since Anaximander's first "map" in the sixth century B.C. The modern versions of these images hinge on Ptolemy's grid, introduced in Western cartography in the early fifteenth century: "The introduction of a graticule of longitude and latitude lines as the basis for determining location and translating the sphere into a two-dimensional map is, writes Denis Cosgrove, by far the most significant feature of modern cartography,"[24] Urban maps are traditionally based on the same principles. Unsurprisingly therefore, contemporary images of the urban on a world scale are often based on traditional cartographic principles. They are planispheres highlighting the largest cities as dots, areas, or diagrams proportional to their size.

The world of cities is, however, not only made of dots on maps; it is also a relational one. Cities are increasingly interconnected and interdependent. As these interurban connections are only partly related to geographical distance – London being more connected to New York than to Cardiff in many ways – traditional cartography is insufficient to portray the global urban ecumene. Contemporary images are thus also often either distorting the Ptolemaic grid or representing topological rather than topographical spaces.[25]

OMA's Visual Language

In its 2004 book, entitled *Content*, the Office for Metropolitan Architecture traces seven years of the agency's work (1997-2004).[26] It is also a manifesto for an architecture beyond rootedness which invites the reader to 'Go East' following what Koolhaas calls the "arrow of innovation."[27] Interesting in the context of this paper is that *Content* is also an iconographic experiment: images, in the broad sense (not only architectural ones), are used in combination with the more proper architectural capacities of the office to produce a "truly contemporary architecture," which OMA defines as follows: "Freed from the obligation to construct, it becomes a way to think anything – a discipline that represents relations, proportions, connections, effects, a diagram of anything".[28] The images in *Content* are therefore the result of research into an aesthetic form that is as fluid and versatile as the multiple and varied objects that this architecture strives to represent (and in some cases to produce). Graphically, *Content* resembles a hybrid between a video game, an American news magazine, and a hijacked advertisement (in the style of *Adbusters*[29]).

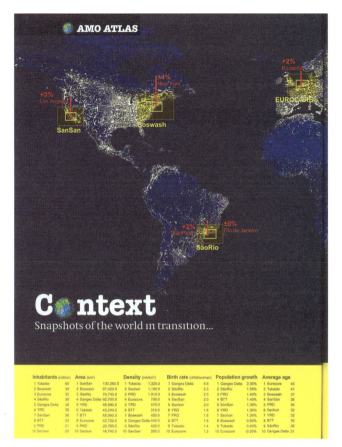

Context
Snapshots of the world in transition...

Inhabitants (million)		Area (km²)		Density (inh/km²)		Birth rate (child/woman)		Population growth		Average age	
1 Tokaido	60	1 SanSan	130,260.0	1 Tokaido	1,320.0	1 Ganges Delta	4.6	1 Ganges Delta	2.30%	1 Eurocore	43
2 Boswash	39	2 Boswash	87,420.0	2 Sechon	1,190.0	2 SãoRio	2.3	2 SãoRio	1.50%	2 Tokaido	41
3 Eurocore	32	3 SãoRio	70,740.0	3 PRD	1,010.0	3 Boswash	2.0	3 PRD	1.40%	3 Boswash	37
4 SãoRio	30	4 Ganges Delta	62,700.0	4 Eurocore	750.0	4 SanSan	2.0	4 BTT	1.40%	4 SanSan	35
5 Ganges Delta	28	5 YRD	46,980.0	5 YRD	570.0	5 Sechon	2.0	5 SanSan	1.30%	5 PRD	34
6 YRD	28	6 Tokaido	45,240.0	6 BTT	519.0	6 YRD	1.8	6 YRD	1.30%	6 Sechon	32
7 SanSan	26	7 BTT	45,060.0	7 Boswash	450.0	7 PRD	1.6	7 Sechon	1.20%	7 YRD	32
8 BTT	23	8 Eurocore	42,730.0	8 Ganges Delta	440.0	8 BTT	1.6	8 Boswash	0.50%	8 BTT	30
9 PRD	21	9 PRD	20,760.0	9 SãoRio	420.0	9 Tokaido	1.4	9 Tokaido	0.40%	9 SãoRio	26
10 Sechon	20	10 Sechon	16,740.0	10 SanSan	200.0	10 Eurocore	1.3	10 Eurocore	-0.20%	10 Ganges Delta	21

The most interesting experiment in *Content* is the attempt to represent urban space on a global scale (figures 3, 4) to describe a spatial order on which to act. Active in each continent and, aiming to think globally in order to act locally, OMA tries to consider each site of intervention (a garden in Paris, an airport in Hong Kong, a media center in San Francisco, etc.) as a specific node in global networks interconnecting people, capital, goods, and information. Those images can therefore be considered as tools for a specific politics of architecture, more precisely a "cosmopolitics,"[30] which attempts to place analysis and action in a global perspective.

The first image (figure 4) is based on altered satellite images of the Earth by night.[31] This background allows us to see and name megalopolises that could not be seen by other methods – for example, "SanSan" (the urban region that stretches from San Francisco to San Diego) and "Tokaïdo"[32] (the urban region from Tokyo to Kobe). This strategy is reinforced by the lists of toponyms at the bottom of the image and the box highlighting them. It is by this simple procedure that OMA constructs a knowledge object, which can also become an object for different types of projects.[33]

The second image (figure 5) takes us into the realm of thematic maps. Instead of social class and cholera incidence information, which was represented on an intra-urban scale in the social cartography of the nineteenth and beginning of the twentieth centuries, these diagrams contain different types of information on a global scale, such as the density of reality television broadcasts and McDonald's outlets, suicide rates, and levels of military expenditure – in other words, information that would usually be absent from the analysis and planning materials used by architects and planners. These thematic maps are there to demonstrate that the type of cosmopolitan urban planning advocated by OMA should incorporate not only new geographic visualizations and dimensions but also new types of information, which only really make sense on a global scale.

OMA's images of the global urban ecumene seem to have two main functions. The first is to publicize the firm's global reach and ambition; the second is to create projectural tools for "glocal" architecture. While these images are probably commercially efficient, it is more difficult to see how they inform architectural projects. Relational images of the urban on a world scale, instead of satellite images or traditional planispheres, are needed to analyze and act on sites as nodes. This search for relational images has been at stake in world city literature.

Images in World City Research
In what is considered the inaugural text of contemporary world city literature, John Friedman's "World city hypothesis," there is a widely diffused image of a network and hierarchy of world cities (figure 6). This emblematic representation of Friedman's fruitful hypothesis was not based on empirical evidence concerning city networks and hierarchies worldwide however. It was simply inspired, according to Abu-Lughod, by the air-route map of Japan Airlines.[34]

Friedman's world-city hierarchy map cancels the contours of continents, and national borders. Nonetheless, it still names continents, and some regions or countries, and maintains locations and topographic distance. This images thus represents a world of networked cities, but one situated on the background of an absent but perceptible planisphere.

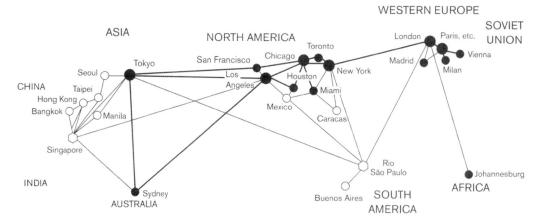

6. The world city hierarchy from (Friedmann 1986)

I think we can understand the important impact that Friedmann's image has had on urban research by the fact that it shows a quasi-postnational image of the world, highlighting a hierarchy of cities. Though very simple, this image, very much like Alberti's *Descriptio*, is a space allowing for new thoughts about the nature of urbanity. With and after Friedmann's *détournement* of JAL's map, researchers working on urban phenomena could better think about cities on a world scale as a system of interrelated, hierarchically organized, and regionalized nodes.[35]

In later works, world-city research focused on global cities as economic command centers. Sassen's seminal book on the global city focuses on New York, Tokyo, and London as individual cities and pays little attention to their interconnectedness.[36] On the basis of this observation, another world city analyst, Peter Taylor, has developed tools for the analysis and visual representation of world city *networks*.[37] His maps have become the trademark of the productive Globalization and World Cities research group (GaWC)[38] of which Taylor is the director. Though not as popular as Friedmann's map, these images shape the way contemporary urban researchers consider the global urban ecumene (figure 7).

A strong advocate of a city-centered understanding of economic development in the *longue durée*, Taylor explicitly produces world maps of cities and not states. He also strives to represent city networks instead of cities as individual places.[39] His map erases, like Friedmann's, national boundaries and gives equal size to each of the 123 most connected cities in the world. His cartogram "solves the problem of depicting an uneven distribution of cities across the world"[40] and preserves more or less its geographical position on a traditional planisphere. Consequently, it is possible with some training to recognise the continents. What this cartogram provides is a base map on which to 'project' all kinds of information concerning different aspects of urban connectivity. Though it graphically does not show *connections*, it shows for each of these cities their *connectivity* – their role in different types of inter-urban networks (figure 8).

These useful cartograms elaborate a vision of the urban world that focuses on economic activities and also on the upper part of the ladder of world cities.[41] As a consequence, the geographical imagination of such images corresponds to a classic developmentally biased conception of the world.

Such images therefore produce, as all images, a reductionist vision of urban globalization and globality. On the other hand, they have encouraged researchers to look more at world cities off those maps, or at "ordinary cities,"[42] somewhat like sailors stimulated to look for

the *terrae incognitae* represented on 16th century maps. But if world-city scholars have recently looked more often at globalizing cities in the South instead of focusing on global cities in the North, they have not yet provided other types images capable of substantially changing our imagination of the global urban ecumene.

If we consider that the role of urban research is to produce a multifaceted and rich understanding of urban phenomena both for scientific and political reasons, this raises an important question. World-city research is indeed embroiled in urban policy worldwide. Hierarchies, rankings, indicators of globality are used in benchmarking and in the elaboration of development strategies. As a result, many public authorities around the world today try to emulate cities figuring prominently on the maps, lists, and diagrams of world-city research. Offering other lists and images is important because it helps open avenues for urban globalisation. It indicates different ways for cities to find their place in the wires and networks of the urban world.

Conclusion

World-scale images of the urban have proliferated recently both in mass media and in academic literature. Some of them play a significant role in the creation of that specific assemblage that I have called the global urban ecumene. Through such images, a consciousness of the urban world scale emerges publicly. Friedmann's world-city hierarchy map contributed to such a process among a public of specialized scholars. OMA's more recent images talk to an audience of architects and individuals interested in architecture. They describe the world as a market and playground for these professionals. They also hint at the necessity to use new tools (thematic world maps, global statistics, etc.) in contemporary architecture.

Images also give specific properties and meanings to global urban assemblages. Peter Taylor and GaWC's cartograms define world cities as concentrating globally active insurance companies, banks, legal consultants, and the like. Other, less academic images associate world cities with gated communities, waterfront developments, Olympic games, etc. Images thus shape our imaginations of the global ecumene. This implies that the activity of producing such images is deeply political. We should therefore be more engaged in the elaboration of new images of the urban world. Those images should show how city authorities and dwellers connect and collaborate also on non-profit grounds (like fair trade,[43] cultural collaboration, etc.) and thereby contribute to reassembling the urban world according to what we wish it should become.

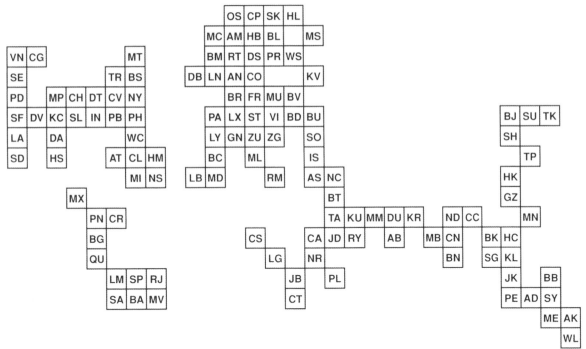

7. An archipelago of world cities (from Taylor 2004)

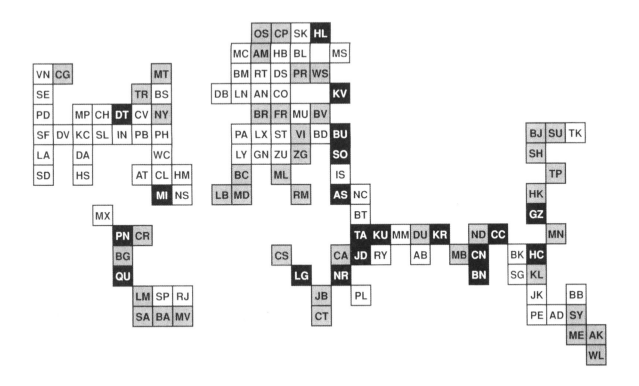

8. Connectivity in terms of advertising (from Taylor 2004)

NOTES

1. The former refers to a human society encompassing the planet, whereas the latter refers to the physical extension of the planet.

2. John Paul Jones III, Sallie A. Marston, "Human Geography Without Scale," *Transactions of the Institute of British Geographers* 30:1, 2005, 416-432.

3. Andrew Jonas, "Pro Scale: Further Reflections on the 'Scale Debate' in Human Geography," *Transactions of the Institute of British Geographers* 31:3, 2006, 399-406.

4. Scott William Hoefle, "Eliminating scale and killing the goose that laid the golden egg?", *Transactions of the Institute of British Geographers* 31:2, 2006, 238-243.

5. Bruno Latour, Reassembling the Social: An introduction to actor-network-theory (Oxford: Clarendon, 2007); Arturo Escobar, "The 'Ontological Turn' in Social Theory: A Commentary on 'Human Geography Without Scale' by Sallie Marston, John Paul Jones II and Keith Woodward," *Transactions of the Institute of British Geographers*, 32:1, 2007, 106-111.

6. By assemblage, I mean the temporary order created by the combination of a series of heterogeneous entities. See Manuel De Landa, *A new philosophy of society: Assemblage theory and social complexity* (London: Continuum, 2006).

7. For the geographer Jacques Lévy, who is faithful to scale, each space is characterised by its specific metric (way of measuring distance), scale and substance, see Jacques Lévy, *L'invention du monde: une géographie de la mondialisation* (Paris: Presses de Sciences Po, 2008).

8. Annick Osmont, *La Banque mondiale et les villes: du développement à l'ajustement* (Paris: Karthala, 2005).

9. Paul Knox and Peter Taylor, "Toward a Geography of the Globalization of Architecture Office Networks," *Journal of Architectural Education* 58, 2005, 23-32.

10. See Saskia Sassen, *The Global City* (New York, London, Tokyo, Princeton: Princeton University Press, 1991); Peter Taylor, *World City Network: A Global Urban Analysis* (London: Routledge, 2004).

11. See Michelle Thompson-Fawcett, "A New Urbanist Diffusion Network: The Americo-European Connection," *Built Environment* 29:3, 2003, 253-270; Blaise Dupuis, "A Swarm Tactic," *Revue Économique et sociale* 67, 2009, 151-155.

12. The impact of our recent access to these resources on our everyday lives' vision of the urban world is still difficult to grasp.

13. For recent theorizations of mobility in these terms, see John Urry, *Mobilities* (Cambridge: Polity Press, 2007); Tim Cresswell, *On the move: mobility in the modern Western world* (London: Routledge, 2006).

14. Michael Guggenheim and Ola Söderström, "Introduction: Mobility and the Transformation of Built Form" in M. Guggenheim and O. Söderström (eds.) *Re-shaping Cities: How Global Mobility Transforms Architecture and Urban Form* (London: Routledge, 2010), 3-19.

15. I use that term in this text because it refers to the urban on a world scale as a space of thought and action.

16. Giorgio de Santillana, "The Role of Art in the Scientific Renaissance" in M. Clagett (ed.) *Critical Problems in the History of Science* (Madison: University of Wisconsin Press, 1959), 3-66.

17. Ola Söderström, "Paper cities: visual thinking in urban planning." *Ecumene* 3:3, 1996, 249-281.

18. Luigi Vagnetti, "La Descriptio Urbis Romae, uno scritto poco noto di Leon Battista Alberti." *Quaderno dell'Istituto di Architettura e Rilievo dei Monumenti di Genova* 1, 1968, 25-59.

19. Ola Söderström, *Des images pour agir : le visuel en urbanisme* (Lausanne: Payot, 2000).

20. Patrizzia Gabellini, *Il disegno urbanistico, Roma, La nuova Italia scientifica*, 1996.

21. Ola Söderström and Markus Zepf, "L'image négociée," *Disp* 134, 1998, 12-19.

22. Public Participation GIS are but one example.

23. Melinda Grubbauer, "The High-Rise Office Tower as Global Type: Exploring the Architectural World of Getty Images and Co" in Guggenheim and Söderström (eds.) *Re-Shaping Cities. How Global Mobility Transforms Architecture and Urban Form* (London: Routledge, 2010), 63-80.

24. Denis Cosgrove, *Geography and vision: seeing, imagining and representing the world* (London: IB Tauris, 2008).

25. See John Allen, "Powerful Geographies: Spatial Shifts in the Architecture of Globalization" in *The Handbook of Power*, Clegg and Haugaard (eds.), (London: Sage, 2008), 157-174.

26. For a more extensive analysis of OMA's *Content*, see Ola Söderström, "De la mégalopole au split screen: trois esthétiques urbaines contemporaines" *Intellectica* 41-42, 2005, 201-224.

27. OMA (2004) *Content* (Köln: Taschen, 2004).

28. Ibid., 20.

29. www.adbusters.org.

30. Ulrich Beck, *The cosmopolitan vision* (Cambridge: Polity Press, 2006).

31. They are altered because, of course, it cannot be night at the same time all over the world, and the cloud that covered certain areas of the globe at the moment the picture was taken was removed.

32. *Tokaido* is not a new toponym, however.

33. This process is in principle no different from the one that enabled Leon Battista Alberti to represent Rome with precision via a single medium.

34. Janet Abu-Lughod, *Before European hegemony: the world system AD 1250-1350* (Oxford: Oxford University Press, 1989).

35. One should also investigate, along the same lines, the role of lists and rankings of world cities.

This has not been done in-depth to my knowledge.

36. The parts of *The Global City* on the strong interdependence of those three cities' real estate markets is an exception.

37. Taylor, (2004).

38. www.lboro.ac.uk/gawc/

39. Peter Taylor, "A new mapping of the world for the new millennium", *The Geographical Journal* 167:3, 2001, 213-222.

40. Taylor, (2004).

41. The number of 123 cities corresponds to those cities that count at least a fifth of London's connectivity as measured by the presence of different types of offices of the top global service firms.

42. Ash Amin and Stephen Graham, "The ordinary city." *Transactions of the Institute of British Geographers* 22:4, 1997, 411-429; John Robinson, "Global and World Cities: A View from off the Map", *International Journal of Urban and Regional Research* 26:3, 2002, 531-554; John Robinson, *Ordinary Cities: Between Modernity and Development* (London: Routledge, 2006).

43. See for instance Alice Malpass, "Fairtrade Urbanism: The Politics of Place Beyond Place in the Bristol Fairtrade City Campaign," *International Journal of Urban and Regional Research* 31:3, 2007, 633-645.

JULIEN DE SMEDT
IS THE FOUNDER AND DIRECTOR OF JDS ARCHITECTS, BASED IN COPENHAGEN AND BRUSSELS, AND CO-FOUNDER OF PLOT. IN ADDITION TO NOTABLE COMPLETED PROJECTS SUCH AS THE HOLMENKOLLEN SKI JUMP IN OSLO AND THE MOUNTAIN AND VM HOUSING COMPLEXES IN COPENHAGEN, JDS HAS ONGOING PROJECTS IN EUROPE, SOUTH AMERICA, AND ASIA THAT RANGE IN SCALE FROM FURNITURE TO URBAN MASTER PLANS.

RYAN NEIHEISER
IS AN ARCHITECT, ENGINEER, AND WRITER WHOSE RECENT WORK ENGAGES ISSUES OF INFRASTRUCTURE, MEMORY, POLITICAL SPACE, AND ENERGY. HE HAS WORKED FOR REM KOOLHAAS/OMA IN ROTTERDAM AND JDS ARCHITECTS IN BRUSSELS, WHERE HE CO-EDITED THE BOOK, *AGENDA: CAN WE SUSTAIN OUR ABILITY TO CRISIS?* HE CURRENTLY LIVES IN NEW YORK CITY AND WORKS AT DILLER SCOFIDIO + RENFRO.

CAN YOU SEE IT FROM OUTER SPACE?

"Sustainable" architecture is everywhere and nowhere. Plagued by the promise of endless technological add-ons, co-opted by the precise ambiguity of corporate advertising campaigns, and commodified by the prescribed checklists and codes that masquerade as design philosophy, "sustainable" design has been rendered impotent, unable to affect the kind of dramatic change necessary to confront the realities of a coordinated energy and climate crisis. However, by combining the best ambitions of architecture (inhabitation, use, and beauty) with the best ambitions of infrastructure (efficiency, scale, and systemization) there might exist the potential for a reconceived and re-empowered form of sustainable design. Two recent projects by JDS Architects, an 1100-meter tower in Shenzhen, China, and a 44-square kilometer zero-energy island zoo off the coast of South Korea, suggest the possibility of an architecture performing at a new scale of perception and influence. One is vertical, one horizontal, and both are big and conceived of as infrastructural architecture that simultaneously instigates systemic efficiencies and enables social inhabitation and use.

Denver, USA; Mission ISS016; Roll E; Frame 26150. Courtesy of the Image Science & Analysis Laboratory, NASA Johnson Space Center. http://eol.jsc.nasa.gov

CAN YOU SEE IT FROM OUTER SPACE?

As usual, the answer is both yes and no. According to astronauts, very little is visible with the naked eye from outer space besides swirls of water, earth, and atmosphere.[1] At the same time, recent developments in satellite technologies have made not only most of the world's man-made development visible from space, it has also made this aerial imagery available to anyone with a computer and access to the Internet. With the democratization of this previously privileged view, we are now able to interrogate the scale and form of our man-made developments and ask: What have we done? What have we made? At the largest scale, at the first level of perception available as one zooms in from outer space, we learn that we have spent the majority of our energy and our effort creating infrastructure.

   Meshes of concrete roads accumulated near the world's largest cities, the manipulated coastline of the Netherlands, intercontinental networks of highway and rail transport as they trail across the relative homogeneity of blank desert expanses, bright blots of accumulated urban street light emerging from the nocturnal darkness, tapestries of well-irrigated and groomed agricultural fields, and even the apparently quite difficult to see Great Wall of China.[2] All of these ultra-objects and mega-traces of human presence – these figures perceptible against the ground of earth's natural landscape – are forms of infrastructure, man-made systems that both enable and describe inhabitation.

London, UK; Mission ISS006; Roll E; Frame: 22939. Courtesy of the Image Science & Analysis Laboratory, NASA Johnson Space Center. http://eol.jsc.nasa.gov

Tokyo, Japan; Mission ISS006; Roll E; Frame 27586. Courtesy of the Image Science & Analysis
Laboratory, NASA Johnson Space Center. http://eol.jsc.nasa.gov

North Sea, http://www.nasaimages.org/luna/servlet/detail/nasaNAS~10~10~73521~178968:
Thames-River-Plume-in-the-North-Sea

THICK, TALL, AND GREEN.

And yet these infrastructures, these newly perceived icons of human development designed
ahead of human inhabitation, outside of concerns for beauty, and with a stubborn single-mind-
edness when it comes to use, can be understood to precede architecture. What if instead,
architecture and infrastructure were conceived of synthetically?

  Bruce Sterling's recent short story, "White Fungus,"[3] imagines the bleak dystopian
extension of the current urban infrastructural logic of choice – horizontal sprawl. New
Jersey and the Eurocore offer only the best examples of this loose infrastructural fabric that
is fast becoming ubiquitous worldwide. The only competing logic could be called vertical
sprawl – the dumb, speculation-driven race to the sky epitomized by many recent cities
throughout Asia and the Middle East. Bland office floors stacked ad infinitum and inhumanly
linked together by Escalade-like elevators speeding along vertical highways and seamlessly
connecting to horizontal highways below. Neither system has much to offer in terms of
sustainability, public space, or monumentality. And architecture, as much as it tries, can do

Collage, courtesy of JDS Architects

Collage, courtesy of JDS Architects

little within this overwhelming infrastructural sprawl to foster such vital moments of efficiency, exchange, and connection.

By imagining architecture at the scale of infrastructure, JDS's proposal for an 1100-meter-tall, 325-meter-wide, park-filled and energy-producing vertical city in Shenzhen (dubbed Shenzhen Logistic City, or SLC) attempts to remedy the failings of both dominant systems of urban sprawl while reasserting the agency of architectural design in shaping our cities. Unlike most skyscraper towers that are merely tall, our tower is tall and thick, interior and exterior, urban and rural, public and private, gritty and green. Its monumentality is achieved both from a distance (a traditional monumentality perceived via the distant static gaze) and from within (perhaps the model for a newer monumentality that emerges from inhabitation, movement, and use). If the horizontal "ruin of the unsustainable" described in Sterling's "White Fungus" fostered a kind of informal urbanism through scarcity and appropriation, we propose that the vertical "infrastructure of the sustainable" in our Shenzhen Logistic City would instigate an alternative kind of informal urbanism through density and diversity. The Shenzhen Logistic City is both an efficiently and systematically designed vertical urban infrastructure and an architectural instigation for multiple spatial experiences, inhabitations, and uses.

Plans, courtesy of JDS Architects

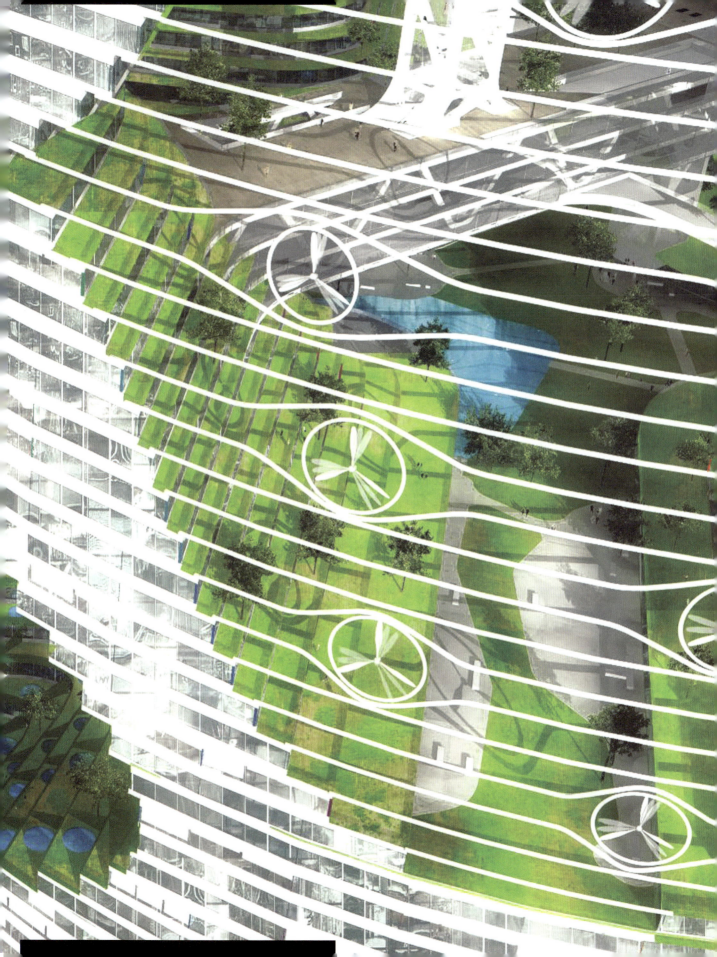

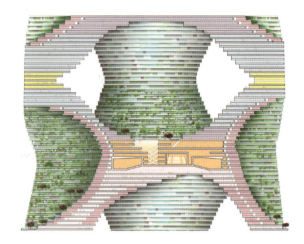

Section, courtesy of JDS Architects

Diagram, courtesy of JDS Architects

Previous: Collage, courtesy of JDS Architects

Collage, courtesy of JDS Architects

Collage, courtesy of JDS Architects

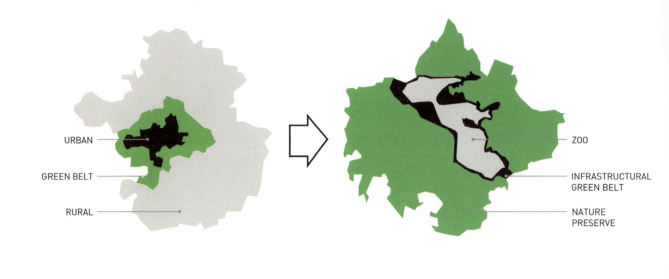

PASSIVE   ACTIVE

Passive to Active diagram, courtesy of JDS Architects

EMPOWERING THE GREEN BELT.

Our proposal for a zero-energy island zoo in South Korea similarly conflates strategies of infrastructural engineering with those of architectural design to more intelligently coordinate the shape of development with the desires for its use. Confronted with the task of developing the undeveloped – the manic infatuation of horizontal sprawl – the question became how to limit development to an absolute minimum while maximizing its productivity and efficiency. We looked to the example of the urban green belt, or growth boundary, an urban planning strategy and form of urban infrastructure that has historically served to passively limit development. Rather than simply establish an edge to development, we would empower the green belt to both concentrate development and enhance surrounding ecologies. Transplanted from the city to nature, our green belt acts as sustainable infrastructure, a machine to both enable development along its length and enhance the ecological health of the surrounding natures. It is a network that collects, organizes, and distributes all of the human development on the island – solar panels, wind turbines, and wave energy converters, but also buildings, roads, public transport, bicycle paths, water cisterns, and waste treatment. It is architecture as infrastructure. Not infrastructure buried below ground, or infrastructure that accomplishes only a single task. This is infrastructure that is present and busy, that multitasks, and that is itself a space of inhabitation and use. It is designed, it is big, and you could probably see it from outer space. But it is also smart, promotes new efficiencies, and instigates a comprehensive ecology of exchange between architecture, infrastructure, and nature.

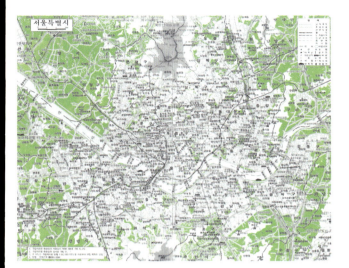

Seoul Green Belt Map, courtesy of JDS Architects

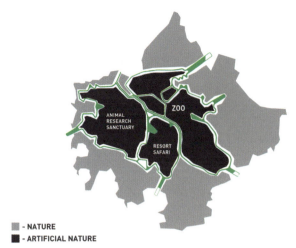

- NATURE
- ARTIFICIAL NATURE

Plan Diagram, courtesy of JDS Architects

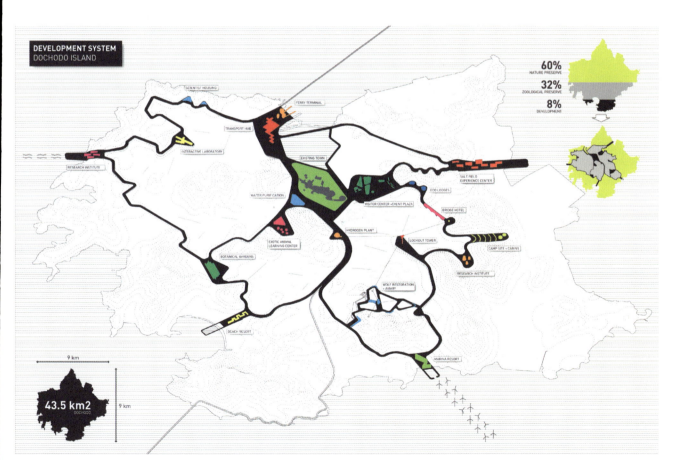

Development Axonometric Projection, courtesy of JDS Architects

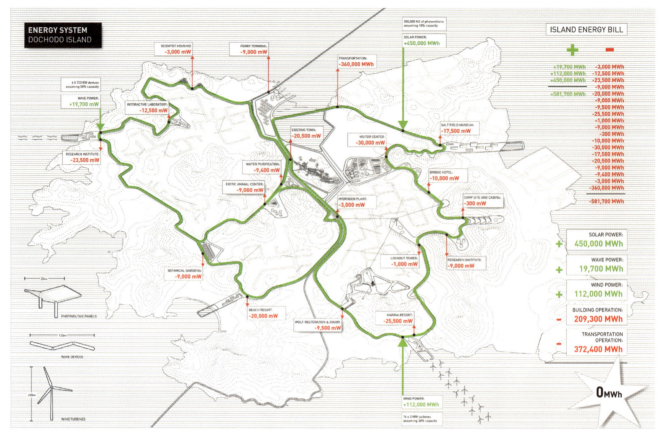

Energy Axonometric Projection, courtesy of JDS Architects

Previous: Island Aerial View, courtesy of JDS Architects

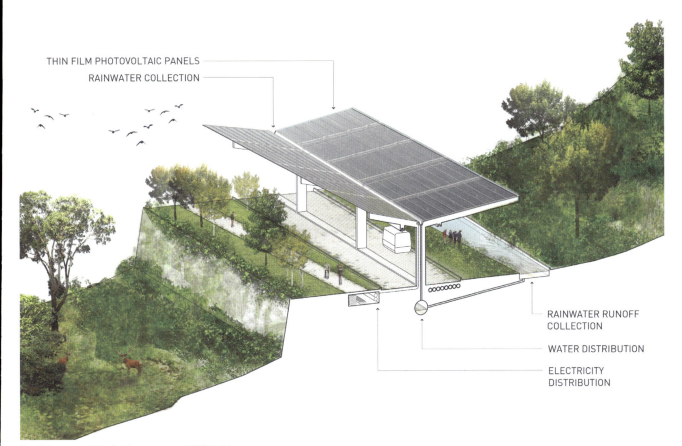

THIN FILM PHOTOVOLTAIC PANELS

RAINWATER COLLECTION

RAINWATER RUNOFF COLLECTION

WATER DISTRIBUTION

ELECTRICITY DISTRIBUTION

Detail Axonometric Projection, courtesy of JDS Architects

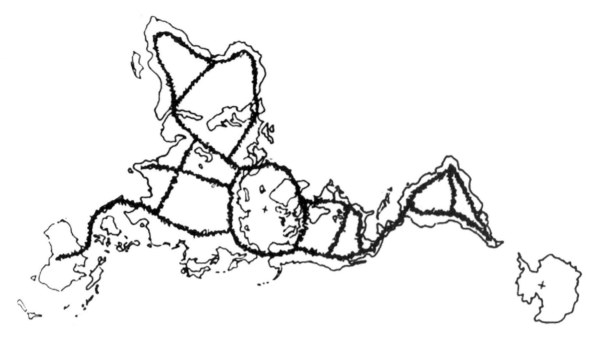

Global Energy Network, Buckminster Fuller.

PERCEIVING A (NEW) NEW DIGITAL ARCHITECTURE.

In the 1970s, Buckminster Fuller imagined a global energy grid to connect the world's disparate electrical production facilities and distribution networks, predicting dramatically enhanced efficiencies. JDS Architects' island energy network and vertical logistic city, at much smaller scales, imagine similarly coordinated efforts at energy production, exchange, and feedback. Forty years after Fuller first imagined his global energy grid, at a moment when a mature information technology (IT) revolution is overlapping with a burgeoning energy technology (ET) revolution, the promise of more sustainable and integrated energy production, distribution, and communication is finally made possible by advances in digital communications and alternate energy technologies. And by combining these new logistical and technological intelligences with all of the messy logics and irrationalities of social exchange, spatial perception, desire, and beauty, a potentially radical new direction for the discipline of architecture begins to emerge.

As opposed to the purely formal possibilities opened up to architecture by new digital modeling techniques of the 1990s (blobs or iterative computational patterns), there might be a newer – more potent, and revolutionary – form of digital architecture that has less to do with digital representation techniques than with a conflation of digital IT logics and energy collection and distribution organizations. If architecture becomes both energy collection and information content production infrastructure (the more advanced equivalent of an inhabitable solar-powered PC), and urban planning takes on the role of organizing systems of energy and information exchange, there are many new and difficult questions that architecture and urbanism will have to grapple with. The space of the Internet and the space of new alternative energy systems are distributed, networked, and often difficult to visualize. What will be the perceptual and social repercussions—from the ground or from the vantage of Google Earth – of this new distributed, sustainable, and digitally enabled network of spatial organization?

NOTES

1. According to Alan Bean, an *Apollo 12* astronaut, "The only thing you can see from the Moon is a beautiful sphere, mostly white, some blue and patches of yellow, and every once in a while some green vegetation. No man-made object is visible at this scale." from, http://www.nasa.gov/vision/space/workinginspace/great_wall.html

2. Former NASA astronaut Jeffrey Hoffman, who flew on five space shuttle missions between 1985 and 1996, says, "I spent a lot of time looking at the Earth from space, including numerous flights over China, and I never saw the wall." From, http://www.scientificamerican.com/article.cfm?id=is-chinas-great-wall-visible-from-space

3. Bruce Sterling, "White Fungus," from *Beyond Magazine*, Issue #1

Previous: Collage, courtesy of JDS Architects

MVRDV WAS SET UP IN ROTTERDAM IN 1993 BY WINY MAAS, JACOB VAN RIJS, AND NATHALIE DE VRIES. IN CLOSE COLLABORATION, THE THREE PRINCIPAL ARCHITECT DIRECTORS PRODUCE DESIGNS AND STUDIES IN THE FIELDS OF ARCHITECTURE, URBANISM, AND LANDSCAPE DESIGN.

CHINA HILLS
A DREAM FOR FUTURE CITIES

In the last twenty years, the incredible economic growth of China has lead to enormous urbanization. Though impressive in size, most of these urban developments are rather monotonous, lacking diversity, individuality, and moreover, relying on external resources.

By 2020, the urban population of China is going to grow significantly: 22 percent of the population (400,000,000 people) will migrate from rural to the urban areas (six percent of the country's surface). These changes for the coming decennia make an evaluation of the recent developments possible and necessary. It questions the typology of the future urbanization. It becomes possible to seize this opportunity to experiment with future cities.

As the urban population grows, the needed programs for new and old housing, offices, forests for leisure as well as oxygen and CO_2 absorption, agriculture, sustainable energy parks and water storages will require more space than the given suitable land.

Since not every part of the country (the deserts, the high mountains) is suitable for agriculture, forestry and urbanization, we then need a total amount of space that equates to two times China's urban areas! This requires not only for an intensification of the forested and agricultural areas, but also for urbanization with a sufficient density with mixed program.

The new urbanization would not only be designed in a true sustainable and autarkic way, but would undertake the task of rebalancing the current ones as well. By incorporating a considerable part of the forests, agriculture and energy production, truly mixed cities will appear. Following this direction in twenty years from now, China could be considered autarkic in ecological terms... Wouldn't that be desirable? What could these new cities look like?

Obviously the required density will lead to higher buildings containing these mixed programs. The current types of towers with their flashy facades do not offer sufficient naturally lit spaces for the needed plantations and energy production. By making spacious terraces, the opportunity for agriculture and energy production is increased. Moreover, this would lead to more attractive liveable areas in highrises. 'Stepped' terraced towers with a rich variety of characters will appear: Green termite 'hills'.

These terraced towers will create giant interior 'grottos' for the bigger darker programs like retail, factories, leisure zones, churches, which could be used as well for storing and cleaning water, cooling capacities, and harvesting dew…

By inserting these new 'hills' in and around the current cities, a sincere Chinese mountain range appears. Where individuality blends with collective responsibilities, architecture melts with urbanism and urbanism turns into landscape architecture…

21世纪初，在人类历史上
第一次世界城市人口（50.8%）
超过农村人口（49.2%）。

In the beginning of the 21st century,
for the first time in history,
the world urban population (50.8%)
is more than the rural (49.2%).

此外，日益增加的需求和
日益减少的资源之间的
差距越来越难以平衡。

Moreover, the world has
to counteract the gap
between increasing demand
and decreasing resources.

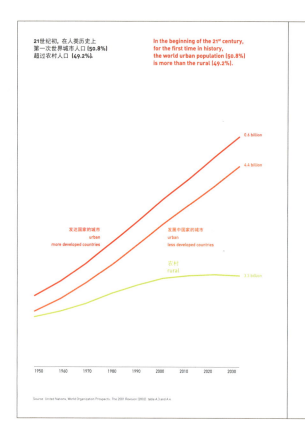

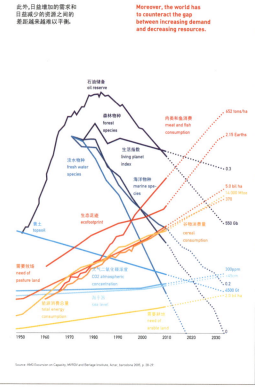

Source: United Nations, World Organization Prospects: The 2001 Revision (2002): table A.3 and A.4

Source: KM3 Excursion on Capacity, MVRDV and Berlage Institute, Actar, barcelona 2005, p. 28-29

中国的城镇人口增长率位于世界第一。

到2020年，将有22%的总人口
从农村到迁移到城市地区。

这个迁移将导致农业和城市的
用地蕨缺。

Within this context, China has
the fastest urban population growth
rates. By 2020, about 22% of total
Chinese population will move from
rural to urban areas. This shift leads
to land shortage in both agricultural
and urban areas.

这个从农村向城市迁移的过程，
可能是中国建立新型城市的最佳时机。

通过加强生态建设，不仅可以
达到自身的可持续发展，也平衡了
现有城市的生态需要。

如果中国可能实现二氧化碳吸收
和粮食的自给自足，这将有贡献于
平衡世界资源的分配。

This rural-urban migration could
represent the perfect opportunity
for China to build responsible and
innovative cities.
By investing more in ecology, these
cities will not only be self sustainable,
but could also compensate the needs of
existing cities.
By being CO2 and food-wise autarkic,
and therefore, contributing to the
rebalancing of the distribution of world
resources, China could be exemplary!

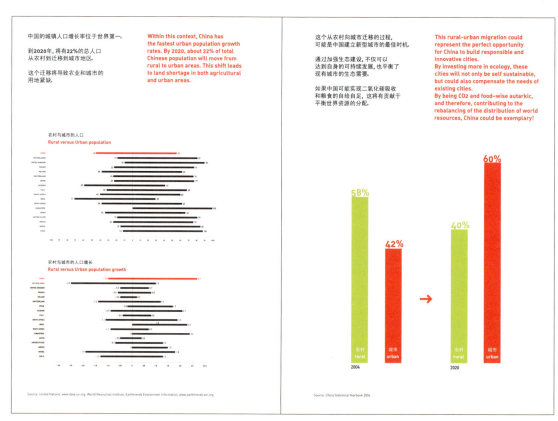

Source: United Nations, www.data.un.org, World Resources Institute, Earthtrends Environment Information, www.earthtrends.wri.org.

Source: China Statistical Yearbook 2006.

如果中国在2020年实现二氧化碳吸收和粮食的自给自足,需要哪些条件?

中国人均需要4 260平方米的土地,包括森林、农业和城镇。

到2020年, 14亿人需要605万平方公里的土地。

How much program does China need to be CO2 and food-wise autarkic by 2020?
Each Chinese person will need 4 260 m² of land including forest, agriculture and built program.
By 2020, the total land needed for 1.4 billion people will be 6 054 108 km².

农业
agriculture
城镇
built-up
森林
forest

1 人
1250平方米 城镇
465平方米 农业
3 545平方米 森林
4 260 平方米 总面积

x 14 亿人口
35万平方公里 城镇
66万平方公里 农业
503万平方公里 森林
605万平方公里 总面积

1 person:
Built-up area: 250 m²
Agriculture: 465 m²
Forest: 3 545 m²
Total land: 4 260 m²

x 1 400 000 000 people
Built-up area: 355 315 km²
Agriculture: 660 886 km²
Forest: 5 037 907 km²
Total land: 6 054 108 km²

约国土面积42%的沙漠和高山不适宜居住和耕作条件。

能否将需要的功能布置在其余国土面积58%的适宜土地上?

Covered by desert and high mountains, 42% of China is less suitable for living and farming.
Could the needed program be placed on the remaining 58% of the country's surface?

58%合适的土地
560万平方公里

58% suitable land
5 597 907 km²

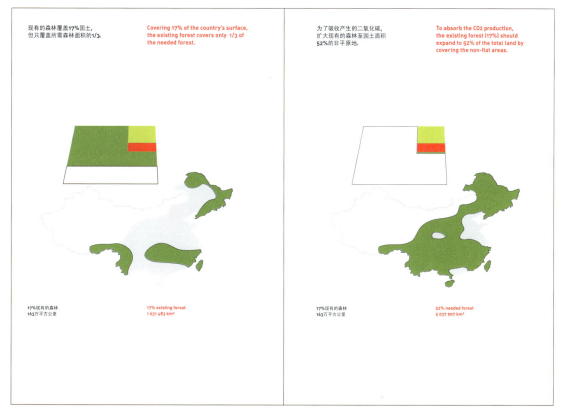

现有的森林覆盖17%国土,但只覆盖所需森林面积的1/3。

Covering 17% of the country's surface, the existing forest covers only 1/3 of the needed forest.

17%现有的森林
163万平方公里

17% existing forest
1 631 483 km²

为了吸收产生的二氧化碳,扩大现有的森林至国土面积52%的非平原地。

To absorb the CO2 production, the existing forest (17%) should expand to 52% of the total land by covering the non-flat areas.

17%现有的森林
163万平方公里

52% needed forest
5 037 907 km²

城镇和农业能否在余下国土
面积**6%**的平原土地上共存？

The remaining 6% of total land is
flatland. Can urbanization and farming
coexist within the available flatland?

为了满足城镇和农业的需求，
中国需要两倍于国土面积6%
的可用平原土地。

中国要满足自给自足，
如何解决土地短缺的矛盾？

To fulfil the agriculture and urban
program demands, China will need
almost twice the remaining 6%
(flatland) of the country's surface.
How could China be autarkic and solve
the land shortage?

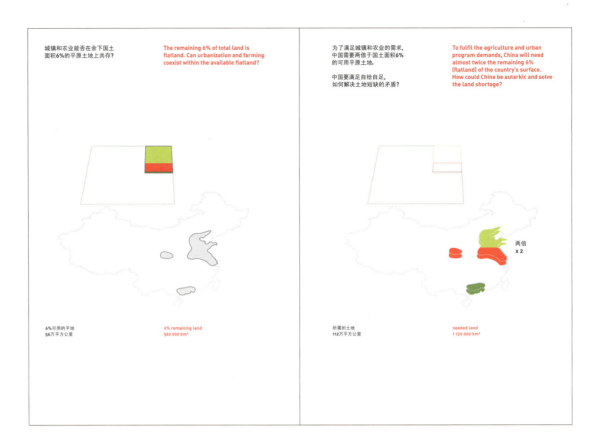

6%可用的平地
56万平方公里

6% remaining land
560 000 km²

所需的土地
112万平方公里

两倍
x 2

needed land
1 120 000 km²

让我们以10万人口城市为单元，
比较不同城市模型所需要的土地。

如果我们采用洛杉矶的密度，
中国需要2.5倍的可用平地。

太多！

Let's look at different city models
and their densities, to compare which
one is more efficient on land
consumption.
If all Chinese population would live
in the same density as Los Angeles,
about 2.5 times the remaining flatland
will be needed.
Too much!

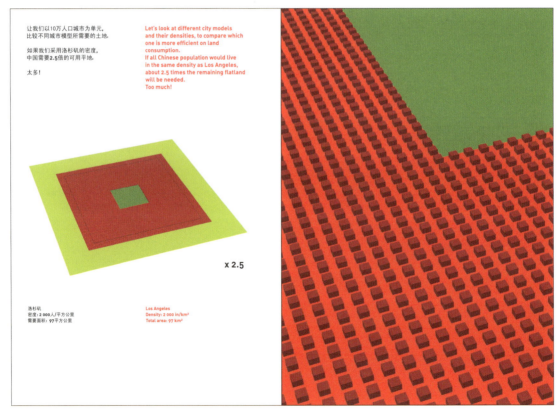

x 2.5

洛杉矶
密度：**2 000人**/平方公里
需要面积：**97**平方公里

Los Angeles
Density: **2 000** in/km²
Total area: **97** km²

如果我们采用柏林的密度，
中国需要**2.0**倍的可用平地。

If all Chinese population would live
in the same density as Berlin,
about 2.0 times the remaining flatland
will be needed.

x 2.0

柏林
密度：**4 000**人/平方公里
需要面积：**71**平方公里

Berlin
Density: **4 000** in/km²
Total area: **71** km²

如果我们采用新加坡的密度，
中国需要**1.5**倍的可用平地。

If all Chinese population would live
in the same density as Singapore,
about 1.5 times the remaining flatland
will be needed.

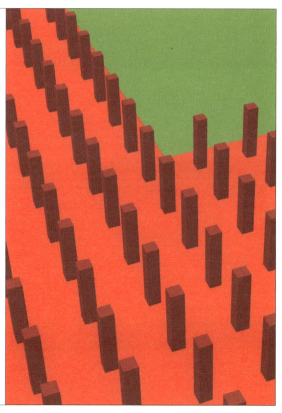

x 1.5

新加坡
密度：**9 000**人/平方公里
需要面积：**58**平方公里

Singapore
Density: **9 000** in/km²
Total area: **58** km²

SCALES OF THE EARTH

即使我们采用上海浦东的密度，
这仍然需要1.3倍的可用平地。

还是不够！

And even if all Chinese population
would live in the same density
as Shanghai Pudong, about 1.3 times
the remaining flatland will be needed.
It will still not fit!

x 1.3

上海浦东
密度：21 000人/平方公里
需要面积：51平方公里

Shanghai
Density: 21 000 in/km²
Total area: 51 km²

我们要怎样做？

如何能够优化城市和农业功能的
共存互补？

公共绿地和50%的农业生产可以
与城市功能结合。

What else could be done?
How could the coexistence of
agriculture and urban program be
optimized?
Parks and 50% of food production
could be integrated on top of the built
program.

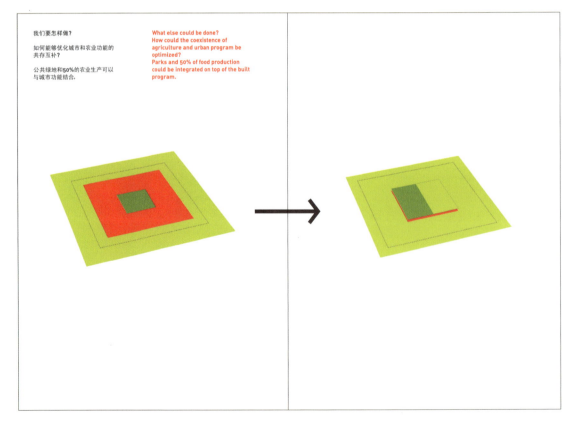

通过不断向三维空间压缩城市体积，达到500米的最大高度，一种新的城市模式能够最大化使用土地。

By pulling this double skin, made of built and green program, towards the sky at the maximum height of 500 metre, the land occupied by the new spatial configuration will dramatically shrink.

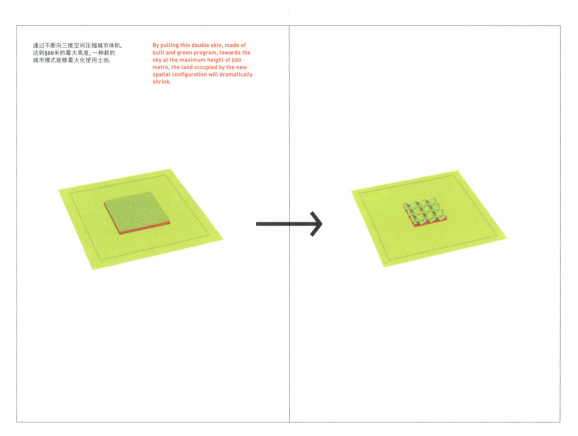

如果所有中国城市都是这种密度，56万平方公里的可用平地将足够！

If all China population will leave in this density (100 000 inh/km²), the available flatland would be enough!

x 1.0

中国山
密度: 100 000人/平方公里
需要面积: 39平方公里

China Hills
Density: 100 000 in/km²
Total area: 39 km²

一系列具有个性特征的
"梯田塔"出现了：绿山。

'Stepped' terraced towers with a rich
variety of characters will appear:
Green termite 'hills'.

为了优化阳光和通风条件，
这些小型城市锥体向北倾斜，
最大化南向立面。

To optimize sun and ventilation
conditions, these compact urban cones
will be tilted towards the north side,
to maximize the southern façades.

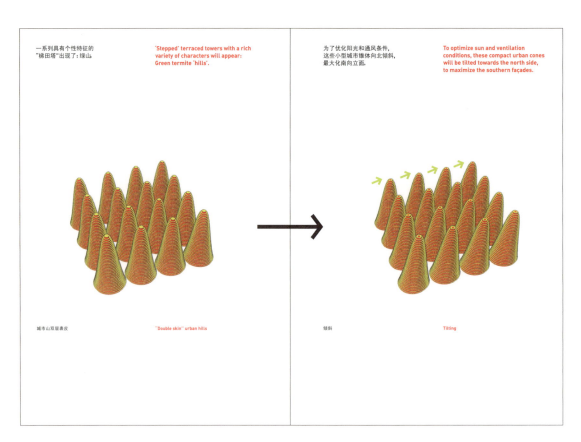

城市山双层表皮

"Double skin" urban hills

倾斜

Tilting

锥体前后移动，
最小化建筑之间阴影。

They will be shifted, to minimize
the building-to-building shadow effect.

每个城市锥体的高度和直径
都有变化，增加露台的效率。

露台大小的不同，
可以种植不同的农作物，
个性化每个山体。

To increase the terraces' efficiency,
each hill would be diversified in height
and diameter from its neighbours.
By differentiating the angle,
different crops could be placed,
characterizing each hill.

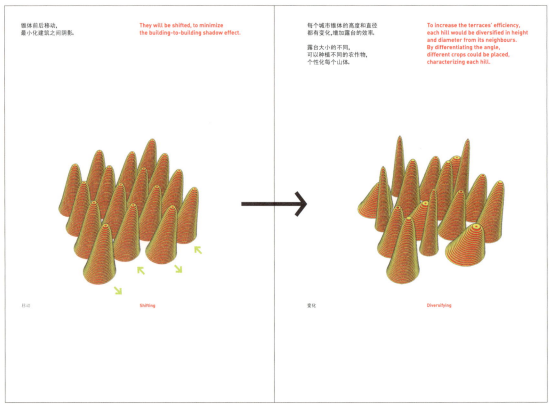

移动

Shifting

变化

Diversifying

融合不同功能的锥体
每组锥体之间和内部的
空间扩大。

By diversifying and merging the cones, each hill could have a different identity and bigger open space could be created inside and outside the cones.

融合 Merging

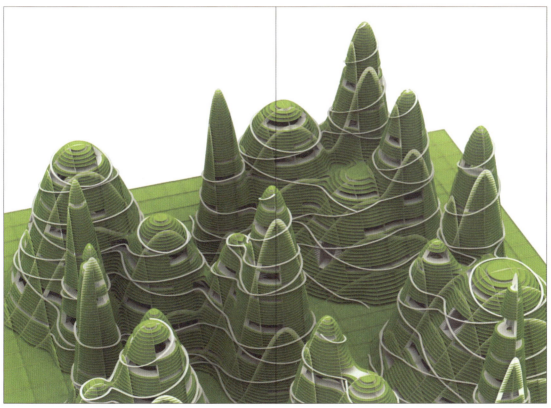

JACK DANGERMOND

FOUNDED ESRI IN 1969 WITH A VISION THAT GIS-BASED ANALYSIS COULD TRANSFORM PLANNING AND ENVIRONMENTAL STUDIES. DANGERMOND GRADUATED WITH A B.S. IN LANDSCAPE ARCHITECTURE FROM CALIFORNIA STATE POLYTECHNIC UNIVERSITY, POMONA AND A MASTER OF ARCHITECTURE DEGREE FROM THE UNIVERSITY OF MINNESOTA. HE WAS ALSO AWARDED A MASTER OF SCIENCE DEGREE IN LANDSCAPE ARCHITECTURE FROM HARVARD UNIVERSITY'S GRADUATE SCHOOL OF DESIGN, WHERE HE WORKED IN THE LABORATORY FOR COMPUTER GRAPHICS AND SPATIAL DESIGN. HE IS ALSO THE RECIPIENT OF TEN HONORARY DOCTORATE DEGREES.

EL HADI JAZAIRY

IS A POST-DOCTORAL FELLOW AT THE HARVARD UNIVERSITY GRADUATE SCHOOL OF DESIGN. HE RECEIVED A DIPLÔME D'ARCHITECTE FROM LA CAMBRE IN BRUSSELS, A MASTER OF ARCHITECTURE FROM CORNELL UNIVERSITY, AND A DOCTORATE OF DESIGN FROM HARVARD UNIVERSITY. HE IS THE DIRECTOR OF THE MULTIDISCIPLINARY FIRM DESIGN EARTH.

GEOGRAPHY BY DESIGN

JACK DANGERMOND INTERVIEWED BY EL HADI JAZAIRY

1. In what ways have geographic information systems had an impact on modes of representation and the operative conceptions of geography and places?

In the computing industry, we look at the legend of Xerox PARC with great admiration. Xerox PARC is where many of the most important innovations in information technology got started. In the geospatial industry, Harvard's Laboratory of Computer Graphics and Spatial Analysis is our Xerox PARC. I think that the things that happened there in the 1960s and beyond forever changed the way we view geography and place.

Geospatial technology has long impacted representation. When we first started making maps with computers at Harvard, it was certainly exciting, but the actual "character' maps we made were very crude by today's standards. Using then state-of-the-art computer mapping techniques, we were still light years behind cartographers who had worked even 500 years before us! And that was a bit frustrating. As geospatial technology advanced, our ability to produce decent-looking maps with computers progressed. In my opinion, it's only recently that computer-based cartography has begun to match or even rival the best "manual" cartography.

To me, the exciting part is not just that computer-based cartography is finally approaching and in some ways exceeded the quality of manual cartography; it's what the future holds in store. Ultimately we don't simply replace paper-and-ink-based maps with maps on computer screens, but we evolve and extend the definition of what a "map" is.

Some of this is already going on today. Beyond the traditional "map," new visualization applications such as Google Earth, Bing Maps, and ArcGIS Explorer have fundamentally changed the way we interact with geography and place. When Stewart Brand lobbied NASA to release the first photograph of earth taken from space, he knew the impact that photograph would have in changing the way we viewed our environment and our relationship with it. Today, anyone with Internet access can get a similar view of the earth, then quickly zoom in to the level of their city, their neighborhood, their house, and even personalize their map with information such as videos and photos, etc. This universal access to geographic knowledge revolutionizes our ability to understand how our world works physically, biologically, and culturally, and mass personalization makes the map relevant to everyone. But who knows how much more our concept of a "map" will evolve in the next twenty, thirty, or fifty years?

And of course GIS is so much more than using computers to automate and customize map products. The technology can be used in many different ways. Much of what distinguishes GIS today and provides exceptional value to users is the ability to perform analysis. The capability to use GIS to ask complex questions related to place and answer them with geographic science has also dramatically changed the way we interact with geography and place.

The ability make rational decisions supported by sound science is crucial today, as our world becomes increasingly complicated and the problems we face become more ominous. And because of accelerating time scales, decisions are not only more complex but need to be made more quickly; and decision-making is becoming more iterative, or "agile", to borrow one of the popular terms of the day. So how do you make better decisions, given that the world is so much more complicated, and your time scale for acting is highly compressed?

One way to get through this is to use decision-support tools, such as GIS – tools that can automate decision-making, suggest courses of action, or at the very least simply organize and structure information in such a way that it is more actionable – making it easier for us to act on because in a sense it has been "pre-processed" by GIS.

2. How do you think that such tools may redefine the practices of architects as they conceive of the geographic as a possible scale, site of intervention, and design approach?

Maps are abstractions of place. So are aerial or satellite images, but imagery is different – I think that for the majority of people today, there is a more instantaneous connection with an image. GIS has already proven successful as a research tool and for performing project work. The big growth opportunity for all of us is for the technology to reach out to "everyone," and we are on the cusp of that happening. As geospatial technology reaches more people, it puts more emphasis on something we've known for a long time: that the transition from paper maps to digital maps makes us rethink "scale."

In a traditional cartographic sense, scale – the relationship between a distance on the map and the actual distance it represents on the ground – is a measure of accuracy. The idea of scale becomes a little abstracted when we move from paper maps (which are static in scale) to digital maps (which are dynamic in scale). Think of a printed map of a city that you used to use for navigation, before in-vehicle GPS devices became so prevalent. It was printed at a certain scale. With computer-based visualization of geographic knowledge, scale is of course dynamic. If you are planning to drive 2,000 miles to visit a relative, the old-fashioned method was to use multiple maps at different scales to get you where you were going – maybe a road atlas to navigate the highways to get you from your city to the destination city, then a more detailed map of the city to get you closer to your specific destination, and then probably a finer map or even some handwritten directions to get you to the exact house. Now, with your GPS, instead of

juggling between three different maps, you're presented with a unified experience that scales dynamically when appropriate.

Our sense of scale has changed due to advances in technology, and it's something we need to think a lot about when distributing geographic knowledge to "everyone." And we, the geospatial professionals, need to think about that because to the average person accessing geospatial data on a cell phone, scale means nothing unless it is done wrong and causes them problems.

Scale is a type of measurement; you can almost think of it as a "rating" of the data, a rating that acts as a guide to how you can use that data and what situations you can use it in. With digital tools, information collected at one scale can now be quickly and easily displayed at another scale. This can result in obvious issues like pixilation during visualization, but it can also have more important implications, such as inaccurate analysis.

We can approach this with techniques such as scale-dependent display, but it really goes a lot further – such as, is the data itself appropriate for this use? Is the intended audience likely to interpret this correctly, and make sound decisions based on it? If not, can I alter the display, analysis, or user experience to ensure it is used properly?

3. What are the characteristics of such an integrated elevated vision, and what geographical knowledge does it bring forth?

Over the last ten years, we've seen a fundamental change in the way GIS is delivered and used, thanks to the Internet. The next ten

Visualization of cellular phone coverage using ESRI's ArcGIS Desktop with the Spatial Analyst and 3D Analyst extensions, and HNIT-BALTIC Cellular Expert extension. Copyright 2009 HNIT-BALTIC, UAB. All rights reserved.

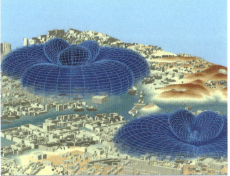

3D view of radio wave propagation modeling using ESRI's ArcGIS Desktop with the 3D Analyst extension and HNIT-BALTIC Cellular Expert extension. Copyright 2009 HNIT-BALTIC, UAB. All rights reserved.

years will see an explosion of faster, more powerful mobile devices, and the line dividing cell phones and personal computers will fade. Mobile devices will continue to grow to support more geospatial functionality, and they will easily connect to GIS systems around the world to use and also create geographic knowledge. Democratization of data – both its widespread use and its universal creation – will result in a new kind of infrastructure: a geospatial infrastructure. Over time, society will become increasingly dependent on this geospatial infrastructure, much as it has become dependent on other, more traditional forms of infrastructure such as electrical grids or highway networks.

When technology is so universally adapted that it can be considered infrastructure, people become highly dependent on it. If your electricity was turned off for a week, how would that impact your life? If all public roads and highways were closed for a month, how would you get by?

Infrastructure is the stuff that is very basic and universal to the way we live, but is often overlooked or almost invisible because it is taken for granted. There's a lot of activity and money spent to build, operate, and maintain this infrastructure, but these activities pale in comparison to the actual use of the infrastructure. You flip a light switch, and the light comes on – you don't need to know the complexities of how the electricity was created and transmitted to your house. I think that's where we are heading with this geographic knowledge infrastructure.

GIS is the technology we have come to rely on to build, operate, and maintain this geographic knowledge infrastructure. In-car navigation applications are probably the furthest along in this regard – as far as geographic knowledge becoming infrastructure. People are becoming increasingly dependent on GPS to get them from point A to point B. I think this is just the tip of the iceberg. As location becomes a core component of more applications we use every day, our dependency on this infrastructure will increase exponentially. And that puts an increased level of responsibility on geospatial professionals who build, operate, and maintain this infrastructure.

Mobile and location-based technologies are also fundamentally changing the way we create geographic knowledge: we're seeing the widespread embracing of crowdsourcing, where the scale of data creators is greater by orders of magnitude. Crowdsourced data is data contributed by non-authoritative sources, e.g., everyday citizens. For example, there are people

– volunteers – updating global base maps right now. The challenge for GIS practitioners is to ensure the usability of this data in a GIS workflow, or to turn this crowdsourced data in to useful geographic knowledge that can easily be consumed by broader segments of society. This can mean checking the "authoritativeness" of the data; it can also mean getting involved in the actual act of data collection, structuring the process to ensure that the data has meaning and is appropriate and authoritative.

GIS practitioners have long been the keepers of purely authoritative data, and are now beginning to take crowdsourced data very seriously. It gives ordinary citizens the opportunity to provide feedback directly to the government. It can significantly augment authoritative data sets at a fraction of the traditional cost. It provides extraordinary opportunities for citizen science. And it can put a virtual "army" of volunteers on a large project in short order.

4. In this data-space, which information is to be retained as relevant? What is the meaning of context? How is such an analytical space to be subsequently interpreted and experienced?

GIS tools supporting crowdsourcing will change the way organizations collect and manage spatial data. For example, new features in ESRI software give users the ability to modify geographic content within any Web mapping application and provide a venue for online communities to become active contributors to geodatabases. Web editing makes it easy to capture ideas and observations for distributed problem solving and extend GIS editing capabilities to more people within the organization. These capabilities allow everyone – from authoritative data editors to citizens on the street – to contribute content to a geodatabase. This will enrich GIS, giving GIS practitioners new types of data to use, manage, interpret, and incorporate into their work. And again I must stress that with this comes a great responsibility on the part of the geospatial professional to make sure the data is used in the correct context.

The issues we have to overcome as an industry and as a society include privacy concerns; data ownership; standards for collecting and structuring the data; and making sure we apply or analyze the data in ways that are appropriate considering the source. These are very complex issues that we need to tackle at the same time we are trying to make everything easier and available to a much broader audience.

Performing spatial analysis, building a spatial data infrastructure… these are difficult, complicated tasks, and they will remain so. In a way, one of our primary responsibilities as geospatial professionals is to hide the complexity. Obviously the capabilities available to a GIS professional or a city planner are going to be very different than those available to a citizen with a cell phone. We need to determine what geographic knowledge is relevant for a given situation, or for a particular audience, and build our applications around that knowledge.

5. Is it fair to think of geography as an objective and universalist field of study? What are the cultural, political, and environmental repercussions of new ways to organize and evaluate potentially counterfactual understandings?

I think that change is inevitable, and not being prepared for change is shortsighted and irresponsible. Many of the things the GIS community is working on – new tools for spatial analysis, for example, or adapting our technology to new platforms such as mobile devices or leveraging new methods such as crowdsourcing – could potentially have huge social or environmental effects, both positive and negative, and this is a responsibility we cannot take lightly.

David Harvey said, "geography is too important to be left to geographers." The combination of increased availability of geographic knowledge and easier access through mobile computers really opens up the use of geographic knowledge to everyone. But that doesn't mean that geographers are no longer relevant. In fact, I think that making geographic knowledge available to the masses means that you need even more geographers.

People already understand maps, and as I said earlier, our definition of "map" is evolving quickly along with the technology. But the map is still our best method for dissemination of geographic knowledge. And when people place all of this new geographic knowledge on a personalized map, and they see environmental problems or economic issues in the context of their neighborhood, their street, their house – this leads to a new level of understanding. They get it, right away. So the ability to take all of this data and put it in context on a dynamic, personalized map is very powerful.

Speaking about ESRI in particular, the company was founded as a socially and environmentally conscious organization. In other words; the company was founded precisely because we thought that GIS technology could be used to positively impact society and the environment – to make the world a better place.

More people using geographic knowledge will result in more highly evolved interfaces. But we must be extremely careful here. Information can so easily be misused. As we get even more information, and make it easily available to so many people, the opportunities for misuse increase exponentially. Even highly trained scientists make mistakes with data, as we've seen — imagine the possibilities for misinterpretation of critical environmental or social data in the hands of an average cell-phone user, who is not trained in things like the scientific method, statistical analysis, etc. I'm not saying that this democratization of geographic knowledge is a bad thing; it's a wonderful thing, and it's something I've personally been wanting for a long time. But our approach needs to be deliberate; we need to deliver the appropriate knowledge, to the right people at the right time, but also we need to package it in a way that gives the best opportunity for correct use and interpretation.

6. What new global issues and debates do such scales of vision raise and how do such visualizations of the Earth-as-home intersect with concerns of ecology and calls for global awareness?

The two big, global issues in my mind are climate change and GeoDesign.

I like to say that climate change is a geographic problem. It's a difficult, complex, politically charged, and vitally important issue. Yet from a knowledge perspective, we are at a distinct disadvantage: at this point in time, we still do not have a clear idea of everything we need to know in order to address the problem in a measured, rational, and above all, scientific manner.

When you think about the multitude of issues surrounding climate change science – from root causes to resultant impacts – geography is clearly an elemental factor in the equation. Every aspect of climate change affects or is affected by geography, be it at a global, regional, or local level. As a tool for helping us to better understand such geographies, GIS is the single most powerful integrating tool for inventorying, analyzing, and ultimately managing this extremely complex problem.

For the last several years, I've been very interested in the idea of GeoDesign – a marriage of design with the analytic power of GIS to create a powerful new environment characterized by fast iterations and

public participation, all supported by a solid scientific base.

Maps are a way to abstract place to make it easier to understand. With GeoDesign, we move beyond understanding place, to designing it. "Where should we locate this new factory?" becomes "How, when, and where can we best achieve the goals of building a new factory within the surrounding environment?" Design should be guided by geographic knowledge. And who's a designer? In a way, we are all designers. Most of us just don't realize it. And we need to get better at it. That doesn't mean we all have to go back to school and study design. But we need a way to integrate design concepts in to what we already do. GeoDesign will give all of us access to better tools to make better design decision.

GeoDesign is a set of methods and tools that allow us to sketch and quickly consider the consequences of alternatives. Just like we navigate to work this way instead of that way, which is a kind of design problem, we'll design the future so it's sustainable, so that it considers all of our geographic knowledge. I want to make this concept of GeoDesign pervasive so people start to make decisions that are based on geographic knowledge. Our future depends on this. Putting geographic knowledge in the hands of everybody, and then giving them the GeoDesign tools that let them design in consideration of all that geographic knowledge is, I think, an important step in human evolution.

7. How do you see the latest concerns of geographic information systems relating to Ian McHarg's initial concepts of designing with nature?

GIS has never strayed too far from McHarg's initial concepts of environmental conservation and using a methodology to do rational planning, taking environmental factors into consideration. Most geospatial professionals clearly understand the notion of map overlay, or polygon processing, having its roots with McHarg's work and being the base theory behind GIS.

GeoDesign is an extension of McHarg's original vision. Or maybe it's just a modern interpretation of McHarg's vision; it's GIS getting "back to its roots." GIS can be used for so many different purposes and for many more applications than McHarg originally envisioned. The technology is making a difference everywhere, and all of those applications have made the technology stronger and better. But I think that maybe we lost a little of our focus for a while, and GeoDesign is an attempt to bring that focus back and

apply the technology to McHarg's vision of designing with nature.

We rarely talk of McHarg without mentioning overlays; the two are often synonymous. Yet usually overlooked in discussions of McHarg's influence on environmental planning and geospatial analysis is the concept of chronology. When looking at geographic overlays of different aspects of a project – comparing them, analyzing them, looking for relationships – McHarg was very interested in the temporal dependencies, or chronology. Causal relationships in geography can sometimes be easily overlooked if time is not taken in to consideration. Placing the overlays in time sequence, as McHarg suggested, can lead to a deeper understanding of structure and meaning in the landscape.

At ESRI, we are putting much effort in to rebuilding our GIS technology to not only handle space but also time – we're adding a robust capability to store and manage temporal data, and we're also working on temporal analysis tools. Adding time capabilities to the equation makes GIS and GeoDesign more comprehensive, moving us closer to a complete system for "designing with nature." And from a GeoDesign perspective, once we have the tools and techniques in place to fully grasp how the past has created the present, we can apply these same tools and techniques to shape our future in a more socially and environmentally responsible manner.

Alan Kay said, "the best way to predict the future is to invent it." GIS has been very focused on analysis and modeling, often in an attempt to "predict the future," which is always difficult. With GeoDesign, we're moving beyond trying to predict the future and toward a mindset where the future can be invented or created in a logical, scientific, and purposeful manner. Carl Steinitz has said: "GeoDesign is geography by design." We're moving beyond a world composed primarily of what you can consider "accidental" geography – things located in a certain place because certain seemingly unrelated decisions were made two, or ten, or twenty-five generations ago. Part of the GeoDesign concept is an up-front understanding of the long-term consequences of our design on society and the environment. That's one big thing we've been lacking.

CHRISTOPHE GIROT
IS FULL PROFESSOR AND CHAIR OF LANDSCAPE ARCHITECTURE AT THE ARCHITECTURE DEPARTMENT OF THE ETH IN ZÜRICH. HIS TEACHING AND RESEARCH INTERESTS SPAN OVER THREE THEMES: NEW TOPOLOGICAL METHODS IN LANDSCAPE DESIGN, LANDSCAPE PERCEPTION AND ANALYSIS THROUGH NEW MEDIA, AND CONTEMPORARY THEORY AND HISTORY OF LANDSCAPE ARCHITECTURE. HIS PROFESSIONAL PRACTICE IS FOCUSED ON LARGE-SCALE LANDSCAPE PROJECTS THAT CONTRIBUTE TO SUSTAINABLE URBAN ENVIRONMENTS.

SCALES OF TOPOLOGY IN LANDSCAPE ARCHITECTURE

Advances in computer technology are challenging some of the most firmly established stepped-scale methods of landscape planning and design, with a new approach to modeling and visualizing that ranges seamlessly from the small object scale to the vaster territorial scale. Recent progress in topological modeling and imaging has in fact enabled an extraordinary convergence between various 3D modeling programs applied to the quantifying, shaping, and plotting of landscape surfaces, sections, and volumes. These topologies are developed, modulated and integrated within the larger 3D framework of a geodesic mesh and are used for a variety of project simulation purposes. Working with tools dependent on GIS frameworks was previously limited by the designers' capacity of modifications and adjustments within the design process. Until now, in terms of communication, we have been confounded with the difficulty of professional collaboration in large-scale landscape design, where the design remains uncoupled to the geodesic information base, preventing vital back-and-forth feedback and adaptation during the various stages of specialist feedback and design optimization. This problem is gradually being resolved through the use of denser GPS-correlated point-cloud scans taken at specific geographic locations (figure 1,2). It is now possible to merge different scales of design within an overall information system using the geodesic point-cloud technique and to develop large-scale landscape projects while maintaining a positive feedback loop that remains true to GPS coordinates. This essay aims to show the scope of work now made possible using this integrated method of topological design.

The Landscape Visualization and Modeling Lab at the ETH has launched landscape visualizing and modeling research at the interface of 3D GIS technology, integrating geo-referenced point-clouds with other parametric tools of design. The results show an extraordinary potential for possible applications in landscape architecture, particularly for projects pertaining to the broader territorial realm. This new combination of techniques is not only of vital importance in the conception of large-scale landscape design and planning projects using CNC modeling, visualizing, and animation techniques (figure 3, 4, 5); it is also helpful in a variety of situations pertaining to design development, communication, and decision-making processes. Three examples of ongoing projects at the LVML show con-

1. On-site in Sigirino gathering detailed landscape data with a 3D photographic laser scanner

2. Single-color point clouds of a forest clearing in Sigirino

3. Students CNC milling a topographical foam process-model of Sion

4. Sigirino site image database generated with image matching software

157

cisely the range of possible applications at various scales of territory.

The Santa Gilla laguna project in Sardinia, first developed as an international workshop studio between the ETH and UNICA in 2008, represents an exemplary case of a large-scale project in landscape architecture for a highly degraded Mediterranean coastal habitat (figure 6). Located within the larger urbanized and industrialized area of Cagliari, the Santa Gilla laguna represents a significant challenge for long-term environmental and economic policy for the region. Two publications about the project describe it in detail. The challenge with this scale of project was the actual topographical variation at the surface of the 700-hectare laguna that barely reached an amplitude of +1/-1 meters. The delicate filigree pattern of the saltwork levees created an embossed relief of paths over the shallow waters, which extended from the beach to the sluices of the River Manu estuary. To be able to coordinate with hydrologists, civil engineers, and planners, it was important to work collaboratively with a collective geographic and topographic database of the entire laguna (figure 7). The proposed landscape project interfaced a precise 3D topographical model of the proposed landscape with existing terrain data, and a broad range of geo-referenced sections were produced throughout the site. The combination of model and sections in turn informed discussions with specialists, oriented specific design choices, and showed options for future phasing and development. The final landscape design proposal was translated into a CNC-milled model, precisely demonstrating how to reestablish a sustainable environment in the Santa Gilla laguna (figure 8). It was demonstrated that equilibrium for the laguna could be reached through innovative topological modulation, soft circulation trails, and appropriate water exchange that improve overall biodiversity and create added value. The pilot project was developed on a 3D GIS base and has evolved into a full-scale research proposal, to be submitted later this year to the European Commission. Due to the huge scales involved, micro changes in topography reflect potentially huge volumes of material, which can be minutely measured in surface comparison volume analysis (figure 9). The precise topological methodology for large-scale landscape architecture shown here will certainly find numerous applications in similar locations on the Mediterranean basin.

Compared to the Santa Gilla laguna site, the Third Rhône River Correction Project in Sion, Switzerland, represents another kind

5. Site video of Sigirino processed with match-moving software for integration into dataset

6. Arial view of Santa Gilla, showing the large-scale coastal landscape

7. Collaborative physical-model design sessions with students and the Santa Gilla local authorities of Santa Gilla

8. Detail of CNC milled model demonstrating various water bodies and landscape structure of the Santa Gilla site

of territorial scale for the LVML. The pilot project is located on the middle segment of the 160-km alpine valley corridor, where the dynamics of the river are set to be entirely recalibrated (figures 10, 11). Together with hydraulic engineers of the Canton of Valais and the City of Sion, the project developed new and more efficient interactive landscape simulations based on a precise 3D GIS database. The method developed at the LVML enables different urban and rural design options to be tested along this particular segment of the river corridor in terms of topology, elevation, and hydraulic efficiency (figure 12). The initial site analysis of the studio participants are cross referenced and combined into a spatial image database, allowing the first impressions of the site to be not only revisited but used as a discrete tool, demonstrating the points of focus, dispersion, and density of interest. The design research looked at the specific relationship between the new calibration requirements of the Rhône River and its possible impact and benefits in terms of livability, environmental quality and image for Sion. The LVML developed a precise topological method that is capable of integrating a better definition of the physical processes at play within the highly urbanized context of Sion. A broad variety of physical factors such as water, people and traffic flow, topography, vegetation, urban growth, and infrastructure were tested. The methodology developed on a geographically referenced geodesic base remains true to the topographic conditions of the existing terrain and is able to operate at all scales of design. The visualization based on this information considerably facilitates the design evaluation of various options and particularly the decision-making process (figure 13), since the absolute comparison of existing and potential terrain modifications can be factually compared and argued. The methodology developed through this pilot project will subsequently be used and tested at other locations along the 160-kilometer stretch of the Third Rhône River Correction Project using variable resolutions of terrain data at strategic locations. Once optimized, the method of intervention will be transferred to other territories presenting similar characteristics outside Switzerland. The Future Cities Project run by the ETH in Singapore will start in the Fall of 2011 with a Landscape Ecology project under the Direction of ETH Professors Christophe Girot and Paolo Burlando on the Ciliwung River watershed in Jakarta testing our capacity for hydrological and terrain modeling at the tropical urban periphery integrating the

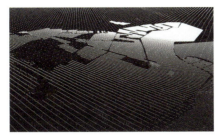

9. Point cloud area-analysis visualisation of the larger territory of Santa Gilla

10. The Sion site within the large-scale linear context of the Rhone valley

11. Large-scale CNC milled foam model of Sion and the Rhone valley context

point cloud surveying technique. The goal of this method is to bring large-scale structural design in landscape architecture back to the forefront of planning methods and development strategies in territories directly affected by increasing watershed discharge due to climate change. The project in Sion provides an effective working method toward more balanced and sustainable landscape topologies for the future.

The artificial 4-million-cubic-meter AlpTransit deposit in Sigirino results from the construction of the NEAT high-velocity rail system, linking Italy to Switzerland. The landscape design of the depot as well as its insertion studies have been developed by Atelier Girot (figure 14). In collaboration with the LVML of the ETH, a geo-referenced point-cloud was taken on site to inform various aspects of topological detailing, ensuring better coherence and connectivity to the outlying terrain (figure 15). It shows a more precise scale of intervention within the territory and how an industrial site located on the alpine Gotthard trail can gradually become an important piece of landscape design at the periphery of Lugano (figure 16). The topological rules for the project were set by the engineers with a general 2/3 slope and rise over the valley floor of 150 meters. The challenge was to reintegrate this project into the surroundings within a highly sensitive cultural and natural setting. Advanced modeling and visualizing techniques were used at every stage of the design process, and this was combined with on-site preparatory tests for artificial substrates and vegetation activators (figure 17). The project is about the adaptation of an artificial topology within the surroundings, subsequently this is where the extreme precision generated by point-cloud scans became essential. The density of technical and visual information inside the point-clouds allowed for highly informed design decisions. The material and physical reality of the massive project are rendered comprehensible and operable from within the design studio itself. During the design and decision-making process, every possible physical, visual, and natural aspect of the project came under scrutiny. The ability to adapt to changing demands in both visual and technical communication, ranging from compaction and effluent analysis to video match-moving visualizations was vital in the five years it took to finalize the concept and get it approved (figure 18). This relative slowness in the making of the project should be considered as a necessary blessing, as the technical and programmatic parameters of the project evolved

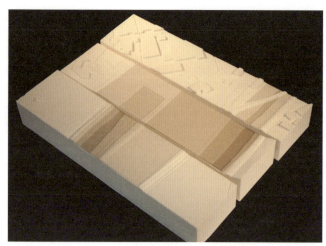

12. Detailed milled model sections of the Rhone river edge

13. Chronological milled model design iterations of the Sion site

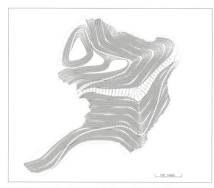

14. Plan of the AlpTransit deposit in Sigirino, Switzerland

parallel to the gradual excavation of tunnel material for deposition. The geo-referenced point-cloud base also allowed the assemblage of landscape photographs (figure 19), enabling a form of site viewing that relates back to the art of site panning and forming a visual history of the transformation of the site.

This selection of examples illustrates the state of advancement of landscape architecture in the domain of topological modeling and visual thinking on the broader territory. In a field of work where 2D layering, projection, and zoning were the rule in the twentieth century, we have now entered an age where geo-referenced 3D visualizing has become the state of the art and an absolute necessity for the dynamic modeling of large-scale projects in landscape architecture.

PROJECT TEAM: ILMAR HURKXKENS, ALEXANDRE KAPELLOS, JAMES MELSOM, AND PASCAL WERNER

NOTES

1. The new Landscape Visualizing and Modeling Laboratory (LVML) of the ETH, created in 2009 and funded by the Swiss National Foundation (SNF), is an interdepartmental research and teaching unit between the Institute of Landscape Architecture (ILA) of Professor Christophe Girot at the Department of Architecture and the PLUS Chair of Professor Adrienne Grêt-Regamey at the Department of Engineering; both are members of the Network City and Landscape (NSL).

2. Santa Gilla, *A New Landscape for the Metropolitan Laguna of Cagliari*, Pamphlet No. 12 ILA ETH, 2009. For more on the Santa Gilla experiment, see: Christophe Girot and Cesarina Siddi, Santa Gilla. *A Laguna in the Metropolitan Landscape of Cagliari. An Experiment for a New Landscape Approach* (Rome: 2009).

3. *Sion sur Rhône. New Landscape Topologies for the Third Rhône River Correction*, Pamphlet No. 13 ILA ETH, 2009.

4. The ETH Institute of Landscape Architecture, under the Chair Professor Girot has developed topological strategies on Swiss waterways since 2005. The first projects published in *Topos* received the design prize at the 2006 Barcelona Biennale. For more information see "New Landscape Topology for Flood Control," *Topos. The International Review of Landscape Architecture and Urban Design*, Challenges, 15 (2007), H. 60, S. 70–76.

5. The Sigirino landscape project was exhibited at the Galerie Lucy Mackintosh in Lausanne in 2009 in a show sponsored by the Fundaçion César Manrique on "Landscape and Territory." A book entitled *Grands Paysages D'Europe*, edited by Lorette Coen and published by the Fundaçion César Manrique, came out in the Fall of 2009.

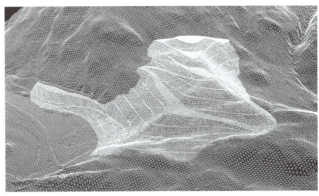

15. Insertion of the AlpTransit deposit into the site of Sigirino

16. View from the Alp Transit deposit site towards Sigirino village

17. Large-scale CNC milled model of the Alp Transit deposit embedded into the larger territory of Monte Ceneri, Ticino

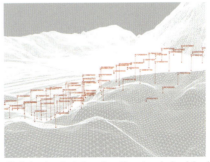

18. Z-depth calculations for effluent analysis of the deposit in Sigirino

19. True–color point cloud model of Alp Transit deposit site, Sigirino

MARK DORRIAN IS PROFESSOR OF ARCHITECTURE RESEARCH AT NEWCASTLE UNIVERSITY AND DIRECTOR OF THE ART, ARCHITECTURE, AND URBANISM ATELIER, METIS. HIS BOOK, WHICH WAS CO-EDITED WITH FRÉDÉRIC POUSIN, LA VUE AÉRIENNE: FRAGMENTS D'UNE HISTOIRE CULTURELLE, WILL BE PUBLISHED BY CNRS EDITIONS IN 2011. HE IS CURRENTLY WORKING ON THE AERIAL VIEW AND ON AIR-CONDITIONING.

ON GOOGLE EARTH

An acquaintance who works in one of the ministries of the French government tells me of a strategy that he has developed to relieve the tedium of his job.[1] On the desk are two computers. The first is reserved for ministerial business, but on the second he launches Google Earth, setting its virtual globe spinning. Thus while one machine presents him with the necessities of the day, glancing at the other offers an imaginative release, allowing him to fantasize that he is flying through the stratosphere, beyond the preoccupations, irritations, and entanglements of earthbound life. If, to quote the authors of *Google: The Missing Manual*, with Google Earth one can "swoop in like Superman from outer space," then my friend's solution is one that permits him to be simultaneously the superhero and his workaday alter ego Clark Kent (and this is something that even Superman himself could not achieve), flying over the planet while, rather more prosaically, continuing to fulfil his bureaucratic obligations below.[2]

One of the curiosities of researching Google Earth is that it can quickly come to seem as if everyone has – like my friend – a Google Earth story to tell. Thus although one usually begins an essay introducing the material to be discussed and expanding upon its less familiar aspects, it is symptomatic – and indeed is a key point of interest – that with Google one does not. There still may be some people on the planet with digital access who do not recognize the name, but they are getting fewer every day.[3] Google, with its extraordinarily dominant Internet search engine, emblematizes globalization. Somewhat like those obscure, singular yet infinitely complex institutions that lie below the surface of science-fiction environments – institutions that are, like God, everywhere and nowhere at the same time and are consequently characterized by the absence of any differentiating noun, so they become known as just "The Corporation" or the like – Google can seem pretty much omnipresent, or at least well on the way to getting there. If totality was one of the dreams of early modernity – Faustian total knowledge, total control, total empowerment – postmodernity has reclaimed it with a vengeance, yet in a new way. The point now is not the reduction of difference through negation and the accumulation of knowledge within some promethean individual but conversely, the ability to navigate (search) difference by managing the interface between things, as enabled by the prosthetic computational power of the processor. So the pyramidal or perhaps helical structures of earlier imaginaries of escalating knowledge tend to give way to a more lateral, archipelago-like distribution in which slow historical ascent becomes superseded by the instantaneity of the network connection – a formation perhaps best indicated by the network pictures or internet maps with which we have become familiar.[4] Thus Google's stated objective to "organise the world's information and make it universally accessible and useful";[5] and thus too a 2006 review essay on Google by John Lanchester for the *London Review of Books* entitled "The Global Id", which thereby characterized it as a kind of collective planetary unconscious.[6]

What strikes one about Google is the constant insistence on the colossal, the gargantuan, and the exorbitant in its agenda, its technology, and its statements. It displays that mixture of the absolute with the seeming negotiation of difference that we tend to describe as holism, which I take to signify a benign encompassing of difference, as opposed to totalism, which is difference's negation. Famously the company was named after the googol, the massive number of 10 to the power of 100 (apparently the even more expansive name "googolplex" – 10 raised to the power of a googol – was first raised as a possibility).[7] The misspelling was by accident, at a stroke draining away some of the (Slavic?) strangeness of the original and endowing the word with a more verb-like quality and a suggestion of the visual, thus associating "ogle" – www.ogleearth.com becoming the address of one of the major Google Earth blogs – and "boggle." And certainly, wide-eyed astonishment seems the order of the day when contemplating this institution that has been ranked as the fastest growing company in the history of the world. Interestingly, when you make a search on Google, you are not in fact searching the internet itself: the technology is much more Borgesian. Instead, Google makes a copy that is constantly being updated of all the pages on the Internet, which are downloaded onto a massive computer cluster that apparently comprises more than one million PCs, assembled, networked, and optimized by the company. The complex is described by the president of Stanford University, himself a Google board member, as "the largest computer system in the world… I don't think there is even anything close."[8] Already, by 2006, a report estimated that Google had more than 450,000 servers distributed across at least twenty-five global locations and connected by a high-capacity fiber optic network; as it concluded, the speed of light ends up being the fundamental constraint.[9] As Google downloads what is in effect the entirety of the Internet, it

"makes an index of every word on a web page, where it stands in relation to other words, whether or not a word is listed in a title, whether it is listed in a special typeface, how frequently it is listed on the page and so on… There are more than a hundred of these criteria, and Google gives a numeric weight to every one of them, for every searchable term on every one of eight billion web pages. When a query arrives – which it does at the rate of many times every second – Google searches the index for the relevant terms, measures the relevance of the results using all its various metrics…, crunches out a single number for each page, and lists them, with the highest score at the top, usually within half a second or so. Even if you didn't know a thing about computers, you could tell that this involved a truly scary amount of computational power."[10]

The figures continue to expand and amaze. In his *Googled: The End of the World as We Know It*, Ken Auletta reports that Google's index contained 1 trillion web pages in 2008, and that in four hours it could index the equivalent of the complete holdings of the Library of Congress.[11]

If, as I have already hinted, Google almost uniquely seems capable of simultaneously encompassing the poles of the universal/singular opposition, then one way in which this is manifested is in the extraordinarily intense subjective identification the company and its services inspire. In October 2006, *The New York Times* ran an article entitled "Planet Google Wants You," which profiled Dan Firger, a law student at New York University and in many ways a typical inhabitant of Planet Google. Six to eight times a day, we are told, his mobile phone rings with text messages from Google reminding him of appointments logged into Google calendar. He searches the web with Google, talks via Google Talk, emails using Gmail, and so on. "I find myself getting sucked down Google's wormhole," he remarks. "It's all part of Google's benign dictatorship of your life."[12] The responses suggest, however, that this "benign dictatorship" is experienced more as an extension, or even a *delivery*, of the self than it is as a transaction with another entity. If the latter is more the mode of experience of Microsoft, computing's so-called Evil Empire and the butt of Google's "Don't be evil" slogan (always "forcing you to do things their way", as one complainant puts it), Google "literally augments your brain. I don't have to remember quite a few things now because Google can remember them for me. Google is an additional memory chip."[13] Ultimately, however, the particular genius of Google is that it does not just facilitate the subject's command of information, but that it assembles and delivers it in a way that leads to a radical identification with what is given. The *New York Times* article closes with a comment by a web designer in California who enthuses: "That's what Google gives you – 'me.'"[14] And so we find that at the same time as Google gives you the world, it also appears to give you "yourself", an effect not unconnected with the company's infamous user-profiling techniques and storage of search histories, rationalized as being necessary for increased search efficiency but also offering sophistication in targeted advertising. When Google invested in the human genetics firm 23andMe in 2007, it was interpreted as a logical step in the quest to expand online user profiling.[15] As *The Guardian* has noted, Google knows more about the United Kingdom's citizens than does MI5, the state security agency.[16]

The dream of total knowledge, which is also a kind of total seeing, is an old theme, but here care has to be taken in distinguishing the particular kind of project that Google represents. In *From Counterculture to Cyberculture*, Fred Smith has examined how the anti-hierarchical and anti-corporate credos of radical 1960s thought fed into the digital discourses of the 1980s and 1990s. And certainly, the holistic ideology of Google's founding partners, Larry Page and Sergey Brin, seems closer to the pan-earth ethic of California hippiedom of the 1960s and 1970s and the hippie-infused West Coast technoculture in which Page and Brin studied than it does to any Enlightenment project.[17] I am thinking here of manifestations such as the *Whole Earth Catalog* – launched in 1968 in Menlo Park, California, where Google's founding partners would set up in a garage thirty years later – with its cover picture of the earth from space, which tried to make the "wisdom" of others (other cultures, peoples, races, places, technologies, etc.) available. In this publication we can see a deeply liberal counterculture, whose watchwords were freedom and individual choice and which – if not exactly consumerist – sought an open access to and participation in the products, techniques, and modalities of life of others that was at least a counterpart to that demanded by market capitalism. In the quest for personal development, there was almost nothing that one could not have, as long as it was not seen to compromise the equivalent pursuits of others. "We are as gods and might as well get good at it," the "Purpose" statement to *The Next Whole Earth Catalog* declared in 1980. In response to the institutional and bureaucratic conditions of formal power structures, the publication aimed to support the developing "realm of intimate personal power" – "the power of individuals to conduct their own education, find their own inspiration, shape their own environment, and share their adventure with whoever is interested."[18]

So where is Google Earth in all this? We have taken this lengthy excursion before returning to Google Earth because it allows us to discern the symbolic dimensions of the program more clearly. Google Earth was released in 2005 and quickly became one of the most remarked upon and – in this era of generalized war and militarization – contentious internet developments. But even in advance of the launch of the program, the name Google Earth seemed highly loaded and symbolically invested. The planet, this earth, when qualified by Google appears to transform into an informational utopia – or even, in Kevin Kelly's eschatological phrase, a new "Eden of everything"[19] – that then exists as the final point on an expanding scale in whose lower reaches those earlier utopias of entertainment and science that were first branded as "lands" and then "worlds" find their place. The virtual globe that Google Earth presents is surely the symbolic counterpart of the corporation's mission to make everything available to you: Google gives you the world, and indeed, after the launch of Google Sky, the cosmos as well. [20]

If we are living, as others have suggested, in the age of the aerial image, then Google Earth is one of the principal phenomena that make it so. Today the aerial view – the image *of* everywhere – seems to *be* everywhere, and it seems plausible to claim that Google Earth is the most prominent manifestation and stimulant of this voracious contemporary appetite for views from above. Relations of all kinds on the ground are increasingly mediated in complex ways from the sky, a situation that Google Earth, through the massive availability of images that it facilitates, has played a key role in bringing about. Much valued for its spectacular and entrancing effects, the aerial view is firmly established as a recurrent feature of popular visual culture, media forms, and touristic installations. When a representative for the London 2012 Olympic Games was interviewed in 2007 on BBC Radio 4, he was asked about the (at that point, still unknown) design for the principal stadium. His symptomatic response was that at least one thing was certain, "it's a media event, so it will look great from the

air." Likewise, tourist concentration in the city is now focused on the London Eye, a massive aerial viewing device marketed as "the way the world sees London" that in 2005 was voted the ultimate world tourist destination (beating such contenders as the Vatican and the Sydney Opera House).[21] At the same time, popular volumes of planetary images proliferate. Often tied to ecological rhetoric – such as Yann Arthus-Bertrand's *The Earth from the Air* – in these books scintillating images of the beauty and diversity of the earth's surface, of extraordinary definition and reproduced with highly saturated colors, achieve a kind of hyperreality that appears simultaneously abstracted and highly palpable and that sublimates both pristine and devastated landscapes alike.[22]

Against this background, the principal question I want to ask of Google Earth is simply, what does it show us? What, and how, do we see when we engage the program? Something that seems to me to be of great interest is its graphic interface, how we operate it, and what happens when we do. In particular I am concerned to think about the ways in which we are solicited by the images on the screen, and the kind of imaginative engagement with them – and by extension, with the earth itself – that they might be said to prompt. Google's mass elevation of the eye of the consumer into space carries with it consequences that demand a reconceptualization of the view from above, one that effectively reverses some of the familiar historical understandings and connotations of aerial vision. Moreover, I am struck by the drift of various developments and trials, in which Google has experimented with ways of more effectively monetizing the program. In an article on the computer game *Spore*, Stephen Johnson has written of what he calls "the long zoom," which he argues to be the characteristic visual paradigm of our time.[23] Exemplifying it by, among other things, Charles and Ray Eames' film *Powers of Ten* (1977) – a connection that is frequently drawn with respect to the Google Earth interface[24] – he stressed its epistemological aspects. The commercial possibilities and evident uses of the "long zoom" in Google Earth, however, suggest another agency, one to do with the establishment of the commodity as the target of the zoom's spatial collapse. The promise here – at least from the point of view of revenue generation – is of a kind of virtuous circle of mutual targeting whereby Google Earth permits the commodity to target, via advertising, the cybertourist cum satellite-consumer, and then in turn to be geospatially targeted by her. A 2006 advertising campaign for Saturn cars, in which Google worked with a San Francisco-based advertising consultancy, is an example. The campaign bundled together various Google products and services "like clickable video clips, Google Earth and the geographic finding of computer users." In an article for *The New York Times*, Stuart Elliot described how the advertisement worked:

> Visitors to a variety of web sites in six cities around the country that are home to 22 Saturn dealerships will see what looks like typical banner ads for Aura, a new Saturn midsize sedan. Clicking on an ad will

produce a view of the earth that zooms in on the dealership nearest to the computer user. The doors to the virtual dealership fly open, revealing the general manager who introduces a brief commercial about [the] Aura. After the spot ends, the general manager returns, standing next to an Aura and offering choices that include spinning the car 360 degrees, inspecting its engine, printing a map with directions to the dealership and visiting the Web sites of Saturn or the dealer.[25]

What happens, then, when we first launch Google Earth? When the program opens and the screen image appears, we find ourselves somewhere in space – not exactly deep space, but far enough away to see the entirely of the globe. In earlier versions of the program, the world appeared with the Americas facing us, in keeping with the U.S.-centric upload of information upon which some technical commentators remarked in early studies (*Google Earth Study: Impacts and Uses for Defence and Security*, for example, produced in 2005 by the French Fleximage, a subsidiary of the European Aeronautic Defence and Space Company). In his 2007 *Google.pedia: The Ultimate Google Resource* Michael Miller makes a bizarre and unironic – but somewhat telling – point regarding this: "Anytime you start Google Earth, the view defaults to the extended zoom of planet Earth, focused on the continent of North America. This is a great place to start because you can get just about anyplace you want from here."[26] The interface works through a principle of grasping, which intensifies the sense of the manipulability of the virtual object: through the hand icon, one can "take hold" of the earth and spin it, or even invert it – a strangely disconcerting experience at first. Notably, at this elevation anyway, we are not moving around the earth; rather we appear to spin the globe in relation to a fixed position that we occupy. The hand cursor is a familiar one, recognizable from other graphics programs (Acrobat, Photoshop, etc.), but here it gains an extra dimension. We are reminded of the cartographic tradition of miniature globes that we place our hands on and revolve. The Google Earth interface offers us a digital simulacrum of these, although with a now strikingly literalized planetary image.

So where exactly are we located when we open Google Earth? The implication is that we are in fact on the moon, or at least on the way there. There is never the registration of any other body, except a generic star pattern, on the graphic interface. More precisely, it might be argued that the Google Earth interface inherits and deploys, as a kind of 'underlay', one of the most popularly recognizable images of the earth: the so-called *Blue Marble* photograph taken by the *Apollo 17* expedition en route to the moon in 1972.[27] In his brilliant commentary on images taken during the Apollo missions, Denis Cosgrove has pointed out the motivating and iconic role they played in emerging ecological discourses.[28] The key point here is the way in which the image of the planet from space produced a new kind of aerial view, one in which the terrestrial surface no longer filled the photographic frame. The world in the image gained a new sense of fragility when the contours of the planet became visible within its frame. The

photographs of a bright earth engirdled by clouds suggested a pristine jewel-like planetary oasis isolated in the vast barrenness of space, a feeling provoked particularly by the famous "Earthrise" image taken from *Apollo 8* (1968), with its view of the distant earth rising above the foreground of the inert lunar desert.[29] As Stewart Brand would comment: "Nowhere in the solar system is the contrast between a living and a dead planet so conspicuous as on the Moon at Earthrise."[30] Moreover, in their liberation of the globe from all cultural signifiers – borderlines, grids, and cartographic codes – the Apollo photographs seemed to show a unified and perhaps even redeemed world purged of conflict, a planet that could be thought of as a single organism.[31]

If we accept that the Google Earth interface in some way inherits and re-performs this image, then in what ways does it differ from it? The Apollo pictures are embedded in a specific history, that of the Cold War space race and manned – and therefore heroic (as articulated through the iconography of the astronaut) – lunar exploration. The pristine singularity of the planet as conveyed by the images was predicated on the singularity of the photographic image-capture event itself, the instantaneous and complete recording of the scene. Conversely, Google Earth presents us with a non-auratic image in which the whole "radiant jewel" of the Apollo images is fragmented – both spatially and temporally – into a panoply of geospatial data sets produced by orbiting satellites and lower-level image-capture devices, which are then digitally sutured together to form the global image. Even with the program's informational layers switched off, we can be under no illusion that this is any kind of "natural" image. With its evidently constructed patchwork, the visual rhetoric of the globe no longer enunciates the "wholeness of the object" but rather the "wholeness of its searchability," for everything that retards vision tends to be drained away. Not only do clouds – 'magical' in the *Apollo 17* image but obscurantist for Google Earth (although they do remain in the program's screen icon, which is a kind of "blue marble" logo) – disperse, but the world ceases to have a dark side, and instead we have an entirely illuminated globe. On Google Earth the darkness of night never falls.[32] This is not a matter of stopping the sun in the sky, but rather of distributing and refracting its agency through the multiple orbiting devices that supply the image data from which the virtual globe is pieced together. This image of a mechanically encircled earth carries none of the sense of specular oscillation provoked by the Apollo images. For crucial to their cultural reception was the spectator's knowledge of what lay outside their frame – and indeed – behind the camera. The sense of the fragility of the planet was echoed and reinforced by the precariousness of the body of its representative, the astronaut who took the photograph. Knowledge of the provisional and contingent sustenance of this little piece of the earth, adrift from the biosphere and looking back at it, deeply intensified the spatial vertigo of these images and their implications.

One powerful effect of the Apollo images was to prompt reflection on the interrelationships among, and interconnectedness of, the planet's inhabitants. The pictorial registration of the earth isolated in the vastness of space suddenly made it seem small and relations on it necessarily close. A similar insistence on a new sense of proximity is evident in many commentaries on not just Google Earth, but on the Google phenomenon more generally. For example, Randall Stross – author of *Planet Google* – writes, "Google has made the earth seem like a single cozy place" and titles his chapter that discusses Google Earth, "Small Planet, After All." [33] Inasmuch as we accept this, then Google Earth – in its construction of a world of always-available proximity, a global totality that is always to hand – appears to produce an intensification of the "one-world effect" of the earlier images of the earth from space. It would be wrong to discount this, and I have heard aid workers, earth-observation scientists, and geographers speak optimistically, inevitably in connection with disaster situations, of the possibilities of the kind of global immediacy, the overcoming of distance between "us" and "them," that Google Earth seems to facilitate. Yet at the same time this raises all kinds of questions, not least those that issue from the gap between the apparent omnipresence available to the Google Earth user and the specific limits of her vicarious experience as constructed by the program. And these in turn prompt the idea that the sense of "global coziness" is likely to be less an effect of the program per se than a relationship with it, one highly dependent on the user's social, political, economic, and geographic situation outside the digital construction.

Equally, the presumption that Google Earth constructs closeness and coziness disregards its more uncanny aspects, the degree to which the sutured virtual globe transforms the world into a "strange planet" rather than a "small planet." One has the impression that, post-Google Earth, the proper realm of the alien is no longer outer space but rather the digital surface of the planet or its newly hollow interior, the entrance to which many internet images captured from Google Earth and posted online claim to have found. On the digital surfaces of Google's planet, strange and uncanny phenomena take shape that are eagerly reported and tracked in various blogs. Peculiar formations are seen to emerge, which beckon alien craft or physiognomically stare back into space and therefore also at the viewer. The apparatus of more earthly plots, plans, and conspiracies also show up in various ways, such as the notorious "black helicopters" (for whose detection on Google Earth *The Register* ran a tongue-in-cheek competition[34]) or the so-called Area 51 military base in Nevada upon which so much speculation has alighted.[35] Even as it builds upon what the images show, conspiracy theory profits from the idea of the constitutive manipulability of the digital image, from the consequent uncertainty over its status, and from what might be described as the question of the "politics of resolution" that Google Earth brings to the fore.

Since its release, much has been made of the national security issues that attend Google Earth, and the company's reply has always been that its global image is constructed of data sets that are already available within the public domain. National and institutional responses to Google Earth have certainly been instructive: complaints have been registered from, among others, South Korea, India, Taiwan, (mis-named as a 'province' of China) and Liverpool, England (because images of the city were not being updated quickly enough to show the results of its ongoing regeneration program – too much still looked like a building site, or had yet to begin).[36] In January 2007, *The Daily Telegraph* reported that Bahrain had blocked access to Google Earth after opposition groups had used it to scrutinize royal palaces and their grounds and calculated that "the ruling Al-Khalifa family owns about 80 per cent of the entire country."[37] The United Kingdom also registered complaints and, according to *The Daily Telegraph* again, British military bases in Iraq were subsequently "blotted out." So too were the Trident nuclear submarine pens in Faslane and the intelligence centre GCHQ, in Cheltenham. According to its research, the paper continued, "the entire aerial footage of Hereford, home to the SAS, has been fuzzed out."[38]

This inevitably suggests that Google Earth might present us with a new kind of political map, one structured according to a different logic than those colored political cartographies, organized by the vectors of national boundaries, with which we are all familiar. Instead, with Google Earth, we have a politics of resolution, or definition, of the image – a new popular political map structured through image resolutions and the upload periodicity of data sets. U.S. Government legislation from the 1990s, for example, prohibits satellite-imaging companies licensed in the U.S. to release imagery of Israeli territory above a certain (low) resolution, unless it is already commercially available elsewhere. (Admittedly, given the rapid international spread of imaging companies and technological developments, this is a restriction that has become increasingly ineffective).[39] The more general point to be made here is that censorship, concealment, or camouflage is not immediately or necessarily legible and tends to differ from the large white spaces of earlier maps, which clearly signal that something is missing or has been excised. With the digital image, the effect is more of a stirring up or a fluctuation in the digital field, not a tear, a blot, or crossing out on top of it.

Yet another, but related, way of understanding the resolution differentials on Google Earth is as a map of (predominantly western) economic and political interests – which is to say, those of the customers of the commercial imaging companies from which Google derives its data sets. Areas that appear in great detail with a fast refresh rate are typically those with high real estate value. Disaster areas, conflict zones, or places where state intelligence has been directed can also suddenly emerge with startling detail. Of an area on the Pakistan-Afghanistan border that "suddenly became as detailed as the images of Manhattan" in March 2007, *Wired* magazine reported, "Turns out, Google gets its images from many of the same satellite companies – DigitalGlobe, TerraMetrics, and others – that provide reconnaissance to U.S. intelligence agencies. And when the CIA requests close-ups of the area around Peshawar in Pakistan's North-West Frontier Province, Google Earth reaps the benefits (although usually six to 18 months later). This is also why remote parts of Asia went hi-res after the Indian Ocean tsunami in 2004 and the Kashmir earthquake in 2005."[40] At the same time, given that high image resolution has tended to intersect with the key locations of the "digital first world," it comes as no surprise that a certain bravado can be attached to image definition in relation to national territories: more than once I have encountered the phrase "third world lo-res," which implies that being first world may come to mean not just having air-conditioned offices and a motorway network, but also having hyper clear territorial images on Google Earth.

And finally, one of the consequences of the popularization, coherence, and availability of geospatial data that Google Earth facilitates is that the surface of the earth begins to address the sky in a new, intentional, way: the terrestrial surface itself becomes manipulated as a media surface, not just virtually on the Google Earth interface, but literally. As the audience of geospatial data is no longer made up of only cartographers, scientists, military strategists, and state operatives but rather – overwhelmingly – consumers, how commodities look from the sky, and how they address it, is a new concern. A newspaper reports that tourists, skeptical of the claims and photographs in holiday brochures, now use Google Earth to see the "reality" of the situation (finding out that the hotel is next to waste dump, or is still under construction, etc.).[41] Moreover, the earth's skin becomes a site for gargantuan advertising landworks addressed to satellites that take up the logic of the "mashup" – the hybridization of text, diagram, and photograph that was pioneered for Google Maps – and transfer it to the terrestrial surface. If the standard narrations of the world-historical effects of digitization tell of the wearing-away of the real by the virtual, these developments give a reverse instance in which – seemingly perversely – the virtual becomes subject to material realization. Navigational technologies that display aerial images consequently register these landworks, not as an additional informational layer that can be switched off but as part of the image layer itself. Thus a massive logo of Colonel Sanders appeared beside a Kentucky Fried Chicken outlet in Tenessee, a locator and brand-icon scaled for the era of "satnav."[42] Anders Albrechtslund reports on a magazine that advertised its 100th issue by constructing a vast reproduction of its cover in the desert near Las Vegas, declaring that it "can be seen from outer space using Google Earth" and calling it "a UFO's-eye view."[43] The aerial view in its contemporary form becomes less, as it has often been thought of in the past, a detached, dispassionate and privileged way of interpreting the world's surface and more a phenomenon that, by its very presence and new mass availability, produces specific, concrete effects upon it.

The most extreme examples of these tendencies though are undoubtedly the recent developments in Dubai, which are calculated to address the global real estate market through the sky. In the vast pictographic constructions of the so-called "Palm trilogy" (the Palm Jumeirah, Palm Jebel Ali, and Palm Deira developments), land-art precedents from the late 1960s and early 1970s such as Robert

Smithson's *Spiral Jetty*, which always had a conceptual relationship with the aerial view, are unraveled and recalibrated for the conditions of the globalized postmodern economy. Clearly related to these are publications such as *The Middle East from Space* (2006), which then naturally takes the form of advertising, displaying the emirate's planetary-scale branding. The volume is published by Motivate Publishing, in which the UAE Minister of State for Finance is a partner and under whose imprint the book by the ruler of Dubai – Sheikh Mohammed Bin Rasheed Al Maktoum – titled *My Vision: Challenges in the Race for Excellence*, appeared the following year.[44]

Perhaps though, from the point of view of Google Earth, it is the development known as The World, lying adjacent to the Palms, which appears the most suggestively articulated in relation to the new conditions and technologies of global aerial vision. The construction, as is well-known, consists of an array of man-made islands fashioned, in Mike Davis' words, "in the shape of an almost finished puzzle of the world."[45] The rhetorical gesture of its government-owned developer, Nakheel, is a little like that of Google itself: to give its customers the world. And perhaps not surprisingly the next step, as with Google's launch of Google Sky, turns out to be the cosmos. Or at least that is what was intended before the current financial crisis, when plans for a development around The World to be called The Universe were unveiled. In 2008 Nakheel announced the development under the banner "Masterplanners of the Universe," but the following year it was placed on hold.[46] As it stands, the curiosity of navigating to The World via the Google Earth interface is of course the reiteration of the global image, the sense of the arrival at a picture of the world that looks back at itself and that is articulated both as a *mise en abîme* and, in its commercial strategy, as a *trompe l'oeil* for investors in the sky. Furthermore, the puzzle-like character of The World to which Davis refers itself gains a reiterative character, given that it is initially encountered in the data set patchwork of the virtual globe that serves as the gateway to the other world toward which we zoom, and to which we will descend to find the patches reinstantiated at another scale, although this time resolved into real-estate parcels.

NOTES

1. This essay was originally presented at a workshop held in Edinburgh on February 3, 2007. This was the first event in the British Academy / Centre national de la recherche scientifique (CNRS) funded research program led by Mark Dorrian and Frédéric Pousin titled "The Aerial View: Spatial Knowledges and Spatial Practices." The text has been revised for publication. For a report on the workshop see Stacy Boldrick, "Reviewing the

Aerial View," *Architectural Research Quarterly*, 11(1) (2007): 11-14.
2. Sarah Milstein, J. D. Biersdorfer, and Matthew MacDonald, *Google: The Missing Manual*, 2nd edition (Beijing, Cambridge.: Pogue Press, O'Reilly, 2006): 108.
3. David Vise singles out South Korea as having been particularly resistant to penetration by Google. David A Vise, "Google," *Foreign Policy*, 154 (2006): 20-24: 20.

4. See, for example, Martin Dodge and Rob Kitchin, *Mapping Cyberspace* (London and New York: Routledge, 2000).
5. http://www.google.com/corporate/ [22.03.10]. Due to be completed in around 300 years, according to Google CEO Eric Schmidt in a presentation to the Association of National Advertisers (USA) in 2005: see, "We'll index the world by 2310, says Google," http://www.theregister.co.uk/2005/10/10/google_index/ [23.03.10]

6. John Lanchester, "The Global Id," *London Review of Books*, 28(2), January 26, 2006, http://www.lrb.co.uk/v28/n02/john-lanchester/the-global-id [23.03.10]

7. David Vise, with Mark Malseed, *The Google Story* (Basingstoke and Oxford: Pan Macmillan, 2008): 39.

8. Cited in Vise, *The Google Story*: 3.

9. John Markoff, "Hiding in Plain Sight, Google Seeks More Power," *The New York Times*, June 14, 2006, http://www.nytimes.com/2006/06/14/technology/14search.html?pagewanted=2&_r=1&ei=5070&en=5f47a9cc1f8a2faf&ex=1189396800 [23.03.10].

10. Lanchester, "The Global Id."

11. Ken Auletta, *Googled: The End of the World as We Know It* (London: Virgin Books, 2010).

12. Alex Williams, "Planet Google Wants You," The *New York Times*, October 15, 2006, http://www.nytimes.com/2006/10/15/fashion/15google.html?ex=1189051200&en=1640e28bbf02e82e&ei=5070 [22.03.10].

13. Ibid.

14. Ibid.

15. Robert Verkaik, "Google Is Watching You," *The Independent*, May 24, 2007: 1-2; 2.

16. Victor Keegan, "That Ringing Sound Is Google on the Phone," *The Guardian* (Technology), September 13, 2007: 4.

17. Fred Smith, *From Counterculture to Cyberculture: Stewart Brand, the Whole Earth Network, and the Rise of Digital Utopianism* (Chicago: University of Chicago Press, 2006).

18. Stewart Brand, ed., *The Next Whole Earth Catalog: Access to Tools* (POINT/Random House, 1981 [4th printing]): 2.

19. Kevin Kelly, "Scan this Book!", *The New York Times Magazine*, May 14, 2006, http://www.nytimes.com/2006/05/14/magazine/14publishing.html?pagewanted=1&_r=1&ei=5070&en=ac7163de40132770&ex=1189051200&adxnnlx=1188918074-MfeDRLvuvFFoXliFxqjuUw [22.03.10]

20. See Susan M. Roberts and Richard H. Schein's discussion of images of the globe in advertisements by geographic information providers, in which they note: "Views from above underscore the advertiser's totalizing claims of complete coverage, of being everywhere." Roberts and Schein, "Earth Shattering: Global Imagery and GIS," in John Pickles, ed., *Ground Truth: The Social Implications of Geographic Information Systems* (New York and London: Guilford Press, 1995): 171-195; 174.

21. Arifa Akbar, "London Eye on Top of the World as It Becomes Best Tourist Attraction," *The Independent*, March 17, 2005: 18-19. See Mark Dorrian, "'The Way the World Sees London': Thoughts on a Millennial Urban Spectacle" in A. Vidler, ed., *Architecture Between Spectacle and Use* (Williamstown: Sterling and Francine Clark Art Institute, and New Haven and London: Yale University Press, 2008): 41-57.

22. For example, the "picture of one of the worst things on the planet: the Athabasca oil sands in Alberta, Canada" selected by Yann Arthus-Bertrand as his best photograph. "What you're looking at is essentially poison and pollution, yet the shot has great beauty." "Yann Arthus-Bertrand's Best Shot," *The Guardian* (G2), September 24, 2009: 23.

23. Steven Johnson, "The Long Zoom," *The New York Times Magazine*, October 8, 2006, http://www.nytimes.com/2006/10/08/magazine/08games.html?_r=2&oref=slogin&pagewanted=all [25.03.10]. I am grateful to Amy Kulper for this reference.

24. For example, Vittoria Di Palma, "Zoom: Google Earth and Global Intimacy," in Vittoria di Palma, Diana Periton, and Marina Lathouri, ed.s, *Intimate Metropolis: Urban Subjects in the Modern City* (London and New York: Routledge, 2009): 239-270.

25. Stuart Elliott, "Marketing on Google: It's Not Just Text Anymore," *The New York Times*, September 22, 2006, http://www.nytimes.com/2006/09/22/business/media/22adco.html?_r=1&ex=1188964800&en=0e8871e885436af5&ei=5070 [27.03.10]

26. Michael Miller, *Google.pedia: The Ultimate Google Resource* (Indianapolis: Que Publishing, 2007): 323.

27. Photograph reference: AS17-148-22727. Vittoria De Palma also discerns a relation between Google Earth and this image in "Zoom: Google Earth and Global Intimacy": 264.

28. Denis Cosgrove, *Apollo's Eye: A Cartographic Genealogy of the Earth in the Western Imagination* (Baltimore and London: Johns Hopkins University Press, 2001): 257-267.

29. Studied by Robert Poole in *Earthrise: How Man First Saw the Earth* (New Haven and London: Yale University Press, 2008).

30. Brand, ed., *The Next Whole Earth Catalog*: 1.

31. On the relation between the Apollo images and James Lovelock's Gaia hypothesis, see Poole, *Earthrise*: 170-189.

32. In later releases, there is an option to switch on a shading effect, which disappears upon zooming in.

33. Randall Stross, *Planet Google: How One Company Is Transforming Our Lives* (London: Atlantic Books, 2009): 131.

34. Lester Haines, "Google Earth: The Black Helicopters Have Landed," *The Register*, October 14, 2005, http://www.theregister.co.uk/2005/10/14/google_earth_competition_results/ [30.03.10]

35. To sample a Google Earth UFO sighting in Area 51, see: http://www.youtube.com/watch?v=ucZKCrMvqu4 [30.03.10]

36. Katie Hafner and Saritha Rai, "Governments Tremble at Google's Bird's-Eye View", *The New York Times*, December 20 (2005) http://www.nytimes.com/2005/12/20/technology/20image.html?_r=1&ei=5070&en=4b89cb0ad323cec6&ex=1189051200&pagewanted=all [30.03.05]; Lester Haines, "Taiwan Huffs and Puffs at Google Earth," *The Register*, October 4, 2005, http://www.theregister.co.uk/2005/10/04/taiwan_google_earth/ [30.03.10]; Lester Haines, "Liverpool Throws Strop at Google Earth," *The Register*, November 27, 2006, http://www.theregister.co.uk/2006/11/27/liverpool_google_earth_outrage/ [30.03.10]

37. "Picture is Not Always Clear", *The Daily Telegraph*, January 13, 2007. http://www.telegraph.co.uk/news/worldnews/1539400/Picture-is-not-always-clear.html [30.03.10]

38. Thomas Harding, "Google Blots Out Iraq Bases on Internet," *The Daily Telegraph*, January 20 (2007) http://www.telegraph.co.uk/news/worldnews/1540039/Google-blots-out-Iraq-bases-on-internet.html [30.03.10]

39. For a report on the appearance of high-resolution images of Israel on Google Earth in 2007, see http://www.informationliberation.com/?id=23961 [30.03.10]

40. On the website they helpfully provided a "Search for bin Laden at Home!" link http://www.wired.com/wired/archive/15.03/start.html?pg=10 [30.03.10]

41. Charles Starmer-Smith, "Zooming In: The World at Your Fingertip," *Daily Telegraph*, November 5, 2005, http://www.telegraph.co.uk/travel/733938/Zooming-in-the-world-at-your-fingertip.html [27.03.10]

42. Lester Haines, "Giant Colonel Sanders Visible from Space," *The Register*, November 17, 2006, http://www.theregister.co.uk/2006/11/17/colonel_sanders_mosaic/ [27.03.10]

43. Anders Albrechtslund, "Surveillance in Searching: A Study into Ethical Aspects of an Emergent Search Culture", unpublished paper, no pagination. I am grateful to the author for providing me with a copy of his essay.

44. http://www.motivatepublishing.com/library/default.asp?categorycode=About_mp&ID=About_mp [30.03.10]

45. Mike Davis, "Does the Road to the Future End at Dubai?," *Log: Observations on Architecture and the Contemporary City*, 6 (2005): 61-64; 61.

46. http://www.nakheel.com/en/news/2008_new_era [30.03.10]

PAUL KINGSBURY IS AN ASSISTANT PROFESSOR IN THE DEPARTMENT OF GEOGRAPHY AT SIMON FRASER UNIVERSITY. SPECIALIZING IN SOCIAL AND CULTURAL GEOGRAPHY, HIS RESEARCH DRAWS ON THE THEORIES OF JACQUES LACAN AND FRIEDRICH NIETZSCHE TO EXAMINE MULTICULTURALISM, CONSUMPTION, POWER, AND AESTHETICS.

JOHN PAUL JONES III IS PROFESSOR OF GEOGRAPHY IN THE SCHOOL OF GEOGRAPHY AND DEVELOPMENT AND DEAN OF THE COLLEGE OF SOCIAL AND BEHAVIORAL SCIENCES AT THE UNIVERSITY OF ARIZONA. HE IS THE RECENT CO-EDITOR OF *THE SAGE HANDBOOK OF SOCIAL GEOGRAPHIES* AND R*ESEARCH METHODS IN GEOGRAPHY: A CRITICAL INTRODUCTION*.

GOOGLE EARTH
AS DIONYSUSPHERE

What were we doing when we unchained this earth from its sun? Where is it moving now? Where are we moving to? Away from all suns? Are we not continually falling? And backwards, sidewards, forwards, in all directions? Is there still an up or down?

—Friedrich Nietzsche[1]

In his 1969-70 seminar, "The Other Side of Psychoanalysis," Jacques Lacan coined the term "alethosphere" to address the Information Age's proliferation of newfangled communication devices such as satellites, computers, and telebanking networks.[2] The neologism "alethosphere," drawing on the Greek *aletheia* (referring to both concealment and truth), is a place where something "gets recorded. If you have a little microphone here, you are plugged into the alethosphere."[3] Lacan notes that even "if you are in a little vehicle that is transporting you to Mars you can still plug into the alethosphere" much like the astronauts who orbited the moon and "had some minor problems at the last minute… with their little machine… By virtue of this [the human voice] they could allow themselves to say nothing but bullshit [*conneries*], such as for example that everything was going well when everything was going poorly. But that's beside the point. The point is that they stayed within the alethosphere."[4]

If Lacan were alive today, he would regard geospatial technologies such as Google Earth (hereafter GE) as a key part of the alethosphere. Lacan's notion of the alethosphere (and his psychoanalytic theories more generally) brings to the fore how social bonds take place through people's *jouissance* (hereafter, enjoyment).[5] As Joan Copjec puts it:

> The ["high-tech heaven" of the alethosphere] myth is probably inspired by the section of *Civilization and Its Discontents* where Freud speaks of modern man's capacity to remake himself as 'a kind of prosthetic God,' to replace every lost appendage or damaged organ with another, superior one endowed with fantastic powers. In this alethosphere … the prosthetically enhanced, plugged-in subject does not need to flee reality in order to indulge his pleasure principle, for he is now able to remould reality in accordance with it.[6]

In this essay, we illustrate the extent to which GE users' experiences are plugged into the enjoyment of what we call the "Dionysusphere."[7] In so doing, we take inspiration from another social theorist who was fascinated by the technological incorporations of pleasure and reality: Walter Benjamin. Benjamin is key to our argument because he focuses on people's practice-based — that is, embodied, psychical, and emotional — interactions with technology. Writing on the rise of popular cinema and the mechanical reproduction of art in Europe during the 1930s, Benjamin affirmed the indeterminacy of technology. That is, Benjamin was careful not to assign any inherent positive (e.g., progressive) or negative (e.g., fascist) tendencies, qualities, or outcomes to cultural media and technology more generally.

Today, the vast majority of contemporary *critical* writings on cartography, Geographical Information Systems (GIS), and a range of other geospatial technologies (GSTs) are caught between a binary of hope and despair. On the one hand is the sprawling literature that highlights the withering of people's democratic rights and freedoms as a result of the rise of GST-driven surveillance and military-industrial imperialism. On the other hand is the well-meaning research that draws on progressive social theories to advocate a GST and GIS-equipped public sphere that can expose (via mapping and spatial analyses) the above problems, as well as enhance local efforts at social and environmental problem solving and justice. We aim to complicate (not deride or overcome) the dualism of hope-fear in the critical studies of GSTs by bringing to the fore Benjamin's open-ended and practice approach to the social dimensions of the rise of new technologies.

We draw on Friedrich Nietzsche's, focusing on Nietzsche's interpretation of Greek tragedy in terms of a mutually affirming dialectical interplay between Apollonian determinations *qua* order, control, and calculation and Dionysian forces *qua* uncertainty, intoxication, and jubilation.[8] We believe that the predominantly Apollonian interpretations of GST (folded into the either-or-ness of conformity versus resistance) risks foreclosing our theoretical and empirical understandings of how GE is actually used in various ways and contexts. We explore how GE is integrated into the Dionysusphere wherein people plug into spaces animated by hallucinatory gazes and the ceaseless movement of desire.

Apollo and Dionysus

First published in 1872, Nietzsche's, *Birth of Tragedy Out of the Spirit of Music*, inquires into the artistic decline of ancient Greek plays as a result of the increasing influence of Socrates' rationalist philosophy. Nietzsche interprets Greek tragedy in terms of two deities: Apollo and Dionysus. For Nietzsche, Apollo and Dionysus are

> Representatives of two art-worlds, which differ in their deepest essence and highest goals. Apollo stands for me as the transfiguring genius of the *principium individuationis*, through whom alone release and redemption in semblance can truly be attained, whereas under the mystical, jubilant shout of Dionysus the spell of individuation is broken, and the path to the Mothers of Being, to the innermost core of things laid open.[9]

Nietzsche argued that the aesthetic brilliance of Greek tragedy resulted from the active synthesis of Apollonian and Dionysian forces. The Apollonian consists of rationality, the plastic arts (e.g., sculpture), orderliness, control, dreaminess, and individualism. Dionysian forces involve passion, music, chaos, intoxication, absurdity, and collective rapture. According to Nietzsche, Greek tragedy was unique because it dialectically fused rather than polarized the duality of Apollo and Dionysus. The analytic categories of Apollo and Dionysus have informed numerous contemporary literary and social theories, as well as spatial theories. Henri Lefebvre, for example, asserts that the "Nietzschean distinction between Apollonian and Dionysian echoes the dual aspect of the living being and its relationship to space – its own space and the other's: violence and stability, excess and equilibrium."[10]

We believe that Apollo and Dionysus can enhance our understandings of GE for three reasons: first, they take seriously the dynamism of social experiences and space; second, they do not rely on the fixity and separateness of users and technology; and third, they exist in creative tension with one another: researchers' overvaluations of the Apollonian dimensions of GSTs can be overcome by elaborating on the Dionysian forces at play in users' interactions with GSTs. Numerous researchers assert that Google Earth is an ideological Apollonian apparatus of techno-culture because it creates a distance between controlling and sober observer(s) and ordered, objectified, and observed subjects.[11] Denis Cosgrove has even dubbed these totalizing and imperial perspectives the "Apollonian Eye."[12] Yet, many researchers oppose such dystopic portrayals by affirming progressive, participatory approaches to GSTs.[13] Thus current appraisals of GSTs are shackled by an oscillatory fear-hope dialectic: GSTs either

control or empower. Not wishing to condemn nor overcome this binary, we wish to elaborate a Dionysian approach to Google Earth to affirm its numerous open-ended, practice-based, and interface-situated dimensions. Our aim is to highlight the extent to which Google Earthlings become enlaced into the Dionysusphere.

The Dionysusphere

For Nietzsche, the Dionysiac is "best conveyed by the analogy of *intoxication*. These Dionysiac stirrings, which, as they grow in intensity, cause subjectivity to vanish to the point of complete self-forgetting… Singing and dancing, man expresses his sense of belonging to a higher community; he has forgotten how to walk and talk and is on the brink of flying and dancing, up and away into the air above."[14]

Similarly, Benjamin affirmed the self-forgetting capacities of cinema and its "unconscious optics," the textual intensities of aphorisms, the seductive commodified urban spaces of Paris, and the intellectual and perceptual liberties afforded by hallucinogenic stimulants.[15] We find parallels between Benjamin's much-celebrated peripatetic figure of the flâneur and the wanderings of GE users. What is more, online forums and blogs about GE exemplify Benjamin's emphasis on how modern media can blur the "distinction between author and public… At any moment the reader [GE user] is ready to turn into a writer [blogger]."[16] The proliferation of online GE forums and blogs, especially those that exemplify the enjoyment of the Dionysusphere (e.g., Ogleearth.com, GoogleEarthHacks.com, and Juicygeography.co.uk), evince the extent to which GSTs such as GE are not simply panoptic devices of surveillance and control but "digital peep-boxes" that can turn looking into ogling, uncertainty into paranoia, and pleasure into intense exhilaration.[17]

The Dionysian Gaze

The Bourne Ultimatum, the latest film in the espionage series based on Robert Ludlum's novels, teems with scenes of assassin Jason Bourne outpacing the panoptic control of cell phone, satellite, GPS, and CCTV technologies.[18] In one memorable scene, CIA agents in a secret London-based CIA substation become increasingly frustrated in their attempts to locate and arrest Bourne and newspaper journalist Simon Ross in the busy Waterloo train station. On a prepaid cell phone, Bourne gives precise instructions (e.g., "Dip left past the photo kiosk") to Ross on how to avoid being spotted by the agents and roaming CCTVs. Surrounded by their wall of computer screens, the agents become increasingly frustrated and then furious as Ross and Bourne continually elude and finally escape their gaze. What is crucial to the scene is the degree to which the agents' failed efforts to apprehend (on and off the screen) Bourne is permeated with frenzied zealousness and mesmerizing enjoyment.

Yet, there are also many instances in which GE users revel in their *inability* to neatly capture and clearly visualize objects, where the GE gaze is defined not so much by high resolutions of mastery but by high dissolutions of speculation.[19] For example, in March 2010, a GE image of a section of seabed, 1,000 kilometers off the coast of Morocco incited numerous online discussions, and newspaper articles about whether Atlantis had finally been found. For many observers, the image's grid structure evinced the street layout of the mythical underwater city. *The Mail Online* report, headlined "Atlantis Revealed at Last… or Just a Load of Old Googles?", noted that "experts were agog, marine biologists baffled and internet bloggers buzzing."[20] The report lamented that there were two problems: "First, the grid of streets, walls and buildings turned out to be the size of Wales. That meant Atlantis was 20 times as big as Greater

1. Signs of ancient ponds

2. Loch Ness Monster

3. A top-ten ranked nude sunbather.

4. A large triangular UFO.

London. More problematic still, the grid of lines doesn't exist on the sea floor. According to Google, the pattern is an 'artifact' of its map-making process."

The website for North America's most popular late-night syndicated radio talk show, *Coast to Coast AM*, included a report on "Ancient Ponds." (figure 1)[21] Listener Dave Mennenoh discovered

a set of ponds close to where I mountain bike [in SE Wisconsin]. I found them on Google Earth when I was mapping out some trail. As you can see from the house at upper right, they are quite large – and likely not noticeable from either road that passes close. To me they look like some ancient symbols, with quite precise shapes – not very natural. I thought someone may recognize one of the symbols or something.

In this example, the GE image materializes a Dionysian gaze that consists of a vertiginous coincidence of too much meaning (for example, there must be something more, something hidden, and something behind the image) and a lack of meaning (e.g., why is this phenomenon occurring? What is it about the image that is suggestive of "X"? Is the phenomenon artificial or natural?). GE can intensify existing social myths about entities that combine a surplus and a paucity of meanings. In August 2009, *The Sun* reported that GE user Jason Cooke had provided "elusive proof" of the existence of the Loch Ness Monster (figure 2).[22] According to the report,

The shape seen on the surface of the 22-mile Scottish loch is 65ft long and appears to have an oval body, a tail and four legs or flippers. Some experts believe Nessie may be a Plesiosaur, an extinct marine reptile with a shape like the Google image. *Security guard Jason, 25, of Nottingham, said: "I couldn't believe it. It's just like the descriptions of Nessie."* Researcher Adrian Shine, of the Loch Ness Project, said: "This is really intriguing. It needs further study."

Dionysian Desire

The GE-inspired website "Ogleearth.com" evinces how GE's practices of looking can morph into the erotic voyeurism of ogling. GE exemplifies what Slavoj Žižek calls an "id machine," that is, a "mechanism that directly materializes" our fantasies and desires.[23] Exemplary here are the many websites dedicated to ranking the "Top Ten Naked People on Google Earth." On Googlesightseeing.com, Alex Turnbull describes the tenth-ranked naked person (figure 3) as follows: "The one that got so many people so hot under the collar. Many people think she's on her front, but personally I remain unconvinced."[24]

Echoing the eclipse of visual resolution by dissolution, GE gives users not merely objects of desire but rather Dionysian objects that cause desire. That is, if GE allowed users to possess via a clear visual definition an object of desire (e.g., a naked person), then users' desire would be extinguished and transformed into mere satisfaction. In contrast, objects that incite desire (or what Lacan calls the "*objet petit a*") are all those GE things that animate the ceaseless movement of desire as part of users' insatiable speculations and doubts about the status of an object. In the Dionysusphere, desire itself becomes the true object of desire: users' activities via web dialogues are directed toward maintaining rather fulfilling desire. For example, a "Googlesightseeer" remarked: "dammit, i still haven't cracked the top ten! i think i'm at #14 right now... i'm gonna have to step up my nudity time on the roof."[25] Another user curtly replied: "at least you are in the top 25!" Echoing the fusion of the Apollonian and the Dionysiand, the website consists of both Dionysians (who assert "How about some pics of people fornicating?! How about some pics of the people who

are watching this blog!!!"[26]) and sarcastic Apollonians (who ridicule such practices with sobering comments such as "Congratulations on conducting this important work that will benefit all humanity," "What an unbelievable waste of time", and "I need the real world.")[27] In response to the Apollonian calls for order, one user replied:

Sort of reminds me of a lady who called the police about a naked man showering who did not have the decency to close the curtain. When the policeman answered that the nearest home was a distance away and that he could not see anything much the women responded that of course you had to use a good set of binoculars.[28]

The UFO (Unidentified Flying Object) is arguably an object that causes desire par excellence. Many Google Earthlings have spotted UFOs on GE such as OriginalDrDil whose Youtube post of "UFOs on Google Earth" has generated (at the time of writing) nearly two million views and almost 4,000 comments (figure 4).[29] On March 30, *The Sun* published an article entitled, "Google Unearthly", with an from Google's Street View program of a "fleet of UFOs in formation" in the sky above a street in Bethnal Green, East London.[30] The "nine silver spheres" "baffled" leading British ufologist Nick Pope, who was "'very excited' by the image, which he labeled 'truly fascinating.'"[31] Qautermas2 noted in a Dionysian manner: "How does that look like anything we know? Not planes in formation, no matter how much you stretch your imagination!!! Strange craft are being reported all the time that bear no resemblance to the explanations offered! Some people will say anything to avoid having to admit they have no idea."[32]

On the question of UFO sightings on gearthblog.com (subtitled "the amazing things about Google Earth™"), GE user "KS" disputed the Apollonian force of rationality configured in a previous blogger's comment ("I wonder whether this says something about the sanity of our society over time?"), with this reply:

Actually, many sane people have seen UFOs, and not just blurry nocturnal objects brought on by perceptual fatigue. I have read hundreds of credible comm/military pilot sightings, which to me suggest that sanity and UFO sightings can coincide. I never doubted my sanity when a large, apparently metallic object flew overhead at low altitude in broad daylight. Btw, this object had very distinctive heat marks along the leading edge of an otherwise clean, metallic surface—such as you could expect for an object that re-entered from high orbit. However, this object was flying at a flat trajectory at low altitude. I won't begin to speculate what this object was, but I no longer doubt these things do happen.[33]

The refusal to "speculate on what the object was" and affirmation of the belief that "these things do happen" evinces how Dionysian desire *takes place* in GE. An object that incites desire is attained or realized not by directly seeking or confronting it. Rather, the UFOs (regardless of their ontological status) reside in the "*curved space of desire*: sometimes the shortest way to realize a desire is to by-pass its object-goal, make a detour, postpone its encounter."[34] Thus the shortest distance between two points on the earth and in the space of desire is not a straight line but via the curve of an arc.

Conclusion

While GE embodies the Dionysian principles of rapture and uncertainty, we are doubtful that GE will spur large-scale social revolution that Walter Benjamin may have hoped for. Nonetheless, Google's Street View does generate some Dionysian activities of resistance. The F.A.T. (Free Art & Technology) web article, "Pantless Germans

Flash Google Street View Car," depicts a brief video set in central Berlin of a gang of young men and women walking parallel to a Google car.[35] During their pursuit of the slow-moving Google car, they mischievously giggle and shout (in thick German accents) "Fuck Google!" Moments later several oncoming pedestrians walk past impassively, giving the Google car the finger. The men eventually drop their pants as the helpless Google car comes to a standstill. Obviously such activities do little to disrupt, let alone prevent, Google's mapping project. Nonetheless, they do incite discussions about the very status of the event. For example, one comment stated: "Fake. That is not a real google streetcar."[36]

Such street-level activities are reminiscent of the political and artistic practices of movements such as the Dadaists, Surrealists, and Situationists. They point towards alternative political positions to researchers' efforts (e.g., under the banners of GIS and society, or participatory GIS) to place GSTs such as GE in the hands of marginalized social groups. Yet these mainstream approaches maintain an Apollonian domination-resistance binary framework that tames our understandings of GE. This essay has attempted to augment this approach by illustrating the extent to which GE spins in a Dionysusphere of giddy gazes and dislocated desires. GE is a spangled orb that not only captures objects in front of satellite lenses but also hooks viewers in front of their glowing monitors. Users would do well to be mindful of the emerging social disorder of Google Earth Addiction (GEA) and the burgeoning websites devoted to GEA therapy.[37] For in the Dionysusphere, the digital divide between user and pusher is indistinguishable: "Yes, my name is Linda, and I'm a Google Earth addict. But I don't want to recover. Does anyone want to join me on a trip around the world? (If you'd like to download Google Earth – it's free – right here – and, in case you're wondering, I'm not on their payroll; I'm just a fan.)"[38]

NOTES

1. Friedrich Nietzsche, *The Gay Science* (New York: Cambridge University Press, 2001), 120.

2. Jacques Lacan, *The Seminar of Jacques Lacan. Book XVII: The Other Side of Psychoanalysis, 1969–1970* (New York: Norton, 2007), 150–163.

3. Ibid., 161.

4. Ibid.

5. For an extended discussion on the social dimensions of jouissance, see: Paul Kingsbury, "Did Somebody Say Jouissance? On Slavoj Žižek, Consumption, and Nationalism," *Emotion, Space and Society*, 1, no. 1 (2008): 48-55.

6. Joan Copjec, "May '68, the emotional month," in *Lacan: The Silent Partners*, ed. Slavoj Žižek (New York: Verso, 2006), 96.

7. This essay build on a much larger argument developed in Paul Kingsbury and John Paul Jones III, "Walter Benjamin's Dionysian Adventures on Google Earth," *Geoforum* 40, no. 4 (2009): 502-513.

8. For an extended discussion on Nietzsche's relevance to geography and aesthetics, see: Paul Kingsbury, "Unearthing Nietzsche's Bomb: Nuance, Explosiveness, Aesthetics," *ACME: An International E Journal for Critical Geographies*, 9, no. 1 (2010): 47-61.

9. Friedrich Nietzsche, *The Birth of Tragedy and Other Writings* (New York: Cambridge University Press, 1999), 76.

10. Henri Lefebvre, *The Production of Space* (Oxford: Blackwell, 1991), 178.

11. For example, see Chad Harris, "The Omniscient #ye: Satellite Imagery, 'Battleship Awareness,' and the Structures of the Imperial Gaze," *Surveillance and Society* 4, nos. 1/2 (2006): 101–122. Brian Klinkenberg, "Geospatial Technologies and the Geographies of Hope and Fear," *Annals of the Association of American Geographers* 97, no. 2 (2007): 350–360.

12. Denis Cosgrove, "Contested Global Visions: One-World, Whole-Earth, and the Apollo Space Photographs," *Annals of the Association of American Geographers* 84, no. 2 (1994): 270–294.

13. Sarah Elwood, "Beyond Cooptation or Resistance: Urban Spatial Politics, Community Organizations, and GIS-Based Spatial Narratives," *Annals of the Association of American Geographers* 96, no. 2 (2006): 323–341.

14. Friedrich Nieztsche, *The Birth of Tragedy and Other Writings* (New York: Cambridge University Press, 1999), 17-18, emphasis in original.

15. Walter Benjamin, *Illuminations* (New York: Schocken Books, 1969), 237.

16. Ibid., 232.

17. Ron Van Lammeren and Aldo Bergsma, "Towards Geodata-Based Communities: Moving from Mapping Tool to Digital Peep-Box," *GIM International* 20, no. 8 (2006): 31-33.

18. *The Bourne Ultimatum*, directed by Paul Greengrass, Universal Pictures, 2007.

19. For an extended discussion on the gaze, see Josh Evans, Valorie Crooks, and Paul Kingsbury, "Theoretical Injections: On the Therapeutic Aesthetics of Medical Spaces," *Social Science & Medicine*, 69, no. 5 (2009): 716-721.

20. http://www.dailymail.co.uk/news/worldnews/article-1150846/Atlantis-revealed--just-load-old-Googles.html.

21. http://www.coasttocoastam.com/photo/photo-of-the-day/41339.

22. http://www.thesun.co.uk/sol/homepage/news/2606683/Loch-Ness-Monster-on-Google-Earth.html.

23. Slavoj Žižek, "The Thing from Inner Space," in *Sexuation*, ed. Renata Salecl (Durham, NC: Duke University Press, 2000), 227-228.

24. http://googlesightseeing.com/2006/11/28/top-10-naked-people-on-google-earth/.

25. http://www.listafterlist.com/tabid/57/listid/8233/The+Web/Top+10+Naked+People+on+Google+Earth.aspx.

26. Ibid.

27. Ibid.

28. Ibid.

29. http://www.youtube.com/watch?v=OZSfTmndqLU.

30. http://www.thesun.co.uk/sol/homepage/news/2348570/UFOs-spotted-in-East-End-on-Google-Street-View.html?allComments=true.

31. Ibid.

32. Ibid.

33. http://www.gearthblog.com/blog/archives/2005/11/ufo_sighting_lo.html.

34. Slavoj Žižek, *How to Read Lacan* (New York: Norton, 2006), 77, emphasis in original.

35. http://fffff.at/pantless-germans-flash-google-street-view-car/.

36. Ibid.

37. For example, see http://www.keegan.org/jeff/googleearth/index.html

38. http://lindaswindow.blogspot.com/2007/12/google-earth-addict.html

THEO DEUTINGER

IS AN AUSTRIAN BORN ARCHITECT WHO LIVES AND WORKS IN ROTTERDAM, WHERE HE HAS OPERATED HIS ARCHITECTURE FIRM TD SINCE 2005. HIS FIELD OF WORK IS NOT BOUND TO ANY SCALE LEVEL, AS HE SEEKS TO COMBINE ARCHITECTURE AND URBAN DESIGN WITH RESEARCH AND CONCEPTUAL THINKING. HE MAINTAINS TEACHING ENGAGEMENTS WITH SEVERAL DUTCH AND INTERNATIONAL ARCHITECTURE SCHOOLS.

LIVING ROOM GEOGRAPHY

Gerardus Mercator, the famous cartographer who coined the term "atlas" for a compilation of maps, described his work as an "imitator of the earth." His contemporary Abraham Ortelius, the publisher of the world's first map compilation in book form, called his work a "theater of the world" (*Theatrum Orbis Terrarum*).[1] World maps, as their origins reveal, are explicit simulations of reality, not an attempt to represent the world but an alternative version of it.

To produce an adequate imitation of the earth requires a thorough triangulation process that translates every coastline, river, and mountain ridge into a series of points that eventually connect as lines on a map. The basis for this enormous enterprise, the triangulation of the earth's surfaces, was the geographical coordinate system, longitudes and latitudes onto which every measured point got tethered. Subsequently the entire globe got captured in a giant web, like an exotic animal. The web in this case functions as the cast of the first earth imitation project. Through unfolding and stretching this web, the first copy of the planet appeared.

The geographical coordinate system is in fact nothing more than a gigantic spreadsheet wrapped around a sphere onto which any kind of information can be charted and with whose help all registered information can be traced. The virtual capacity of this spreadsheet is infinite. At the 1884 International Meridian Conference[2] the placement of the earth's spreadsheet was standardized by setting the position of the zero meridian to Greenwich, England, just as people began to worry about the finiteness of the planets resources.[3] The world's first national park was created at Yellowstone in the United States in 1872. In 1889, the Foundation for the Protection of Birds was established in the United Kingdom.

During Europe's colonialism era, every unique feature on earth was collected, labeled, and allocated to specific categories in universities, zoos and museums. The entire globe and its possessions were claimed, disassembled, shipped, and reconstructed according to ascendant scientific methods. This process reached its climax at the end of the nineteenth century, slightly relapsed during modernity, and then was turned inside out during the last third of the twentieth century.

The number of exotic species one might find today in a zoo pales in comparison to that of species inhabiting nature reserves and protected landscapes around the world. Zoos have evolved from being prisons to refuges and mainly function as incubator for endangered species that will eventually be released into the wild. Similarly, one finds the most extraordinary culture and art pieces of the world not in museums but marked as World Heritage buildings, protected cities, and designated landscapes. Fossils and cultural relics are now often left unexcavated and simply registered by their exact GPS coordinates to record their existence and while extending better protection in their indigenous environment.

Earth itself has turned into a giant zoo and a vast museum navigable through the use of the spreadsheet (geographical coordinate system), together with the image of the earth that functions as its way-finding tool. The image of the earth overlaid by the spreadsheet reflects what Heidegger described as *Weltbild*, "not an image of the world, but the world understood as image."[4] The earth is increasingly considered a tool, an object, which, after getting to know it, we have begun to use it. The sphere we sought to index and categorize turned into a giant classification system for everything and everybody on the planet. As a faithful imitation of the earth, this catalog with its worldwide image and its worldwide web of coordinates was the precursor of the Internet.

In 1966 the writer Stewart Brand led a public campaign to pressure NASA to release a satellite photograph of the Earth that was rumored to exist. Brand's later work would marry the image of the earth with the contents of a catalog. His most memorable project was *The Whole Earth Catalog*, an American counterculture publication first issued in 1968. This serial opus' aim was to offer "a catalog so that anyone on Earth can pick up a telephone and find out the complete information on anything." In his June 2005 commencement speech at Stanford University, Steve Jobs compared *The Whole Earth Catalog* to the Internet search engine Google. Kevin Kelly, founder of *WIRED* magazine, went further to suggest that "it is no coincidence that *The Whole Earth* catalogs disappeared as soon as the Web and blogs arrived. Everything the *Whole Earth* catalogs did, the web does better."

Thus the Internet itself is nothing more than another refinement of earth imitation, the continuing spreadsheet accessible to everybody, constantly updated and enriched with additional information. For a long period the true shape of the Internet was unclear, but the launch of Google Earth in 2005, and other similar programs, forced the curtain to fall and reveal the true face of the Internet: earth itself. For the user, from now on the imitator, the World Wide Web changed dramatically, as anyone who adds something to the Web turns from a simple editor into a geographer. Everything of interest can be inscribed and documented "on site." Geography as science got popularized and a new profession appeared: the living room geographer.

While the technical replication of the globe was advanced by navigators of the high seas, the living-room geographers sit in their private atmospheres reporting on the world outside, which starts at their front door. The desktop in any person's living room turns into the base camp for expeditions into reality. Excursions are documented by text, image, and video and get added to the online earth. Every day millions of explorers enrich the latest earth imitation with new observations, feelings, and events.

The Internet is the first earth imitation that allows annotation by all earth inhabitants. Everything seems to be of interest, and everything seems to be equally important. What the Internet does not offer does not exist, and the less frequently something is mentioned, the more likely it is that it will disappear. The representation and reproduction of a place are personalized and individualized. Nobody keeps an overview and nobody is giving order to the whole. If one were to print

out all images of the Eiffel Tower in Paris that circulate on the Web, the pile would probably be larger than the actual tower. But exactly in this mess lies the power of the imitation. Yet individuality is only seemingly leading, since with its totality of individual contributions, the Internet is unconsciously becoming the world's most communal project ever. This new imitation project is in fact the earth's first social earth imitation project and has little in common with any earth imitation projects before it. With the perfect replication of the image of the earth through the satellite imagery, the earth and its imitation near a merger, and a new social and subjective project begins.

The more information fed into the Internet, the more emotionally attached its connected users are to it. Peter Sloterdijk states, "Globalization is the time in which ideas got replaced by interests."[5] This social earth imitation project has become the perfect indicator of global interests. The more information added, the less overview any person can have, and yet the more accurately an image can be traced. Unlike the triangulation points that map mountaintops, the triangulation points of the Internet are constantly moving and gaining or losing relevance. This mapping project can never end.

At the level of the city, this means that after knowing how places are shaped, we slowly start to understand how places are perceived and used without having to be there. It also means that while a city's form might be stable, its use can change with ever-increasing speed. The crux is to find the right triangulation points in the city in order to be able to generate accurate maps and diagrams of the social imitation project. These new layers on top of the urban fabric are refining the understanding of the city and at the same time introducing new and more powerful planning tools. The Internet will never replace the opinion of the people, just as world map never replaced the features of the planet it represented. But this earth-imitation will make the people's interests increasingly more legible, just as the world map made space fathomable.

Finally, through increasing ability in the manipulation of satellite imagery, the earth itself will turn into the most accurate and current map. With the introduction of a future Echtzeit version of Google-Earth, users become the actors in a real-time atlas. Ortelius' *Theatrum Orbis Terrarum*, 440 years old, comes to life.

NOTES

1. *Theatrum Orbis Terrarum* ("Theater of the World") is considered to be the first modern atlas, compiled by Abraham Ortelius and published in 1570 in Antwerp, Belgium.
2. International Meridian Conference in Washington, 1884.
3. The creation of the world's first national park at Yellowstone; USA in 1872 or the foundation of the Royal Society for the Protection of Birds; UK (1889).
4. "Daß die Welt zum Bild wird, ist ein und derselbe Vorgang mit dem, daß der Mensch innerhalb des Seienden zum Subjectum wird." *Martin Heidegger: Holzwege* (Frankfurt, 1950), 90ff.
5. Peter Sloterdijk, *Spharen III*, (Frankfurt: Suhrkamp Verlag Frankfurt Am Main, 2003).

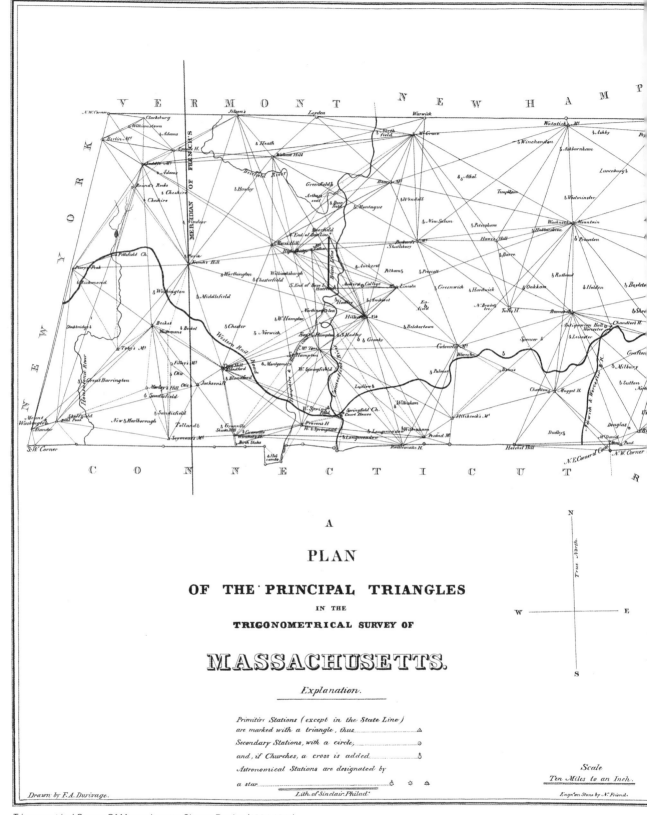

Trigonometrical Survey Of Massachusetts, Simeon Borden (1834-1841)

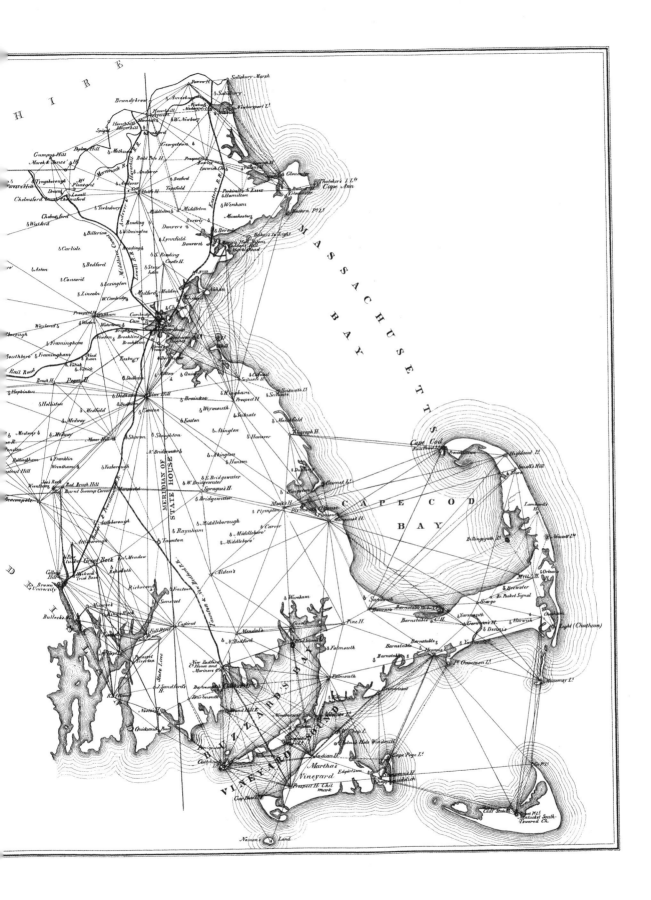

WHAT ARE
YOU
LOOKING AT?

071. farm1.static.flickr.com/1/124659356_bbe1e5b661_o_d.jpg, http://www.flickr.com/photos/
       nolifebeforecoffee/124659356/sizes/o/in/set-72157603316890957/
072. courtesy El Bee, Hong Kong
073. techolive.com/wp-content/uploads/2009/06/dscf9448.jpg
074. furnituretrader.com.au/images/thumbnails/123.jpg
075. emeraldinsight.com/fig/2720070603002.png
076. courtesy El Bee, Toronto

077. upload.wikimedia.org/wikipedia/commons/5/55/Meissner_effect_p1390048.jpg

078. furnituretrader.com.au/images/thumbnails/123.jpg

079. rescue007.org/images/McDonald.jpg

080. photolib.noaa.gov/700s/theb0976.jpg

081. courtesy El Bee, New York

082. courtesy El Bee, Hong Kong

083. anonymous surveillance camera capture
084. courtesy El Bee, New York
085. courtesy El Bee, Hong Kong
086. courtesy El Bee, Hong Kong
087. anonymous surveillance camera capture

088

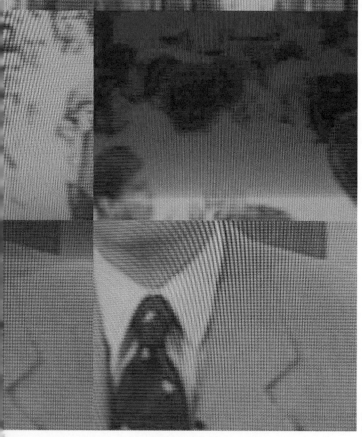

089

088. courtesy El Bee, Hong Kong
089. identinet.files.wordpress.com/2009/01/surveillance1.jpg